The Dialogue of Negation

The Dialogue of Negation

Debates on Hegemony
in Russia and the West

Jeremy Lester

Pluto Press

LONDON • STERLING, VIRGINIA

First published 2000 by Pluto Press
345 Archway Road, London N6 5AA
and 22883 Quicksilver Drive, Sterling, VA 20166–2012, USA

British Library Cataloguing in Publication Data
A catalogue record for this book is available from the British Library

ISBN 0 7453 1630 1 hbk

Library of Congress Cataloging in Publication Data

Lester, Jeremy.
    The dialogue of negation : debates on hegemony in Russia and the West /
Jeremy Lester.
        p. cm.
    Includes bibliographical references.
    ISBN 0–7453–1630–1 (hc.)
    1. Power (Social sciences) 2. Political science—Philosophy. 3. Gramsci,
Antonio, 1891–1937—Contributions in political science. I. Title.

JC330 .L47 2000
320.1'092—dc21   99–056757

Designed and produced for Pluto Press by
Chase Production Services, Chadlington, OX7 3LN
Typeset from disk by Marina Typesetting, Minsk, Belarus
Printed in the European Union by T. J. International, Padstow

Contents

Preface

Some of the material contained in the opening sections of this book was initially written for incorporation in my earlier study of hegemonic struggle in contemporary Russia, *Modern Tsars and Princes*.[1] On very sound advice from friends and colleagues who read the early drafts, it was suggested that much of this material would in fact be far more suited to a separate study in its own right, analysing the conceptual evolution of hegemony and bringing matters right up to the present. This new book is the product of that advice.

Few can doubt that the notion of hegemony has attained a wide degree of popular usage over the last thirty years. If, back in 1965 in his major work *For Marx*, Louis Althusser could lament that no one had as yet taken up and followed through the necessary development of this remarkable example 'of a theoretical solution in outline to the problems of the interpenetration of the economic and the political',[2] it was a lament that was to be quickly rectified. In the intervening years, hegemony-centred studies have been a veritable growth industry.

Old laments, however, have given way to new ones. For one thing, the conceptual rigour of many of these studies leaves an awful lot to be desired. And for another thing – though this is more an ideological lamentation than anything else – many of the more recent studies have either completely ignored, downgraded, belittled or transcended the input of the theorist who did most to provide the concept with its new-found status. The theorist in question, of course, is Antonio Gramsci and the trend has its roots in Althusser himself, notwithstanding all the compliments he invariably paid to Gramsci, and notwithstanding the fact that this was the beginning of a dramatic rise in Gramsci's world-wide popularity and influence. If the present study, then, is first and foremost a historical and conceptual analysis of hegemony, it is also to be acknowledged right from the outset that it is written in the desire to restore the very specific Gramscian-*Marxist* interpretation and usage of hegemony – and perhaps more crucially in the current climate, *counter-hegemony* – to centre stage.

The very specific purposes and aims of the study are detailed in the Introduction. Two other features of its approach and content, however, are worth emphasising now, for it is these two features which define its breadth and depth of coverage. The first concerns the way in which the notion of hegemony has accompanied the temporal movement from pre-modern to modern and now to (supposedly) postmodern structural settings, and the way in which a study of its contours and remit can provide a vital contribution to our understanding of this very complex process. Secondly – and very much connected with the above – is the geographical movement and interaction of the concept between East and West, and its capacity to contribute to our understanding of the shared and different traditions which dialectically link and divide East and West, Russia and the rest of Europe. Both of these phenomena, to be sure, have been intrinsic areas of interest in earlier studies of hegemony, but not quite in the manner or the extent as in the present study.

Over the course of the book's evolution, I have incurred a debt of inspirational and motivational gratitude to a great many people, too numerous to list. For his warmth, generosity and openness, I would particularly like to express my thanks to Giuliano Gramsci – Antonio Gramsci's last surviving son – who made my visits to Moscow such a worthwhile experience; to Roger Simon for his advice and encouragement on an earlier draft; and to Gemma, my wife, for continued patience, tolerance and support. For the others, I hope it will suffice as a mark of gratitude if I dedicate the book to my comrades in both East and West for whom the struggle for hegemony still continues. We may not always agree on specific tactics, but the overall strategy and the goals will always unite us. As Gramsci himself once commented: 'life is always revolution'.

Introduction: Hegemony and the Project of Modernity

> And so, walking or quickening his pace, he goes his way, for ever in search. In search of what? ... He is looking for that indefinable something we may be allowed to call 'modernity', for want of a better term to express the idea in question. The aim for him is to extract from fashion the poetry that resides in its historical envelope, to distil the eternal from the transitory.
>
> Charles Baudelaire, *The Painter of Modern Life*

1

In a review of *Modern Tsars and Princes: The Struggle for Hegemony in Russia*, one commentator was keen to stress that: 'It is very much to be hoped that potential readers of [Lester's] book will not be put off by the frightening word, "hegemony", in [the] subtitle.'[1] Not surprisingly, the use of the word 'frightening' here somewhat took me aback at first. It was certainly not the usual nor the expected adjective one would have immediately thought of applying in the kind of context one was dealing with here. So, why was it being used? And with what kind of connotations, hidden or otherwise, in the subconscious of this particular reviewer?

I suppose one aspect of the fear which can be generated by the mere mention of the term hegemony might feasibly relate to some kind of intrinsic conceptual complexity. Certainly many of the specialist political and philosophical dictionaries which include the term are apt to refer explicitly to its difficulties of comprehension and understanding, although quite why this is the case is never properly explained. On the other hand, one should also recognise that there are many others who go to the opposite extreme, emphasising and indeed celebrating the concept's unusual simplicity. If there is any intrinsic complexity about hegemony, these analysts would argue, it is not so much to be found in its theoretical construction, so much as in its practical, realisable attainability. Paraphrasing Bertolt Brecht, there is undeniably a sense in which hegemony (like Brecht's 'communism') is one of those simple things which anyone can grasp, yet because of its very simplicity, that is why it is so difficult to achieve.

Another possible aspect of hegemony's apparent 'frightening' status might relate to its perceived *dictatorial* implications. There is certainly no denying that in many of its earlier, pre-Gramscian incarnations, as will be highlighted a little later on, it was very closely intertwined with connotations of dictatorship and imperialism. But then, the notion of hegemony under review was entirely based on a Gramscian understanding, one which clearly differentiated hegemony from outright dictatorship. So what was there to be so preoccupied about?

This leaves one remaining option. What I am most inclined to infer from the reviewer's use of the word 'frightening' in its direct association with hegemony is its intrinsic modern-day connections with theories and strategies directly associated with the left. In other words, there was an ingrained ideological hostility to the use of a concept so closely identified with political forces not of the reviewer's own liking and taste.

If indeed this was the basis of his expressions of fear, he would be far from alone in sharing such hostilities to the notion of hegemony. It is perhaps sufficient, as well as very appropriate given the specific Russian context here, to remember that only a couple of years earlier such a doyen of the opposition of the international left, General Auguste Pinochet, had specifically warned the new post-communist leaders in Russia of the continuing threat they faced from a new type of communism which was threatening the stability of the entire capitalist world. This communist threat, he asserted, came in the more 'respectable' guise of 'Gramscism', which he went on to define as 'Marxism in a new dress'. This threat was all the more dangerous because, through its notion of hegemony and other such 'disguises in sheep's clothing', it was much more able than previous communist doctrines to penetrate the consciousness of a society's intellectual class as well as the ordinary masses.[2]

The irony here – at least in terms of the reviewer's ingrained fear of hegemony because of its left-wing connections – is, I am sure, not lost on anybody. Although he is perfectly correct to be aware of the concept's almost exclusive modern-day associations with left-wing thinkers and activists, there is almost certainly no denying that its more general principles have been much more effectively used to help define the depth of consensual entrenchment of *liberalism* and *capitalism* throughout the twentieth century. 'Frightened' is therefore the last thing anyone on the Western – though not, of course, the Latin American – right should be, since they have been far better practitioners of hegemony than their ideological opponents.

Thus far we have ascertained that the concept of hegemony, in certain quarters at least, is evocatively frightening; that it is perhaps complex, yet simple and irredeemably difficult at one and the same time; and that it also has a habit of encouraging a playful sense of irony. What else can we say about hegemony? Why does it merit a whole book devoted to an emphasis of its importance? Before embarking on a much more specific account of its conceptual significance, let us pursue for just a little while longer the playful sense of irony which we have identified as being an integral accompaniment to a study of hegemony.

Whatever else we can say about the meaning and importance of hegemony, few can deny that it is one of those terms today which is used perennially in everyday political usage, but which all too often is unaccompanied by any real, or at least sufficient, explanatory meaning. In many instances hegemony has assumed the appearance of a taken-for-granted concept, and it is precisely here that the more discerning analyst will immediately spot the irony and the paradox. At its empirical best, there is no better tool than the concept of hegemony to demystify the plethora of things around us which achieve an unwarranted and reductionist status of naturalness because of their own sheer taken-for-grantedness. Hegemony, therefore, is in danger of acquiring the very attributes of the disease which in many cases it set out to cure. Instead of demystifying, it has increasingly become embalmed in its own mystificatory logic.

Anyway, let us now, temporarily at least, leave the terrain of hegemonic irony and explore further some of the underlying foundations of its richly-deserved conceptual importance. The first thing which I think needs to be emphasised is that the modern-day conceptual and empirical application of hegemony possesses virtually no boundaries. To put it succinctly, it is an immensely adaptable concept which is highly extensive in scope, capable of addressing not only macrological forms of practices and phenomena, but just as importantly, micrological phenomena as well, helping us 'to understand the most minute operations and experiences of everyday life'.[3] To take just a few examples out of literally hundreds: it has been used as a conceptual background and framework for analysing the process of identity formation amongst Afro-Brazilian activists in Rio de Janeiro and São Paulo; to investigate the process of ideological exchange between religious and secular thinkers in the context of the cultural and political changes which have taken place in Iran since the 1950s; as a framework for analysing the formation of opposition attitudes by striking National Health Service ancillary workers in Britain towards privatisation; as well as to analyse the literary writings of a number of emerging African writers such as Ngugi wa Thiongó.

Moreover, as we can see from even this cursory outline of its scope, the transcendence of geographical boundaries is also accompanied by the transcendence of disciplinary boundaries. There is virtually no domain in the social sciences and humanities today which has not utilised and employed a notion of hegemony within its recent research framework. Nor is its use limited to the traditionally dominant realms of history, political science, philosophy, economics, literary criticism and aesthetics. Other realms, such as psychoanalysis and social psychology, have also enriched their research frameworks and their nomenclature by an inclusion of a notion of hegemony, suitably adapted to their specific requirements.

A second factor very much underpinning the importance of hegemony in modern times is the crucially significant way it has been able to span and synthesise the domains of theory and practice. Put in another way, I do not think it would be too much of an exaggeration to say that the notion of hegemony is one of the best examples of *praxis* that has (ever) been developed. Certainly, from the vantage point of the left, it has made an enormous contribution to the movement away from overly-determinist conceptions of economism and historicism, and has successfully restored the primacy of *will*, which, after all, was the essential centrepiece of Marx's own prioritisation of praxis as the key to revolutionary change.

As for the very practical consequences of hegemonic-based (or more accurately speaking *counter*-hegemonic) strategies, this, in true praxis fashion, has generated all manner of (self) creative activity, energy and experimentation. One certainly does not have to look further than modern-day Latin America to see some of the fruits of this strategy. And it is undoubtedly no accident that right-wing dictators, such as the aforementioned General Pinochet of Chile, should be the most vocal in their outspoken concern of the growing threat of left opposition movements who successfully utilise such praxis-oriented, counter-hegemonic strategies.[4] Ultimately, of course, one hopes that it is through the actual implementation of a creative, empowering, counter-hegemonic process that one will also come to understand what the full scope of a *new* hegemonic project might look like, both in terms of the ideas as well as the institutions which would need to sustain any new hegemony.

Having referred to hegemony's ability to synthesise the domains of theory and practice, let us now turn to important features of the concept in the separate realms of philosophy and politics. On the purely philosophical front, the notion of hegemony has been able to provide some very important insights in a number of significant areas. First and foremost, it has contributed to the perennial debate on the nature of the relationship between human subjectivity (humans as actual agents of change) and the more objective processes of social change, as well as on the related question of how agents can actually be activated and mobilised in any given context. Without doubt, most modern conceptions of hegemony tend invariably to be extremely anti-positivist in their scope and remit and give a lot of credence to the conviction that moral choices should be an intrinsic component of the social sciences.

In addition to this, the problematic of hegemony is one which would intrinsically deal with important questions of representation. Similarly, its remit would encapsulate fundamental questions on the nature and scope of the relationship between epistemological constructions and the subject to which any kind of conception of knowledge is addressed, with one possible aim here being to show the way in which the nature of any knowledge 'is determined by both the act of addressing and the subject that is addressed' in the hegemonic process.[5] Last, but not least, there is arguably no better concept than hegemony for highlighting the kind of role played by intellectuals in the overall determination of certain types of power relationships.

Turning to the domain of politics, the conceptual impact of hegemony has, if anything, been even greater in modern times, having provided a whole multitude of analysts with not only the central category for an essential theorisation of politics, but having also provided the scope to witness the increasing ontological primacy of politics. Two related elements can be highlighted in particular here. One is the way in which the concept has been very usefully employed to determine the precise contours and boundaries of the actual activity called 'politics'. As Benedetto Fontana has argued, for example, the basic issue of how one seeks to formulate and construct a sociopolitical space whose essential defining characteristics delineate it properly as 'political' lies precisely at the very heart of hegemony's task. By means of the concept of hegemony, the political 'assumes a purposive and prefigurative character ... And to the extent that such a prefiguration necessitates the engagement of the conscious will within a world-in-becoming, the political is an innovating and creative form of activity.'[6] In an evolutionary context, Fontana is surely correct when he argues that the historical development and elaboration of hegemony has very much contributed to the formation of 'the people' (in a generic sense) as a vital category of politics. In the Italian context which lies at the centre of his research, he has clearly shown that the transformation of the *volgo* and the *moltitudine* into a far more determinate *popolo* was very much a product of the increasing impact of hegemony. Similarly, as will be highlighted in much greater detail in Chapter 1, it is certainly no coincidence that the emergence of a notion of hegemony in the realms of Russian Social Democracy in the latter part of the nineteenth century was very closely correlated with a brand new emphasis (in the Russian tradition) on the significance of politics.

The role of hegemony here, however, is by no means restricted to a formulation of the contours of the political. Much more crucially, its maturing conceptual and empirical remit has also provided the scope for a fundamental widening of the transcendental horizon of politics. As Stuart Hall has noted, in a modern-day context it is impossible to reduce the realm of politics to the occupancy of the state or even to any notion of electoral or party-based activity. These remain crucially significant. But, as notions of hegemony have been able to demonstrate, the basic rhythms, forms, antagonisms and sites of political activity are now far more varied, and failure to recognise this would be unforgivable.[7] As the horizon of politics has expanded in this way, so the pivotal relationship between forms of coercion and consent has likewise undergone fundamental changes. Again, then, it is precisely the nature of this relationship which so characterises the essential problematic of hegemony.

In its whole conceptual approach to politics, one of the main tasks of any hegemonic-based study is to try to assist the analyst to understand the essential depths of acceptance and stability underpinning a given social order. In the process, however, what the notion of hegemony can also achieve (perhaps more than any other conceptual framework) is an understanding as well of the ways in which change and *crisis* are likewise intrinsic features of any systemic order which must be continually addressed. Hegemony, in other words, possesses a double bind. It demonstrates that there is a dialectical relationship between stasis and change, integration and disintegration, permanency and flux, as well as a permanent juxtaposition between old and new, decay and growth. Similarly, it provides a framework for understanding the key process of social disaggregation and any ensuing form of *re*-aggregation.

The final justification for a study exclusively devoted to hegemony, which I think clearly needs stressing in terms of setting the scene for what is to follow, is arguably the most crucial point of all. As it will be making a regular appearance, however, throughout the course of the book, let me restrict what I have to say now to just the following: the concept of hegemony provides us, I think, with the most *integrated* picture of the reality and workings of power in the modern world. As we have already seen, first and foremost this means political power. Notwithstanding the primacy of politics, however, the richest and most rewarding studies on hegemony are undoubtedly those which give full credence to the 'transpolitical' dimension of its scope. What one is really seeking through the conceptual use of hegemony is the manner in which political power interacts and interconnects with the realms of culture, philosophy, ideology, economics and the social realm in its entirety. Indeed, if I may be so bold as to put it this way, the concept of hegemony is like a good impressionist painting: it brings a wholeness to all the individual brush strokes on the canvas. What would otherwise appear haphazard and random can all of a sudden be transformed into a harmonious, unified form. The point to stress, however, is that there is structure only in the whole. In the parts there is no form in themselves, no shape, no context. Hegemony's task is to bring the parts together, to illuminate what would otherwise be a hazy blur and silence.

2

Having outlined the main reasons for regarding the concept of hegemony so highly, and having emphasised its vital importance in our capacity to understand the modern nature of power in all its possible aspects, let me now add one absolutely crucial clarificatory addendum to all of this. Many, if not all, of these points of celebratory reference and conceptual importance are due very specifically to Antonio Gramsci's highly unique and evocative formulation of hegemony. It is therefore Gramsci's interpretation of hegemony which lies at the heart of the present study and around which nearly all of the debates on hegemony will take place. To borrow the terminology of Michel Foucault in his wonderfully penetrating study *The Archaeology of Knowledge,* there is absolutely no doubt that Gramsci's understanding and use of hegemony marks a decisive 'threshold' in the historical status of the concept. This threshold is followed by a 'rupture' and concludes in a wholesale 'transformation' of the concept.[8] From the moment of Gramsci onwards, the meaning of hegemony is able to enter a new phase of development, a new time, which distinguishes it from many of its previous empirical origins and original motivations, and which to a large extent as well 'cleanses it' from a great deal of its earlier 'imaginary complicities'.

Gramsci's innovatory significance notwithstanding, it is nevertheless important at this stage in the study to bear in mind that hegemony possessed an extremely long pre-Gramscian history of its own, which is certainly worth excavating and analysing for its own intrinsic interest. After all, through a study of the function of words, their emotive content, and the lexical and situational context in which they occur, it is certainly possible to gain vital insights into the state of collective awareness at any given moment in time. Likewise, again with reference to Foucault's epistemological archaeology, the etymological analysis of a term can also give us crucial insights on its forms of succession, its implications, its demonstrative reasoning, its spatial distribution, its dependencies and the type of progressive specification to which it was subject. It can tell us about its forms of coexistence and its field of presence. It can tell us whether it had any hidden meanings which can be traced back to its origins; the extent to which it was perhaps subject to mere repetition, and what the nature of its principles of exclusion were. It can also enlighten us on its 'field of concomitance', its field of memory, and perhaps most crucially of all, the 'procedures of intervention' to which it was subject.

When looking for the archaeological roots of hegemony, what more appropriate place to commence than ancient Greece – that veritable yardstick against which we rightly measure the self-knowledge of the modern era. Known in its original Greek derivation as ηγεμονια, the first thing that immediately strikes one about its origins and evolution is the indubitable connection it has with that most unique of classical institutions – the *polis*. The freedom which each and every individual polis claimed for itself made for a special, yet extremely, uneasy kind of relationship when it came to the inter-state domain. At some point it was thus inevitable that the freedom of one polis was always going to be reflected against the freedom of every other polis, and it was precisely this complex dialectic which ultimately shaped the emergence of hegemony. Indeed, it would not be unfair to say that if it was the peculiar nature of the existence of the polis which created the scope for the emergence of hegemony, so also the failure of the principles of hegemony at this time ultimately helped to destroy the essential features of the polis.

If anything can be said to capture the essence of the meaning and practice of hegemony in its earliest usage, it would be the degree to which it always found itself located (or trapped) within a continuum, whereby its task was to balance the different poles of the extremes by a continuous and complex process of oscillation. We can see this at work in purely conceptual terms by the manner in which hegemony came to signify and represent a difficult balancing act between the poles of leadership and direction on the one side, and domination and supremacy on the other. Both were integral features of hegemony and both were inextricably linked, as well as locked, in perpetual strife and combat.

We can also see the complexities of this balancing act at work in the practical domain as well. In the very earliest renditions of hegemony, the term was applied to the process of alliance building between city states. 'Hegemonial' alliances essentially stemmed from earlier forms of alliances such as the Amphictyony and the Symacchy. Where the first was almost exclusively based on tribal kinship and/or religious ties, and the second was dominated by military requirements, a hegemonial alliance was often far looser in form, but also much broader in scope. Military needs, to be sure, were most often considered paramount, but not exclusively so.

The first organised alliances (properly speaking, and distinct from those which occurred in myths and legends) date from the middle of the sixth century BC when the Peloponnesian League was first inaugurated. In his own historical account of this period, Victor Ehrenberg characterises the ensuing one hundred years or more as a time dominated by an overwhelming 'struggle for Hegemony' in the region; a period which culminates in the final demise of hegemonial aspirations towards the latter part of the fifth century BC, and especially with the rise of Macedonian influence and eventual supremacy.[9] What is most important to witness in this struggle for hegemony, however, is not just the way in which a struggle ensues for the unification of different city states in the practical sense of creating new alliances. Just as importantly, it was also a struggle for paramountcy between the internal features which characterised hegemony in the first place: leadership as against domination, direction as against supremacy.

The attempt to create hegemonial alliances at this time comprised a variety of essential characteristics. As has already been indicated, the institutional basis of such an alliance was usually represented in the guise of a 'League'. The hegemonic state and its allies were linked either by oaths or treaties on a *bilateral* basis, usually for an unstipulated time. The primary duty of the Hegemon was to protect the allies, while for the latter the main duty was to follow the Hegemon in time of war. It was thus both an offensive as well as defensive alliance, created partly for expansionist ambitions, but also for the enhancement of peace and good order. Separate alliances amongst and between the allies were nearly always tolerated as long as this did not adversely affect the Hegemon's own militaristic ambitions. Similarly, at times when the League as a whole was not engaged in military combat with an external force, the Hegemon would not necessarily involve itself in disputes between its allies, even if this led to outright military conflict between them.

Key functions which were considered most vital for sustaining the unity of an alliance were always firmly delineated in the domain of the most powerful state, and it was these functions which were considered to be 'hegemonic' ones. At the same time, at least at first, strong degrees of autonomy were nearly always granted to the subservient entities in recognition of the fact that this too might assist the requirement of a more voluntary-based alliance. After all, as no less an authority than Aristotle pointed out, the main defining feature of *hegemonia* as a form of rule was that it should be firmly oriented 'to the interest of the led, and not to the establishment of a general system of slavery'.[10]

As for the underlying basis of such alliances, again both contemporary commentators and later historians have tended to focus on a variety of factors to explain the type of conditions which were necessary to sustain a viable hegemony over and above outright military control. Such factors, for example, range from favourable geographical and climatic conditions, to the successful inculcation of religious ideas and notions of racial supremacy, as well as claims of superiority based on the supposed epic deeds of a state's ancestors: what one commentator has called the already conscious use of history as 'a happy hunting-ground for edifying stories'.[11]

In addition, and not surprisingly, a state's economic potential was similarly a crucial factor here, especially when considered in conjunction with the growing power of the urban city over the rural countryside. Aristides, for example, is not alone when he supposedly exhorted the Athenians to 'grasp hegemony' by encouraging its people to leave the fields and live in the city.[12]

Last, but not least, the notion of *logos* was also regularly invoked to define criteria and characteristics of hegemonic power. An absolutely central interpretative category of all classical Greek culture, *logos* essentially possessed two, not necessarily mutually compatible, meanings, both of which were utilised to good hegemonic advantage. The first, perhaps best associated with Isocrates, emphasised the significance of *logos* in terms of discourse, and the whole domain of speech and language (*logos hegemon panton* – 'speech and language are the ruler and guide of all things').[13] The second interpreted *logos* as reason, and the subsequent capacity of rationalism to impose an ordered structure of hegemony is best associated with the school of Platonism.

Up until now, the emphasis has been placed on the rather benign, even progressive, features of hegemonial alliances at this time. However, by far the most pertinent defining feature of all attempts to create hegemony in the ancient Greek world was the apparent unstoppable tendency which always witnessed, sooner or later, the practical abrogation and annulment of the autonomy of the allies *vis-à-vis* the Hegemon. In other words, it rarely took long for a hegemonial alliance to become an *arche* – a united *empire* based on outright coercion and control. Ultimately, the two principles of hegemony and autonomy were never able to reach a final harmony. Indeed, as William Ferguson has noted, this was surely the *reductio ad absurdam* of the entire system of hegemonies at this time. Hegemonies which were created amongst individual city states with the primary purpose of warding off the challenge posed by an aggressive imperial power (Persia), ultimately, and perhaps inevitably, resorted to the same methods of imperialism as the first course of defence.[14]

One of the paramount ironies of this process can also be seen in the fact that it was the 'democracy' of Athens within the framework of the Delian League (created towards the beginning of the fifth century BC and made up of approximately 150 cities), which inaugurated this transition from hegemony to outright imperialism long before the 'timarchic' system of Sparta (and Athens' great rival) pursued similar tendencies within the Peloponnesian League.

The first effective move in the transition to imperialism came when Athens began to monopolise the financial activities of the Delian League (in 454 BC), and not only started to raise tributes and taxes from the 'allies', but also imposed her own system of coinage, weights and measures. Control of the purse-strings was then followed by a series of other measures which frequently set the pattern for imperialist tendencies in many of the other hegemonic-based Leagues as well. The essential characteristic at work here could not have been clearer. Where hegemony had at least attempted to give credence to the principle of unity within diversity, the new-style imperialism rested squarely on uniformity. Similarly, earlier hegemonic-based notions of allies and 'friendship' *(philia)* linking the different states together were comprehensively transformed now into 'subjects', as Athens became increasingly conscious of her role as the new 'mistress' of the Empire. Certainly by the time of Pericles, obedience had totally displaced any notion of friendship as the defining norm of inter-state relations.

With similar processes occurring in all the other Leagues and alliances, it is thus clear that by the latter part of the fifth century BC the very notion of attempting to unify the heterogeneous Greek states by means of a process of (benign) hegemony had been recognised as an abject failure. From now on, imperial notions of unity in the Greek and Hellenistic world were to predominate and, of course, there was no better testament of this in the next century than the exploits of Alexander the Great. It is precisely at this point that one can also witness the definitive decline of the ancient Greek polis. If in the early part of the fifth century the city state had been pervaded by the conviction that there was no greater humiliation which could befall it than to be subject to the dominion of another city or the will of a foreign ruler, from the end of the century onwards the new type of Hellenistic city could not have represented a greater contrast. As Ferguson thus very astutely noted in relation to Alexander the Great's political legacy, based on an arguably perverse, if 'genial', adaptation of Aristotle's ideas of state-building, Alexander had successfully discovered the means to legitimise a new approach to despotism:

> It was a means of uniting cities or provinces in an indissoluble whole while preserving, on the one hand, the superiority and freedom of action of the suzerain, be it an emperor or a republic, and, on the other hand, the self-respect of the inferior states, without which their status was politically intolerable. Deification of rulers did the impossible: it

reconciled completely the antinomy between the city-state and imperialism. It resolved the antagonism into two harmonious duties; the duty
of the ruler to command and of the subject to obey. To Alexander the
Great governments have been in serious debt for over two thousand
years.[15]

In Roman times, the nature of the new Empire meant that there was even
less scope now for formal notions of hegemonial-type alliances. Whatever the successes of Alexander, it was only really with the triumph of
Rome that imperialism attained its logical end – no other variant of imperialism, either before or since in the history of the world, has ever really
equalled it.

A similar picture can be seen throughout the long centuries of the medieval period. Hegemony, if used at all in any kind of exponential form, is
used merely as an adjunct of imperialism, the 'hegemonial idea of empire'.
That is to say, it is used to define the nature, and perhaps scope and strength,
of imperial power in any given context, but certainly not as a distinctive
alternative to an imperial structure of power in its own right. In some
usages, the connotations are more positive than others. According to Alcuin,
one of Charlemagne's key intellectual advisers, the main criterion of an
imperium was the amalgamation of different *gentes* perpetually divided by
language and race, and in this context he was particularly impressed by
the 'peace of hegemons' which had been imposed in Britain.[16] Elsewhere,
the notion of hegemony was often invoked at this time to portray the often
bitter struggle between the spiritual and secular powers for ultimate control within the *imperium*.

For the next concerted period of hegemony's application and usage, we
must advance to the middle of the nineteenth century, and specifically to
intellectual circles located in Prussia and Piedmont. The new geographical location, of course, is no accident. As the pressure for German and
Italian unification begins to rise to a crescendo, Prussian and Piedmontese
intellectuals in support of such a process – and acting very much with the
interests of their own states in mind – are once again turning to the origins
of the ancient Greek understanding of hegemony as a deliberate means of
underpinning their own state's respective position of supremacy.

The kind of meaning given to the process of hegemony in the intellectual
circles of these two states, however, is, in some areas at least, significantly
different, and if nothing else this in itself can certainly tell us an awful lot
about the ultimate process of German and Italian unification and the kind
of traditions it established. Not for the first, or indeed last, time, the ultimate point of divergence centred on the complex relationship any notion

of hegemony was deemed to have with leadership on the one hand, and outright forms of (military) domination and dictatorship on the other.

Turning to the Prussian/German tradition first, hegemony is seen as a key principle of the German Historicist school of thought, associated first and foremost with Leopold von Ranke. For Ranke, the notion of hegemony is now decisively stripped bare of all its superfluities. In his eyes, it is reducible to nothing more than naked military and political power (with social and economic factors being at best subservient trifles), whereby the only agent of hegemony in world history which really counts is the state, or, to be even more accurate, the very large state. As Peter Gay has pointed out, this was after all 'the age of the great powers, and Ranke wrote their history in the confident conviction that he was concentrating on the main theme. The important powers were important quite simply because they were important. Ranke's God was bored by losers.'[17]

Such a focus on the all-encompassing role of the state was hardly out of the ordinary in nineteenth-century Prussian intellectual circles. An unstinting faith and confidence in its abilities and its potential had long since been the norm, and had very much contributed to the dominant view that the state was nothing less than the pivotal factor of human history. Nor was it just an embodiment of explicit coercive power. For Ranke (clearly following in the footsteps of Hegel), it was also the highest embodiment of morality. International struggles for power are ethical struggles, and to any victor in war must be assigned a superior moral energy and status. It is for this reason that all Ranke's states are distinguished by the requirements of a *raison d'état* and one which is far more unfettered by the constraints of internal processes than had previously been outlined in, say, the writings of von Humboldt.

What essentially mattered most for Ranke was the principle of state action in the domain of foreign policy – it is here, then, that the logic of hegemony could be most firmly identified as the key benchmark of success. In the clash for world influence and supremacy, hegemonic success went to those states which were able and willing to use the powers at their disposal to acquire colonies and dependent, client territories. Without such imperial aspirations, no state would be in a position to command the kind of natural and human resources required for the maintenance, or, the further pursuit, of hegemony. At the same time, however, the struggle for hegemony was constantly being counterposed by the requirements for equilibrium, or, 'a proper balance in the network of competing great powers'. History, therefore, was ultimately reducible to these two great forces: hegemony and equilibrium. While the first was always tentative, the second was itself perennially unstable, and it was the constant interaction and alternation between the two which essentially drove History forward.

For the most part, of course, Ranke himself was writing at a time when there was an essential trough in the overall fortunes of German power abroad. It did not take too long to see, however, that this was a trough behind which a new great wave of movement towards hegemony had been building up. The first product of that new wave was Bismarck. Undoubtedly the ultimate beneficiary was Adolf Hitler.[18]

When it comes to the case of Italy, just as Ranke stands out in Prussia as the great 'ideologue' of German hegemony, so here too one figure more than others dominates the process in which direct connections are made between hegemony and the emerging construction of unification – Vincenzo Gioberti. A philosopher by training and background, Gioberti was an influential figure in the Risorgimento throughout the 1840s until his death in 1852. In the last year of his life he was ordained a priest – for much of the preceding time he had aimed, unsuccessfully, to rally the Papacy to the nationalist cause in the forlorn hope that the Church would stand at the head of the unification process.

Following the failure of the 1848 revolution and the growing disenchantment towards Rome which set in as a result, many of Gioberti's former priorities, if not the ideas themselves, now began to undergo a fundamental seachange.[19] First and foremost, what Gioberti now starts to do is to place far more emphasis on the singular capabilities of Piedmont, which now not only had to be the 'arm' of the nation, but its 'brain' as well. And it is in these later writings on Piedmont, particularly in *The Civil Renewal of Italy* in 1851, that the notion of hegemony and its integral relationship with the unification cause now takes on an absolutely pivotal role.

Always a firm believer in the idea of a federal form of unification, Piedmont is nevertheless now given the specific task of forging a new hegemony by Gioberti, because without such an hegemony there would be no redemption or national genesis for the country. Above all, there had to be a realignment of social forces which could unite the liberal bourgeois intelligentsia with key sections of the popular masses.

For Gioberti, the primary significance of hegemony needed to be taken directly from its earliest origins in ancient Greece. Indeed, on a number of occasions, Piedmont's task is directly correlated with that of Athens at the beginning of the fifth century BC. Hegemony, in other words, is understood as 'a form of primacy, of supremacy of the majority, not underpinned by legalistic or juridical foundations, but properly speaking of a moral efficacy which one component part of a linguistic and national community is able to exercise over the others'.[20]

Similarly, as with the ancient Greeks, while military supremacy is the key factor here, hegemony should also encompass a recognition of other forms of superiority strong enough to make the reliance on coercion and outright force a matter of last resort only. For the ancient Greeks this had been achieved by the superiority of Athenian culture, while in more modern times religion had acted as the main bond. Consequently, two contradictory modes of hegemony have always existed: an 'ordinary' mode which has been characterised by the more indirect, moral supremacy of a given state where hegemony can be seen as more synonymous with 'influence', and an 'extraordinary' mode where the greater superiority of a state's military might has been the main force preserving hegemonic status. The latter, however, should always be viewed as a transition to the former if a genuine form of hegemony is to be maintained for any length of time.

For Gioberti, therefore, military primacy and moral hegemony are the two essential coefficients of any national doctrine and both must be in place for any successful policy of unification. Moreover, history demonstrates that in each case of national unification and consolidation, one province or one city has always emerged as the central embodiment of hegemony, without which a permanent status of national unity would be impossible to sustain. Just as importantly, history also demonstrates that force is the primary mover in the creation of national unity; the recognised dominance of a city or a province is not awarded to it by any process of election, but must be grasped when the internal and external situation is at its most propitious. The contradictory tensions of any hegemonic doctrine or process is thus a constant, integral feature. One cannot escape the fact that in any initial 'moment' of hegemony, coercion and dictatorship are required elements, although wherever possible the basis of any dictatorship should be underpinned not just by the forces of necessity but legitimacy as well.

As we have already seen, however, in the case of any desired Piedmontese hegemony, the ultimate outcome should be a form of Italian unification which would allow a high degree of autonomy to constituent parts. Gioberti, in other words, remained convinced that this form of hegemony would be far more attractive than a Mazzinian approach to unification, or, what would be the other major alternative, a unification forced on Italy by a dominant foreign power. For this reason, he also remained convinced that any 'hegemonic dictatorship' acquired by Piedmont would ultimately receive the consent of the other major Italian principalities. Whether she liked it or not, Piedmont had a 'hegemonic duty' which she could not refuse to accept. If she did refuse, the alternative would be the imposition of a 'false hegemony'. In the first case, it would be a hegemony of those who sincerely loved the cause of Italian patriotism, in the latter, a hegemony based on lies and deceit.[21]

Long ridiculed by many contemporaries and later analysts alike for his extremely convoluted theoretical style, as well as the inconsistency and frequent absurdity of many of his more fanciful ideas, Gioberti is nevertheless at least credited with making the notion of *Italy* legitimate. In his own assessment in the *Prison Notebooks,* Gramsci's primary interest in Gioberti, it has to be said, is the manner in which he can be considered an Italian parallel to Proudhon in France. However, whenever the comparison is made the reader is left in no doubt that Gioberti comes out more favourably than Proudhon, largely thanks to the far more radical position he took up after 1848. Indeed, on a number of occasions Gramsci's explicit praise of Gioberti is extremely fulsome, calling some of his ideas a highly pertinent mixture of originality as well as ones which successfully lent a new sense of pride and respectability to Italian aspirations for national unity, unlike those of Mazzini which were too often 'woolly' and which had all the appearance of 'empty chatter'. More significantly, at one point Gramsci even equates Gioberti's philosophy and general conception of life as a prime illustration of the hegemony of a directive centre over an intellectual class, 'which offers to its adherents an intellectual "dignity" providing a principle of differentiation from the old ideologies which dominated by coercion, and an element of struggle against them ...'.[22] What was Gioberti's real undoing, argues Gramsci, was that his 'great programme' (along with the great programme of Mazzini) inevitably had to give way in the end to the political realism and empiricism of Cavour.[23]

For the purposes of the present study, Gioberti's real significance can be seen in the fact that through his 'rediscovery' and his constant employment of the notion of hegemony in his later writings, this undoubtedly represents one of the main terminological stimulants (if not necessarily conceptual influences) on Gramsci's own decision to make hegemony such a pivotal element of his entire political theory.

The other immediate, and far more vital influence on Gramsci, meanwhile, can be traced to the way in which the notion of hegemony had also been utilised in Russian Social Democratic circles ever since the 1880s; more 'vital' because this was the first overt usage of hegemony within a strictly *Marxist* framework. As this debate, however, really marks the start of the thoroughgoing investigation of the *modern* conceptual significance of hegemony, it is best that we break off the chronological historical excursus here and deal much more fully with the Russian origins of the debate in Chapter 1. What I think we can at least continue to do while in this introductory mode is to set the scene for Chapter 1 by briefly exploring some of the possible *motivations* for the emergence of a debate on hegemony in the hitherto totally different context of late nineteenth-century Russia.

In attempting to explain why the notion of hegemony 'suddenly' made its appearance on the Russian Marxist scene at this time, a number of reasons have been put forward by various commentators. One study, however, stands out from the rest, both in terms of its depth of conceptual engagement as well as in the nature of its broader conclusions: Ernesto Laclau's and Chantal Mouffe's *Hegemony and Socialist Strategy: Towards A Radical Democratic Politics*.[24]

A thoroughgoing critical debate with a great many aspects of this 'post-Marxist' tract will in fact feature regularly throughout the course of the present study. But for now let me limit myself to the very specific issue at hand; namely, the 'genealogical' roots of hegemony in Russia. I would like at this stage to raise two fundamental challenges to the analytical approach taken by Laclau and Mouffe. The first challenge is of a methodological nature. Throughout their analysis, Laclau and Mouffe make repeated references to the very positive way in which they too have been influenced by Foucault's emphasis on epistemological archaeology. This can clearly be seen, for example, in the manner of their very use of a term like 'genealogy' in relation to hegemony, as well as in their much wider support and application of Foucault's conviction in the power of discourse.

This influence notwithstanding, however, at the very outset of their study, and in blatant contravention it seems to me of everything which a Foucauldian genealogy demands, they boldly announce that they are deliberately avoiding the temptation to go back to the origins of hegemony. Instead, they prefer simply to 'pierce a moment in time' in order 'to detect the presence of that void which the logic of hegemony will attempt to fill'.[25] In the process of doing this, two things are immediately apparent. By not excavating the archaeological roots of hegemony and by commencing their study at an already established point in the term's existence, they cannot help but introduce a good degree of distortion into their analysis. Following on from this, one would have to say that this distortion is very deliberate. By piercing the moment of time which they do, it does not take too long to realise just how convenient this is for their ensuing theoretical and political aims.

And it is precisely here that the second challenge or criticism can be made. According to Laclau and Mouffe, the underlying significance of the origin of hegemony is not so much the 'majestic unfolding' of its identity, so much as the fact that it is a fundamental 'response to a crisis'.[26] This crisis, they go on to inform us, is a crisis of Marxism, the parameters of which were very clearly described by Thomas Masaryk in 1898. First, the crisis consisted of 'the new awareness of the opacity of the social, of the complexities and resistances of an increasingly organized capitalism'. Secondly, there was the ever-increasing 'fragmentation of the different positions of social agents which, according to the classical paradigm [of Marxism] should have been united'. From this moment on, Laclau and Mouffe inform us, 'the problem of Marxism has been *to think those discontinuities* and, at the same time, to find *forms reconstituting* the unity of scattered and heterogeneous elements.'[27] Hegemony's emergence, therefore, is designed 'to fill a hiatus that has opened in the chain of historical necessity'.[28]

Now, let us be clear that there is undoubtedly a lot of relevance here in Laclau and Mouffe's analysis, which certainly goes some way in explaining the kind of influences which impacted on Gramsci's thought processes. However, our concern at the moment – and it is supposedly Laclau and Mouffe's concern as well – is to understand the motivations for the emergence of hegemony as a conceptual tool in Marxist circles, *not* just in the West, but even more particularly in Russia. Its appearance there *pre-dates* its conceptual usage in Western Marxist circles by at least three decades, and also pre-dates any notion of a specific 'crisis of Marxism' by more than a decade.

What, then, are the consequences of this? The first thing which I think needs to be stressed is that even assuming that we accept the correctness of this apparent crisis of Marxism at this time, it is a crisis very much of *Western* Marxist circles, which can only possibly have an impact on the conceptual development of hegemony *after* it has already entered the theoretical and practical domain. That is to say, one can acknowledge that such a crisis affected the way hegemony developed in a Western context, but this clearly and self-evidently does not in itself explain its origins in Russia in the mid-1880s; especially when one bears in mind that it is first and foremost associated with the likes of Georgii Plekhanov, a very orthodox Marxist.

Secondly, if one can talk about hegemony's Marxist origins in relation to a 'crisis', in Russia's case it is not so much a crisis of Marxist theory trying to face up to an increasingly organised and established capitalism, so much as it is a very creative response to a different kind of crisis altogether: the crisis of an *emerging,* structurally very weak and insecure Russian capitalism, trying desperately to impose itself in the conditions of a *pre-modern* sociopolitical context and in conjunction with extremely *uneven* forms of development.

To be fair to Laclau and Mouffe, they are not entirely unaware of this different kind of crisis in Russia, but they then go on to describe it as a 'crisis or collapse of what would have been a "normal" historical development'.[29]

And quite clearly, the assumption of normality here is extremely erroneous. From its very inception, there was nothing 'normal' about the developmental course of Russian capitalism and Russian modernity. Indeed, the presumption of normality on Laclau and Mouffe's part is precisely the kind of reductionist, unilinear and determinist form of argument which they categorically reject throughout the rest of their study as the worst perversity of the Marxist approach. In short, the emergence of hegemony in Russia has little or nothing to do with a crisis of Marxist theory, but is instead a response to a crisis of an altogether different kind, the circumstances of which were very unique to Russia and certainly not compatible with earlier developmental processes in the more 'advanced' parts of the West.

As will be highlighted in Chapter 1, as conceived by the Russian Marxists, hegemony has a distinctly temporary air about it, something which is at best tactically contingent or supplemental. It was only with Gramsci – stemming to some extent from the overall crisis of Marxist theory in the West at this time – that hegemony really achieves a more solid, substantive conceptual basis. But crisis or no crisis of Marxist theory, without Gramsci's appreciation and understanding of the very specific and very different Russian roots of hegemony, the concept would have looked a lot different.

3

With the outline of the main evolutionary background of hegemony now complete, let us turn finally to the key aims of the present study. Three major tasks warrant particular mention. The first is very much a direct consequence of the theme which was introduced immediately above: to analyse the way in which the concept of hegemony has interacted between East and West. The notion of interaction here, it should be immediately stressed, implies a great deal more than comparison. As has already been indicated, the East–West motif was absolutely crucial in the origins of the modern notion of hegemony; it remained important in certain key areas throughout the Soviet period (primarily in an oppositional capacity, it has to be said), and now that the Soviet Union has ceased to exist, it has once again taken on enormous *intermediary* significance. Our concern, then, is to appreciate the extent to which this can be considered an interaction of *compatibles*. Is it a mutual process of interactive dialogue? Is it a conceptual form of interaction which speaks a commonly understood language; or at least, to use a key Gramscian term, a language which is organically *translatable?*

Underpinning this part of the study is also a desire to engage with Fernand Braudel's claim (along with others) that Russia, in all manner of ways, should be considered 'the Other Europe'.[30] What are the myriad implications behind this construction of otherness? Is it perhaps simply a desire to reinvoke that age-old notion of antagonism between East and West – the one representing and personifying despotism and the other freedom – which goes back as far as Herodotus, the very founder of History? Or is it more complex than that? As Gramsci himself pointed out, for example, at one level linguistic constructions like 'East' and 'West' are perhaps nothing more than 'historico-cultural' products, largely defined by cognitive processes. After all, 'outside of real history every point on the earth is East and West at the same time'.[31] Having said that, however, within the scope of real history, it is very hard not to acknowledge the almost undeniable sense in which East and West clearly do correspond to concrete facts which thereby allow us to 'objectivise' the reality of any differentiation.[32]

Moreover, continuing with Braudel's terminology for the time being, from the perspective of a shared left ideology, does Russia still remain the 'other'? Was Henri Lefebvre, for instance, right when he argued that any dialogue between Eastern and Western Marxists would always be highly problematic given that in the East a language is used which is essentially 'unreflective' and very much oriented to conditions of struggle and defining ways of behaviour, whereas in the West it is far more imbued with rationalism, a search for objectivism in terms of logical prerequisites, and above all much prefers 'signifying to deciding', even to the point of making a fetish of the process of signifying *per se*.[33]

Similarly, given the context in which we are working in, how does the condition of 'uneven and combined development' affect the nature and manner of the translatability of concepts? To what extent is hegemony capable of transcending the boundaries of pre-modern, modern and (possible) postmodern social systems?

No one has thus far captured the importance of the conceptual interaction of hegemony between East and West more than Perry Anderson. Deconstructing the logic of the concept, Anderson not only highlighted the centrality of this theme in Gramsci's own prison writings, but he also drew attention to the aporias involved in the process of interaction, as well as some of the evident political and ideological risks.[34] Not that Anderson was totally uncritical of Gramsci's formulation of the East–West dialectic. Notwithstanding the 'intensity' and 'originality' of Gramsci's enquiry, he laments that 'Gramsci never finally succeeded in arriving at an adequate Marxist account of the distinction between East and West.'[35] And his failure, according to Anderson, was due to one overriding factor: he too readily assumed the simultaneity of the key concepts in his geographical comparison (especially the concept of the state), which thus led him to ignore the essential conundrum that there was no social or historical *temporal* compatibility between East and West.

This, I have to say, is not a criticism I find in any way compelling. Gramsci was clearly not unaware of the socio-economic gulf which separated East and West. Nor was he unaware of the fundamental consequences which stemmed from a recognition that the Russian state was still essentially mired in a condition of feudal or Asiatic autocracy, as distinct from the bourgeois democratic condition of the Western state, something which even his earliest writings very astutely attested to, and which his notion of translatability also very clearly appreciated. Anderson may well be right in highlighting some of the debilitating antinomies in Gramsci's prison writings (which is hardly surprising given the conditions Gramsci faced), but I think Anderson clearly overreaches the critical potential on this vital issue, a matter which will be dealt with further in Chapter 2.

Having raised Anderson's critique of Gramsci, this leads me nicely on to the second of the general aims of the present study: a broad defence of Gramsci, especially as regards his own conception of hegemony and not least its continued relevance today, both in our overall understanding of what is happening around us, as well as the more specific task of formulating a suitable strategy for the left to pursue – in both East and West.

At one level, this is a defence of Gramsci from those who, no matter how much they profess to admire him, have nevertheless attacked or criticised him from a whole range of different Marxist perspectives, a prime example here being Louis Althusser (see Chapter 4).

What most motivates the ambition to defend Gramsci and his conception of hegemony, however, is arrived at when one considers two other types of critical assessment. First, a defence of Gramsci is certainly needed against those theorists (such as Laclau and Mouffe) who would like the left to adopt a post-Marxist understanding of the conceptual and strategic importance of hegemony. More especially, it is a vehement defence of Gramsci against those who would actually appropriate him in a very *positive* way in their post-Marxist ambitions; that is to say, who see Gramsci as the quintessential post-Marxist of his own time and era (an assertion which at least is *not* made by Laclau and Mouffe).

Elsewhere in the present study, a defence of Gramsci will also be made, sometimes implicitly, at other times explicitly, against a whole series of other allegations which are highly pertinent to the ongoing debate about the precise meaning and significance of hegemony. By far the most absurd of these allegations, I would contend, comes from those commentators who view Gramsci's concept of hegemony as nothing more than 'a totalitarian thought … clothed in liberal guise',[36] a view which is palpably inaccurate on both fronts.

If the above represents one strand in the Western critique of Gramsci, we must likewise not forget the underlying critical reception many of his ideas associated with hegemony were greeted with by Stalinist sympathisers and other official ideologues of the old Soviet regime. This criticism was denoted by official silence in some instances (which in itself spoke volumes of course), and by the occasional surreptitious charge of near-heresy in others (a subject which will form the backdrop to the analysis in Chapter 3).

Arguably a more substantial accusation against Gramsci is that his brand of Marxism ultimately represents a fundamental return to an outmoded, outdated philosophical *idealism*. Certain key elements of the defence here will be dealt with in Chapters 2 and 4 (with the latter drawing heavily on the interpretations of Jacques Texier, especially in his encounter with Norberto Bobbio).

Not unrelated to this broad anti-Marxist stance, but somewhat leading the accusation in a different direction, is another claim very closely associated with Ernesto Laclau and Chantal Mouffe. Underpinning the very foundations of their post-Marxist convictions is the pivotal assertion that with the very introduction of hegemony into the Marxist domain (be it in Russia at the end of the nineteenth century or in the West towards the beginning of the twentieth century), this thereby intrinsically produced 'a logic of the social' which was totally *incompatible* with the basic categories of classical Marxist theory.[37]

By providing a defence on these issues, it is certainly not my intention to envelop Gramsci in a shroud of infallibility. Nor do I wish to clothe him in a very narrow interpretative straitjacket. To do such a thing would offend against virtually everything he stood for. Similarly, it is not my intention to use the platform of defence purely in a negative or negating manner. If and where there is a legitimate defence of Gramsci and his ideas on hegemony, one is at least hopeful that such a defence can at the same time serve as a very positive and constructive celebration of a form of Marxism which can continue to offer a great deal for a much more discerning modern-day audience on the left.

Take, for example, the kind of defence one can apply to the very form, nature and style of his theoretical writings, particularly his prison writings which have often been criticised for their frequent slippages, inconsistencies, contradictions, antinomies, indiscipline, repetition and basic lack of intellectual rigour. To counteract such charges by reference to the debilitating conditions of a fascist jail is precisely the kind of defence, no matter how relevant and valid, which is steeped in negativity. Much better, then, to emphasise the enormous *positive* features on display here. Whenever one reads the *Prison Notebooks,* for example, one cannot escape being drawn into an immense *creative* engagement. The unfinished, spontaneous and *ad hoc* nature of these notes requires the reader to immerse him/herself in an all-embracing creative relationship with the author. Far from being a mere passive recipient of a well-worked out schema of ideas, the reader is instead a fundamental part of the very thought processes of the author, a witness at the beginning of the creative thinking process and an active agent in the ultimate destination which has been mapped out. What we find in Gramsci, therefore, is a lack of dogma and a lack of rigidity which was (and almost certainly remains) second to none – not only in the Communist movement but beyond.[38] Earlier we identified some of the ironies associated with the concept of hegemony. Can there possibly be a greater irony than to end up saluting the intellectual style of the greatest modern exponent of hegemony for the benefits and rewards it brings to his readers, knowing full well that those benefits came about because of his confinement in a fascist jail, and more to the point, a confinement which ultimately killed him?

Moreover, whilst on the broad subject of Gramsci's manner of intellectual composition, it is also useful to remember another extremely positive attribute of the way in which his theory of hegemony was actually formulated. As Perry Anderson has so cogently pointed out:

> Gramsci's theory of hegemony … was based, not only on personal participation in contemporary political conflicts, but also on an extremely close, comparative enquiry into the European past. In other words, it was the product of scientific study of empirical material, in the classic sense in which this was practised by the founders of historical materialism. This was not to be true of any other major thematic innovation in Western Marxism.[39]

And so we come to the final major task of the present study. If we are specifically setting out to defend Gramsci's conception of hegemony, then I think it unavoidably follows that we must also set out to defend *modernity,* for it is within the parameters of modernity (rather than pre- or postmodernity) that socialism – that search for a new civilisation – undoubtedly has the best (the only?) possibility of success.

The question of Gramsci's relationship with modernity is undoubtedly an extremely complex one. At one level, it is possible to argue that Gramsci was someone living on the cusp of the fully fledged modern experience; that is to say, he had a sense of inhabiting the time and space of two dichotomous life worlds. To one side of him, there was the (pre-modern) past which had not yet faded away into the fullness of the twilight. Indeed, echoes and images of this past are clearly seen in many aspects of his thought, especially in his constant evocation of *organicity*. To the other side of him lay a (modern) future, the contours of which were becoming increasingly clear. Thus, as Renate Holub rightly points out, nearly all of Gramsci's writings, albeit perhaps quite unconsciously at times, can be situated in his efforts to understand the major phenomena of modernity: to come to terms 'with the effects of technological modernization on the structure of the social, familial and, above all, cultural world'.[40] In the process of coming to understand the new forces at work, and especially in applying their criteria in the whole realm of knowledge and culture, the picture that undoubtedly emerges is of a theorist with a 'maturing and continuously evolving' sense of attachment to modernity.

Of course, such a claim should not detract from the very serious reservations Gramsci also alluded to, reservations which likewise accrued from his very specific contextual location in the early part of the twentieth century which thereby gave him such obvious opportunities to conceptualise the inherent dangers of modernity.[41] But ultimately it was the potential, and the principle of hope, which accompanied the adventure of modernity, which most influenced Gramsci (as indeed it was to influence the likes of Bertolt Brecht and Ernst Bloch). As he so cogently put it in one of his prison notes: '... people aspire to the adventure which is "beautiful" and interesting because it is the result of their own free initiative, in the face of the adventure which is "ugly" and revolting, because of conditions which are not proposed but imposed by others'.[42]

By introducing the notion of modernity at this particular juncture, there is a clear recognition that perhaps far more complications than solutions are actually being raised here, particularly in today's academic environment of conceptual overkill. To help matters a little, then, let us explore more fully the notion of modernity which is being used here and the nature of the defence which is to be given.

Following Henri Lefebvre – in contrast, for example, to Theodor Adorno on this issue – we need first of all to differentiate modernity from modernism. Far from being seen as correlative with each other, Lefebvre instead views these terms as essentially antithetical, whereby the former encapsulates a sense of critical reflection in contrast to the latter's overpowering sense of certainty and arrogance:

> By modernism, we mean the consciousness which successive ages, periods and generations had of themselves ... of triumphalist images and

projections of self. It is made up of many illusions, plus a modicum of insight. Modernism is a sociological and ideological fact. Its pretensions and fanciful projects can be seen in the press *in statu nascendi*. Exhibitions are mounted to reconstruct it.

By modernity, however, we understand the beginnings of a reflective process, a more-or-less advanced attempt at critique and auto-critique, a bid for knowledge. We contact it in a series of texts and documents which bear the mark of their era and yet go beyond the provocation of fashion and the stimulation of novelty. Modernity differs from modernism just as a concept which is being formulated in society differs from social phenomena themselves, just as a thought differs from actual events.[43]

Second, given the concentration on the political throughout the present study, the notion of modernity is being used as a very broad set of political indicators. As for the kind of qualities one has in mind here one should certainly single out, if only in passing at this stage, the attributes of universalism, heroism (in the shape of the so-called historical 'grand narratives' which are the product of modernity), collectivism, institutionalism and libertarianism. In addition, one should also not forget such crucial features as the emergence of the *self* as the main subject of agency within modernity, as well as the emergence of a very distinctive kind of new, enlarged public space in which political contestation and the search for new forms of legitimacy can now take place. And last, but by no means least, there are the enormous political effects of the modern turn to rationalism: in the manner in which, for example, human coexistence is redefined and renegotiated according to principles of 'symmetric reciprocity'; as well as the way in which modernity uses reason to create its own normativity exclusively *'out of itself'*.[44] Indeed, it is precisely through this process, one could argue, that the logic of hegemony makes its appearance on the modern stage.

Virtually all of these qualities, of course, are ones that postmodernists would wish to condemn to the proverbial dustbin of history, along with the category of history itself. As Jacques Derrida has written, for example, modernity is nothing more than 'an imperative for totalitarianism';[45] or to use the more lyrical tones of Jay Bernstein, 'the site of beauty bereaved'.[46] Indeed, now that communism has collapsed in the East, we are repeatedly told that the ghost of modernity can finally be exorcised in the West as well. As Zygmunt Bauman has critically noted:

Social engineering, the principle of communal responsibility for individual fate, the duty to provide commonly for single survivals, the

tendency to view personal tragedies as social problems, the command-
ment to strive collectively for shared justice – all such moral precepts as
used to legitimize (some say motivate) modern practices have been compromised beyond repair by the spectacular collapse of the communist
system. No scruples. No supra-individual commitments contaminating
individual enjoyment. The past has descended to its grave in disgrace.[47]

In their place, postmodernists would much prefer to espouse such things
as privacy, subjectivism, localism, difference, plurality and simulacra. As
Chapter 5 hopes to show, however, any notion of constructing a new
hegemony (at least for the left) on such foundations is surely a delusion of
the worst kind. What in effect it leads to is the 'privatisation of dissent'
and a form of social monadic isolationism. To borrow Max Weber's well-
known metaphor, however bad the 'iron cage' of modernity might be, there
is at least the in-built possibility of release, an option which is far better
than the advice that one should simply relax inside the cage since all possibility of escape is futile.

Third, and finally, to quote Marshall Berman amongst others, the notion
of modernity is also being used as a 'mode of vital experience'; an 'experience of space and time, of the self and others, of life's possibilities and
perils'.[48] It is here, I think, that the full remit of modernity opens up in
front of us (just as it did for Gramsci and for Marx before him).

If anything can be said to characterise the 'modern' condition, it is
undoubtedly its overwhelming sense of disorientation, dualism and its state
of contradictoriness. No one, of course, captured this better or more elo-
quently than Marx through his motifs of things pregnant with their contrary
and of solids melting into air. If this is one side of the modern condition,
however, there is also another one. What modernity also produced was
the intellectual (as well as the material) tools and scope to become aware
and conscious of these contradictions, as well as the hope and conviction
that the contradictions could be overcome. The key here, of course, was
the dialectic: the dominant methodology of the whole of modernity, which
would both ensure the discovery and conceptualisation of the essential
contradictions of modern life as well as their transcendence into a higher
form of unity, totality, coherence and solidity.

As Berman thus notes, these two sides of modernity represent nothing
less than 'a paradoxical unity': a unity of disunity in which the forces of
disintegration and renewal are in perpetual struggle with each other. Its
tone is one of irony which speaks of the devastations of modernity being
overcome by the intrinsic, unfulfilled potential of modernity, of the hope
'that the modernities of tomorrow and the day after tomorrow will heal

the wounds that wreck the modern men and women of today'. And it is an awareness that the most thoroughgoing critique of modernity can only possibly come 'from those who most ardently embrace its adventure and romance'.[49]

It is precisely this set of paradigms, therefore, that the left must continue to engage with and work to accordingly, as Gramsci himself did with his logic of hegemony. Only by attempting to give credence to the transcendence of contradictions within modernity; only by retaining the conviction that to understand is also to unify, can the left retain its vibrancy and its creativity. To renege on this task, as postmodernists impel us to do, would leave the left sterile. Moreover, without the sustenance of its 'grand narratives' and hopes, it would undoubtedly succumb (as we can see already) to an all-consuming boredom.

A prevailing sense of irony, then, may well be the dominant attribute of modernity. But better a sense of ironic commitment within the parameters of modernity than the kind of 'comic agnosticism' that has become one of the defining features of postmodernism.[50] As Lefebvre reminds us, better a consciousness endowed with irony than one that is not, because without the method of irony there is no real scope either for critical intellectual reflection or the necessity of opting and the sense of risk that every option involves:

> The meaning of history, man's history, must be understood and vanquished; it is not written in advance by a destiny or a determinism; meanwhile, the possible and the impossible come face to face; the possible may fail, but it *was* possible; the irony of history is unfathomable, yet the gap between what was intended and what is achieved can be reduced, otherwise revolution would always be meaningless. Irony is not meaningless.[51]

It is a viewpoint, of course, that Gramsci would have entirely shared.

Having started our search for the origins of hegemony in Ancient Greece, let us also end there. In light of our understanding of modernity and the manner in which it should be defended, perhaps the real modern hero of the left should be none other than Sisyphus. As Albert Camus wrote of this 'proletarian of the gods' who is both so powerless and rebellious: 'At each of those moments when [Sisyphus] leaves the heights and gradually sinks towards the lairs of the gods, he is superior to his fate. He is stronger than his rock.' The myth here, Camus argues, is tragic only at the rare moments when it becomes conscious: 'Sisyphus … knows the whole extent of his wretched condition, it is what he thinks of during his descent. [Nevertheless the] lucidity that was to constitute his torture at the same time crowns his victory. There is no fate that cannot be surmounted by scorn.' For these reasons: 'One must imagine Sisyphus happy.' After all, the struggle itself back towards the heights 'is enough to fill a man's heart'.[52]

1 The Russian Origins of Hegemony

> There was no bourgeoisie, the need was not for it:
> For the revolution they needed capitalism,
> So they could make it in the name of a proletariat.
>
> Maksimilian Voloshin, *Bourgeoisie*

Russian Exceptionalism and the Development of Capitalism

In connecting the concept of hegemony with the rise of Russian Social Democracy at the end of the nineteenth century, two factors stand out above all others. Very much interconnected with each other, they revolve around the initial evolution of capitalism in the country (and the accompanying socio-economic changes) and the widespread debate concerning Russia's desire and capacity to maintain a process of 'exceptionalism', first and foremost towards the Western mode of civilisation.

A sense of Russian exceptionalism with regards to the West had been proverbial ever since the Mongol invasions, and notwithstanding the efforts of modernising Tsars like Peter the Great, had remained an important legitimating factor for most Russian rulers. Not for them were the slowly evolving yardsticks of European rationality needed to give credence to their political or cultural psyche. Fyodor Tyutchev might well have over-exaggerated the situation when he claimed in his most celebrated poem that there was absolutely no capacity to fathom Russia with the mind, and that one was therefore only left with an irrepressible 'belief' in her uniqueness. Where he was accurate, however, was in the conviction that none of the yardsticks ever quite squared up to the reality of Russia. To understand Russia always meant changing the yardsticks in some shape or form.

This essential belief in an exceptional Russia was designated in a whole spectrum of different areas, ranging from structures of one kind or another, to broad and expansive developmental patterns. Above all, however, it was most commonly designated by the nature of the relationship which existed between state and society. Here was a relationship as unique to Russia in the early-to-mid nineteenth-century world of Western capitalism as it had been unique to the fifteenth-century world of Western feudalism.

A useful guide to comprehending this relationship is Max Weber's notion of patrimonialism. Although it is of strictly limited use in understanding the evolutionary process of Russian state power, its implicit *cultural* interpretation of that power certainly has considerable relevance.[1] Not only was the state–society relationship in Russia one in which the state possessed an effective monopoly on all political authority, public information, economic resources and wholesale trade; it was also a relationship which created no space whatsoever for individual or group (estate) rights. It was one where every individual – serf, noble or government bureaucrat – was bound to the state in unlimited service. More to the point, it was a relationship which viewed the state, through the person of the ruler, as not only sovereign but *proprietor* of the realm as well. In short, it was a relationship of bondage and subservience. As Boris Chicherin wrote in 1858: 'All without exception were obliged to serve the State for the term of their lifetimes, each in his allotted place.'[2]

Not only was the state all-powerful in relation to society, it was also, in effect, *independent* of it as well. Within such a rigid scheme of subservience, it was simply impossible for any really effective rival power-centres to emerge. Even the Russian nobility could not evolve a homogeneous class identity similar, say, to the European feudal aristocracy, which might possibly serve as a counterweight to the power of the state. It simply did not possess the kind of corporate privileges which would provide it with such an identity. Even after they were officially liberated from state service in 1762 and were allowed to possess landed property of their own, the formal rights of the Russian landed aristocracy were never really enshrined on a firm legal basis. By the very process of contracting out of the traditional Russian social system, their newly acquired private property and continued existence as a class became ever more dependent on the state and continued service to it. This fate was also to befall the peasants a century later.

Such grants of freedom to Russian social classes as occurred in the eighteenth and nineteenth centuries, then, did not by themselves fundamentally alter the basic relationship that had always existed between state and society. What did begin to alter the relationship, however, was the added ingredient of a gradual transition to capitalism. With widespread changes in the economic substructure of Russian society, its social composition now took on a whole new significance.

Two primary reasons have often been cited by historians to explain the Russian state's new-found commitment to a rapid process of capitalisation: the need to maintain the country's international standing, together with the need to provide greater domestic financial stability. Whichever one of these reasons one prioritises, there can be little doubt that the catalyst occurred in 1855 with the fall of Sevastopol. The hypertrophic concentration of power in the hands of the Russian monarchy had always been accompanied by a long, sustained and largely successful process of territorial expansion. With Russia's defeat in the Crimean War, this connection was fatally undermined, and it was on the foundations of this crisis that a new phase of modernisation now began.

One of the first tangible consequences was, of course, the Emancipation Act of 1861. Restricted though it may have been in its real emancipatory effects, it did undoubtedly have major social consequences, which were in good part born out of its very restrictiveness.

First of all, it without doubt aggravated conflicts which had long been in place between the nobility and the state. By the measures of the Act, the old authority of the landowners was considerably reduced as the peasants were now granted new entitlements over the land they cultivated. Attempts to compensate the landowners – by means of monetary incentives, as well as by the introduction of new organs of self-administration (the *zemstvo*) – did little to offset such grievances. If anything, they exacerbated them. As for the former serfs themselves, they too inevitably felt cheated by the new economic burdens which were imposed on them, and now that the 'mystique' of the old order was showing the first signs of decomposition, their new sense of pent-up grievances were clearly ripe for a whole range of possible articulations. If the landowners and the peasants had their own separate antagonistic grievances to bear, they were at least at one in their hostility to another major consequence of the 1861 Act – the emergence of a much stronger, richer class of peasants in the guise of the *kulaks*.

In the manufacturing domain, meanwhile, the process of modernisation – in the form of industrialisation and urbanisation – was having an equally dislocative social effect. As Perry Anderson has pointed out, after having gone a good way in relinquishing its grip on the agricultural sector, it was almost as though the Russian state sought compensation and consolation for this by massively entrenching itself in industry.[3] And as the motor of the industrialisation programme itself, it was inevitable that it would be the state which would be the main procreator of new class formations in this sector. Certainly the Russian bourgeoisie which appeared at this time was very much a conscious product of its creation. Without the finances of the state, its protective tariffs, its deliberate destruction of handicraft production, and its overall paternalism, the emergence of a Russian bourgeoisie, to put it very mildly, would have been a lot more difficult. The increasing success of its generation, however, was at the same time not without its contradictions. The state and the bourgeoisie may have been structurally dependent on each other, but this was very much a symbiosis which had the potential right from the very start of weakening and ultimately destroying both sides. In particular, the state was to learn that controlling the bourgeoisie was a very different matter from controlling the nobility. For all of the financial resources thrown at industrialisation and capitalisation, the project also depended on the innovative and creative resources of the new bourgeois elite. But it was precisely these capacities which were being stifled by the state's reluctance to relinquish any degree of control. Similarly, it was inevitable that at some point in time, the interests of the two parties would have to diverge dramatically over the question of private ownership of the means of production. On top of this, the almost total reliance by the state on foreign loans at this time was certainly bound to suffocate the domestic room for manoeuvrability. The resulting overblown tax burden in particular could not do otherwise than block the development of the internal capitalist market, without which long-term investment was unimaginable.

Whatever problems the state faced with its new bourgeois offspring, they quickly paled into insignificance with the traumas aroused by the other social incarnation of capitalism's birth – the industrial working class. If the bourgeoisie was incomparable with the nobility as an embodiment of a dominant social group willing to succumb to absolute state control in a purely docile and servile manner, the comparison between the working class and the peasantry as embodiments of subaltern social forces could not have been wider. Where the enslavement of the latter and its ingrained love of order and stability had always been a major pillar of the absolute state, the personality features of the former were preconditioned to bring disorder and instability. This was not necessarily because of any peculiar 'psychological' features it may have had, but more from the fact that its very structure, organisation and cultural outlook were to be very much shaped in this way by the unique environment into which it was born, and within which its very survival depended. As Tim McDaniel has argued, the very process of a state-induced capitalism in Russia at this time was itself responsible for engendering extraordinary degrees of worker militancy and solidarity, degrees of militancy and solidarity certainly well beyond levels found in other capitalist countries.[4]

Finally, one should not forget the intelligentsia. Prior to the emergence of capitalist structures in Russia, the intelligentsia had largely been an alienated, rootless caste; a constant source of criticism to the existing 'patrimonial' structure, but one which lacked the power and the resources of a well-defined, cohesive social interest standing behind it. As the process of capitalisation developed, however, and with it the dissolution of former estates and castes and their replacement by new groups far less subservient to the state, so the Russian intelligentsia was provided with a whole new *raison d'être*. A need for a new, far greater secularised system of higher education, a need for a whole new breed of experts to run and service the new industrial economy, together with a growing recognition of the benefits of a well-read and educated general public, all created brand new opportunities for the intelligentsia to make their mark on this newly evolving society. At the same time, it likewise created opportunities for the newly emerging social groups and classes to accrue their own 'opinion-moulders' of society.

In previous eras, the Russian state had always managed in the end to integrate the various competing dynamics of the modernisation process into a fairly coherent structure, one which kept its degree of absolute control largely intact. The burning question from the second half of the nineteenth century onwards was: how and by what means would the present modernisation process be brought under similar forms of control? Three options were open to the state: absorption, accommodation and resistance. At various times all three options were tried. In the end all three failed.

Of the three, absorption was needless to say the state's preference; it was, after all, the one that had traditionally been used with considerable success in the past, and in a whole series of ways – for example, the *Zubatovshchina* – was repeatedly tried over the ensuing years. Resistance was the state's second preference. The least preferred option, meanwhile, was accommodation, or at least any serious process of accommodation towards the new social interests which had been generated. Accommodation ultimately meant introducing a real degree of politics into the traditional state–society relationship. It implied a new scope for the free play of autonomous interests and opinions, whereby former mechanisms of control would have to be turned into mechanisms of communication, and former processes of exclusion would have to be transformed into processes of inclusion. Control and exclusion had been the hallmarks of the state's all-pervasive concentration of power, but even in the past they had also been shown to be a testimony of the state's underlying fragility. If the fragile condition of the state was not to prevail, it clearly had to forego the old notion that politics was nothing more than an administrative task which could be best carried out by an omnipotent arbiter.

The reluctance to pay the going 'market price' of politics proved in the end to be a main watershed in the demise of the old style Tsarist-based exceptionalism in Russia. It also proved to be a key watershed in the emergence of a totally different kind of Russian exceptionalism – Bolshevism.

Plekhanov and the Concept of Hegemony

The non-Western exceptionalism personified in the 'official' structure of relations between state and society in the Russian tradition was often matched by a deeply inherent exceptionalism in many of the attempts to overcome that tradition. As the slow evolution of Russian development was ever more sanctified into an all-embracing Russian 'Idea', it was not only the conservative Slavophile tendencies in Russian intellectual circles that came to embrace its spectre for their own purposes. Many progressive radical thinkers and activists began to embrace their own version of this new messianism as well, particularly in the third quarter of the nineteenth century.

The spiritual essence of the oppositional exceptionalism of this era was the aversion to the principle of politics representing the art of the possible. Politics as a means was never part of the vocabulary of this new generation of radicals. There was only the politics of the end, the goal. Indeed, everything was always posited in *absolute* terms: 'absolute freedom, absolute equality [and] absolute happiness. Anything less than the Absolute was inconceivable'; and above all, pragmatism was to be regarded 'as an invention of the devil'.[5]

The Absolute of all absolutes, meanwhile, was the 'people'. Just as the official Russian tradition had succeeded in atomising the people *en masse* to the dictates and needs of the Tsarist state, so the radical exceptionalists likewise retained a concept of an atomised people as a collective homogenous unit, though a people that was now deified on the altar of Russia's future salvation and happiness. Indeed, no matter how much the people failed in practice to live up to the expectations of the radical exceptionalists, the term was nevertheless constantly proclaimed with religious-like fervour.

The underlying strategy of this radical exceptionalism encompassed the twin themes of sweeping away the old order and tradition by political terror (and assassinations), together with the inauguration of a new order by cultural re-education in the form of the 'going to the people' movement. Any notion, meanwhile, of Russia following a Western path of capitalist modernisation was rejected, partly on the practical basis that it would be totally impossible to create the requisite infrastructure for this kind of development and, more importantly, on the spiritual basis that the people would simply not accept its inherent attributes of injustice, inequality, and social fragmentation. As Szamuely has so aptly commented, for the radical exceptionalists '[the] horrors of industrial capitalism ... fulfilled the same function [for them] ... as the lurid portrayal of Hell did in medieval Christian theology'.[6] The inhumanity of the system, the abhorrent nature of bourgeois rule, and the contemptible style of middle-class life were all considered paths down which Russia had no reason and no need to travel. A new road to Calvary was the only solution.

It was set against the failure of the oppositional exceptionalists, espe-cially after the assassination of Tsar Alexander II in 1881, that a new form of opposition to the Russian tradition was inaugurated: orthodox Russian Marxism in the form of Social Democracy and in the person of Georgii Plekhanov. Exiled to Geneva in January 1880 for his radical espousal of Populist exceptionalism throughout the previous decade, Plekhanov's expe-rience with Western life and conditions was to have a dramatic effect on his way of thinking. First and foremost, Plekhanov was introduced, more fully than he had been before, to the ideas and writings of Marx and Engels. Through his discovery of the 'universal', 'scientific' foundations of Marx-ist thought, Plekhanov now began to move slowly away from his former exceptional ideas about Russia to a position which accepted Russia's inevi-table 'Europeanisation of social life'.

Describing his reaction to the theories of Marx to an 'Ariadne thread', which led him 'out of the labyrinth of contradictions' into which his thought had been driven under the influence of earlier exceptionalist mentors like Chernyshevsky and Bakunin,[7] Plekhanov quickly came to the opinion that Russia's initial experience of capitalism was neither transitory nor wholly negative. Russian society, he argued, had already begun to cut 'the Gordian knot' of its own tradition, and the only possible outcome of the transi-tional phase it was now going through would be the establishment of a bourgeois-constitutional order, in essence no different from that existing in the West.

The irony of Plekhanov's emphatic conviction of the inevitability of universal laws of development applying to Russia in the same manner as they once applied to the West, was certainly not lost on many of his con-temporaries. Just at the time when Plekhanov had discovered the orthodox Marx and Engels, so Marx and Engels had themselves given more credence than they had ever previously done to the notion that Russia indeed was an exceptional civilisation with its own unique laws of development, a unique civilisation that might well progress from a semi-Asiatic mode of production to socialism in one historical leap on the basis of its commune tradition.[8] Being 'more Marxist than Marx', however, was an accusation that Plekhanov was going to get used to.

In his first major works in exile, Plekhanov's primary task was to try to expose, once and for all, the fallacy of the exceptionalist standpoint amongst the opposition forces. As his main weapon, he turned to an analysis of the development of capitalism in Russia and the effect this was having on the old social relationships. Taking issue with the Populist notion that Western-style capitalism was no more than 'an artificial transplant' which Russian traditions would easily withstand, Plekhanov countered with his belief that capitalism had in fact already taken root in Russia, and its seeds were beginning to affect virtually all aspects of her economic life. In *Our Differences*, written in 1885, a whole host of facts and statistics were cited in order to demonstrate such things as the penetration of foreign capital into Russia, the ever-growing dependence of the small handicraft industry on commercial capital, the process of 'proletarianisation' of the craftworkers and the transformation of small handicraft production into a domestic system of large-scale production.[9] The result of all this, Plekhanov went on, had been the creation of new bourgeois and proletarian classes, as well as a system of production predominantly oriented to the newly created urban centres.

As for the peasant commune, meanwhile – the source of all hope for the Populists and most other exceptionalist forces – this too had succumbed to the penetration of capitalist forces. Again, citing a wealth of statistical information, Plekhanov was adamant that by means of the development of a money economy and commodity production, the old system of communal land tenure had been effectively undermined from within, and in its place a new form of *private* ownership was beginning to emerge.

In what was seen as a final *coup de grâce* to the radical exceptionalist forces, Plekhanov also turned his attention to the likely effects a sudden curtailment of this process of development would have, both on society as a whole and on those who might envisage leading a revolutionary *coup d'état*, either in the name of a socialism that artificially speeded up Russia's modernisation, or, in the name of a socialism that prevented that very process of modernisation. Writing now in ever more orthodox Marxist tones, Plekhanov was adamant that it was impossible to 'create, by decrees, conditions alien to the very character of existing economic relations'. Everything, he went on, would combine to defeat a movement prematurely interfering in a process of capitalist development that was already well under way. Its own unpreparedness, the hostility of the higher estates and the rural bourgeoisie, the people's indifference to its organisational plans, and the underdeveloped state of economic relations in general were objective factors that could not be overcome, irrespective of the degree of revolutionary desire.[10] As for the leader of such an attempt, he necessarily would find himself in an insoluble dilemma. Citing a passage from Engels' *The Peasant War in Germany*, Plekhanov asserted:

What he *can* do contradicts all his previous actions, principles and immediate interests of his party, and what he *ought* to do cannot be done. In a word, he is compelled to represent not his party or his class, but the class for whose domination the movement is then ripe. In the interests of the movement he is compelled to advance the interests of an alien class, and to feed his own class with phrases and promises, and with the asservation that the interests of that alien class are their own interests. Whoever is put into this awkward position is irrevocably lost.[11]

Should a revolutionary elite try to maintain control in such a situation, then this would merely result 'in a political monster similar to the ancient Chinese or Peruvian empires', in other words, to a renewal of Tsarist despotism with nothing more than a different lining.[12] In the objective conditions prevailing in Russia, therefore, new types of struggle were required to inflict a defeat on the entrenched old order. At the heart of these new struggles, *political* activities would now have to play a predominant role; and part and parcel of any new-style political struggle would be the attempt to secure a dominant position of class hegemony – *gegemoniya*.[13]

When it comes to a dissection of this newly introduced principle of hegemony in Russian oppositional affairs, its linkage with an emphasis on the importance of strictly political activities is very crucial. Placing politics at the forefront of the anti-Tsarist struggle had been a primary concern of Plekhanov's ever since he had read *The Communist Manifesto* in the early months of his Genevan exile. In an introduction to his own translation of this work in 1882, Plekhanov was now convinced that future social changes in Russia could only come by means of a long drawn-out process of political struggle that would parallel the economic changes being introduced by the development of capitalist productive relations. The old terrorist methods of struggle had brought no sympathy whatsoever from any of Russia's social forces, and by the very process of terrorist activity, any thought about creating a much broader social movement of reform had been subsumed under the simple cult of destruction.[14]

A year later, meanwhile, in his *Socialism and the Political Struggle*, Plekhanov returned to an attack on the tactics pursued by his former Populist allies. Once again criticising the former total rejection of having anything to do with politics, Plekhanov was now adamant that *only* a political struggle geared towards the creation of a broad emancipation movement would have the strength to destroy the social edifice of absolutism. Likening politics to 'an earthquake that could destroy a poultry house', Plekhanov was convinced that political practice had to overcome the erroneous ideals of the old Populist believers.[15]

Politics was not something that existed in a social vacuum, however, and for Plekhanov, of course, the new emphasis on political struggle was inseparable from the emphasis on *class* struggle. For a new class trying to break free from the chains of the old order, the political struggle had to be the main mechanism for achieving emancipation. Upon achieving political domination, a hegemonic class would be in a position of carrying out a deep-seated reconstruction of society, and would also have the weapon of state power to secure it against the blows of reaction.

Clearly, then, as a committed orthodox Marxist, Plekhanov was convinced that the long-term political future of Russia now lay with the emerging proletarian class. If, in the eyes of the old Populists, it was the people that had been seen as the repository of absolute justice, absolute freedom and absolute human happiness, they now had to be replaced by the proletariat.

While the long-term future belonged to the proletariat, however, Plekhanov's Marxist orthodoxy could not belie the fact that the *short-term* future had to lie with the hegemony of the bourgeoisie. It was this class which possessed the only effective means and resources to counter the old traditions still governing Russia, and it was this class whose interests were most directly being affected by a lack of recognised social and political rights, which could be put at the service of their ever-expanding economic interests. As he wrote in *Our Differences:*

> Our bourgeoisie is now undergoing an important metamorphosis; it has developed lungs which require the fresh air of political self government, but at the same time its gills, with which it still breathes in the troubled water of decaying absolutism, have not yet completely atrophied. Its roots are still in the soil of the old regime, but its crown has already attained a development which shows that it absolutely needs to be transplanted.[16]

Still, despite the recognition that bourgeois hegemony would be the logical outcome of the future disintegration of the old order, Plekhanov had at least consoled himself and his orthodox Marxist supporters with the possibility of *accelerating* the conditions for the future proletarian hegemony. This was largely to be achieved by two main processes. First, while always insisting that the interests of the new bourgeoisie remained fundamentally incompatible with the continuation of the old-style absolutism, and that therefore a political conflict between the two was unavoidable, Plekhanov was nevertheless convinced that the bourgeoisie would never be in a position to inflict a defeat on absolutism *by itself.* Political freedom, he regularly told his supporters, could only be attained by a mutual alliance of the new social forces against the old, and this would inevitably be a matter of great significance for the proletariat and its own process of development. Reminding his audiences that Marxist theory dictated a bourgeois-democratic regime as the first progressive step for Russia's modernisation (or Europeanisation), he also reminded them that the proletariat had a unique chance to secure suitable practical benefits for itself, if it agreed to render its services to the cause of bourgeois hegemony. First and foremost, civil rights under a new bourgeois regime should be universally granted by means of a formal constitution. The proletariat should openly be allowed to set up party organisations and trade unions, and should also have access to the media in getting its message across. By such means, the social emancipation of the Russian working class could well follow quite quickly upon the fall of absolutism, and in the very process of assisting the creation of bourgeois hegemony, the conditions for a future proletarian hegemony would also be established.[17]

As for the second strategic plank of a future proletarian hegemony, this, if anything, was seen as even more crucial. So as to avoid being the tool of the bourgeoisie, and so as to avoid being subsumed under any future bourgeois hegemony – a fate which had befallen most of the Western working class in Plekhanov's view – the Russian proletariat should engage in the coming struggle for the overthrow of absolutism as 'an independent and self-interested force'. To achieve this, a special role would have to be played by the socialist intelligentsia, upon whom lay the task of correctly channelling the consciousness of the proletariat.[18]

This implicit linkage between hegemony and consciousness, so important in the later Leninist (and, of course, Gramscian) framework of analysis, was first posited by Plekhanov in the early 1880s. The socialist intelligentsia, he wrote in *Socialism and the Political Struggle:*

> ... must become the leader of the working class in the impending emancipation movement, [it must] explain to it its political and economic interests and also the interdependence of those interests and [it] must prepare them to play an independent role in the social life of Russia. They must exert all their energy so that in the very opening period of the constitutional life of Russia our working class will be able to come forward as a separate party with a definite social and political programme. The detailed elaboration of that programme must, of course, be left to the workers themselves, but the intelligentsia must elucidate for them its principal points ...[19]

Plekhanov, it is fair to say, never did square the circle of precisely how the workers were to engage in the detailed elaboration of the programme and how the intelligentsia were to elucidate it. Only Lenin was able to resolve this division of labour. Nevertheless, as already emphasised, an important linkage had been made between a process designed to culminate in political domination (hegemony) by a leading class, and the manner in which that class achieved its consciousness.

Although Plekhanov never left a clearly worked-out definition of hegemony in his writings, it is quite clear that the term had enormous strategic influence on his understanding of precisely how the working class was to attain power in Russia in the future. Its association with such things as the primacy of political struggle, temporary class alliances, the maintenance of class autonomy within any alliance, and the importance of consciousness being formed by intellectuals, are all significant landmarks, not only in his own limited use of hegemony, but in establishing the future reference points of a term which was indeed to acquire enormous significance under future Russian revolutionary thinkers, most notably, of course, Lenin himself.

Hegemony and Leninist Exceptionalism

According to one of Plekhanov's biographers, when Lenin first met the 'father' of Russian Marxism in his Genevan exile in May 1895, the young revolutionary idealist was by no means in full agreement with Plekhanov's strategy of attaining class hegemony. A central plank of disagreement between the two revolved around their view of the importance to be attached to the newly emerging bourgeois class and their liberal brethren. Whereas Lenin, equating Russian liberals with Western liberals, was firmly convinced that the bourgeoisie was much more inclined to be a major force supporting a basic status quo in Russia, Plekhanov, as we have already seen, was of the opinion that for as long as absolutism continued to exist in Russia, the bourgeoisie would inevitably have a revolutionary role to play. While 'you turn your back to the liberals', he is reported to have told Lenin, 'I prefer to turn my face towards them.'[20]

Such disagreements were apparently smoothed over by the end of the meeting, with Lenin admitting the error of his ways at no substantial cost to their relationship. Indeed, over the next few years or so, the two men were to work very closely together, specifically on the project of establishing an independent Russian Social Democratic newspaper, a task, in Lenin's words, which was absolutely crucial to establishing the basis of Plekhanov's now 'famous' mode of hegemony.[21]

Above all, Lenin's broad acceptance of the Plekhanovite strategy of class hegemony was most noticeable in their joint struggle against the economist/corporatist tendency that was now beginning to appear within Russian Social Democracy, a tendency which negated the core of hegemonic strategy by its disinclination to engage in political struggles and its reductionist espousal of pure and simple economic-based struggles solely within the workplace. In works such as *The Tasks of the Russian Social Democrats* (1898) and *What is to be Done?* (1902), as well as others at this time, Lenin forcefully lent his voice of support to the old Plekhanovite emphasis on the primary need for the new social classes to involve themselves directly with political activities as a means of advancing the broad democratic cause. More specifically, Lenin was likewise adamant that the working class, albeit from an independent standpoint, had to set itself the task of helping to create a bourgeois-constitutional order, by means of which the working class would be given the tools and the political space to then go on and work for its own future hegemony. Last, but by no means least, Lenin was also at one with Plekhanov on the significance that should be attached to a new socialist intelligentsia in preparing the relevant kind of class consciousness for the coming phases of hegemonic struggle – the bourgeois hegemonic phase first, and then the proletarian hegemonic phase that would follow.

On all of these issues Lenin and Plekhanov were seemingly in full agreement, and for most commentators the fundamental differences that emerged between the two were only noticeable after the 1903 Congress of the Russian Social Democratic Labour Party and the abject failure of the 'bourgeois' revolution of 1905. While this is true in terms of dating the origin of their *personal* rift, from the perspective of their theoretical and strategic differences towards class hegemony, it is significant to note that even while Lenin was giving firm support to the Plekhanovite line of hegemony after 1895, he was at the same time often espousing various nuances that were almost certainly bound to leave him in disagreement with Plekhanov at some stage in the future. The 1903/1905 dividing line, in other words, has to be seen as the *continuation* of their theoretical and strategic differences, rather than the beginning.

What was quite clear from a very early stage was that Lenin's exceptional strength of 'revolutionary will' would inevitably come up against the rigorously deterministic framework within which Plekhanov (and the other pioneers of Russian Marxism) had set the Social Democratic movement. Lenin was always going to find it difficult to accept the kind of hegemony that Plekhanov had envisaged for Russian Social Democracy, both as regards the kind of allies the new working class should seek, as well as the *nature* of the alliances it should accept.[22] Whether Plekhanov personally recognised it or not prior to 1903/1905, there is no escaping the fact that a form of Leninist exceptionalism was on the cards from the very beginning. And the component parts of Plekhanov's broad evolution of a strategy of hegemony were to play a large part in the subsequent development of this new form of radical exceptionalism.

The first nuance of difference espoused by Lenin concerned the objectives to be gained by engaging in political struggle. As we have already seen, although Lenin was an ardent supporter of Plekhanov's emphasis on the need to engage directly in political struggle, it was nevertheless quite clear that he had a somewhat different conception of politics in mind. Writing in *What is to be Done?*, Lenin was adamant that 'there is politics and politics'.[23] Going on to explain what he meant by this distinction, he quoted a passage from the first edition of *Iskra:* 'Social Democracy does not tie its hands, it does not restrict its activities to some one preconceived plan or method of political struggle; it recognises all means of struggle, as long as they correspond to the forces at the disposal of the Party.'[24]

As it stood, this object of politics was not all that different from the kind of ideas Plekhanov had been espousing ever since his 'conversion' to Marxism in the early 1880s. In conjunction with other of his writings, however, Lenin's advocacy of a narrow behaviouralist, rather than a broader procedural, approach to politics did represent a clear difference of attitude.

As early as 1898, in his pamphlet *The Tasks of the Russian Social Democrats,* Lenin had made it clear that working-class engagement in political activity had nothing to do with a genuine articulation of recognised different interests, nor with a process of building alliances through consensual arrangements. No political alliances, he argued,

> ... can, or should, lead to compromises or concessions on matters of theory, programme or banner ... [This] attitude of the working class, as a fighter against the autocracy, towards all the other social classes and groups in the political opposition is very precisely determined ... Moreover, the Social Democrats render this support in order to expedite the fall of the common enemy, but expect nothing *for themselves* from these temporary allies, and concede nothing to them.[25]

Lenin's notion of the Social Democrats expecting 'nothing for themselves' from the political alliance they entered into was not strictly true, of course. Writing to his fellow Social Democratic revolutionary, Aleksandr Potresov, in January 1899, Lenin readily admits that the Social Democrats must 'utilise' any allies that they might have dealings with in order to secure Social Democratic ends.[26] In essence, then, from the very beginning, whenever Lenin spoke of politics as an adjunct of securing class hegemony and leadership, he invariably had in mind a process of 'utilisation' or 'assimilation'. Hegemony as a form of *consent*, however, was rarely, if ever, at this time, implied.

Indeed, political hegemony established on this kind of basis was a constant theme in his writings right up to the 1917 revolution and beyond, as witnessed, for example, in the political content of his highly renowned work *Imperialism, The Highest Stage of Capitalism*, published in 1917 itself.[27] It was also the issue over which he split ranks with many former Social Democratic allies, not least with the aforementioned Potresov, who from 1903 onwards, openly accused Lenin of his 'primitive interpretation of the idea of hegemony', and for his peremptory attempts to seek to 'assimilate' rather than ally with potential supporters from other social groups and classes.[28]

This association of hegemony with such things as assimilation and utilisation of other political and social forces was not in itself, however, at the heart of Lenin's rupture with Plekhanov. The real bone of contention concerned two other factors of growing antagonism between them. The first, which was at least directly connected with the above, concerned the manner in which Lenin's own understanding of hegemony was meant to apply *over* the working class itself by means of the new type of party organisation that was set up following the 1903 congress. Lenin's views on the need for the creation of a specific type of centralised, vanguard party organisation as a means of fostering the ultimate goal of class hegemony for the proletariat had been definitively set out in his 1902 pamphlet *What is to be Done?*. At the time, this had drawn little criticism from Plekhanov since it was primarily viewed as an important contribution in the much broader struggle against economism. It was only later, however, following the actual establishment of this kind of party organisation after 1903, that Plekhanov truly appreciated the significance of what Lenin had done, and how the notion of hegemony had now been applied as an internal class principle.

At the heart of Lenin's narrower application of hegemony over the working class itself was the crucially important matter of attaining the right kind of class consciousness. Lenin, following Plekhanov himself, had argued that consciousness could only be brought to the working class from without, by intellectuals, or at least by those who understood the universal laws of social development. History demonstrated that left to their own devices, the working class themselves would not attain the kind of consciousness that was needed to prepare them for their ultimate destiny of class hegemony; they would be restricted to a consciousness that would simply perpetuate the bourgeois-capitalist phase of historical development.[29] Plekhanov, as we have seen, had made this very connection himself, but had skirted round the consequences of following this piece of logic through to the end, since it quite clearly implied a potential reversal of the

Marxist, materialist dictum that being determines consciousness. Lenin, however, was less bound by such theoretical niceties. As had already been demonstrated in his understanding of politics, everything had to be subsumed to the attainment of class hegemony, and if this meant recognising that a specific vanguard possessed the wherewithal to achieve this, rather than leaving it to the masses themselves, then so be it. The working class, in the process of struggling for its class' hegemony, would have to accept the hegemonic leadership of this vanguard.

For all of Plekhanov's criticisms now – that Lenin had 'excluded socialism from the mass and the mass from socialism', and that 'the proletariat, instead of serving as the conscious, historical agent of the socialist revolution, would merely be utilised by the party to achieve *its* ends',[30] – one cannot help concluding that Lenin here was simply following through some of the logical connotations of Plekhanov's own understanding of the relationship between hegemony and consciousness. It is also significant to note here that it was precisely this issue of the relationship between the leadership and the masses which came to preoccupy a great deal of Gramsci's attention.

The *real* decisive break in the relationship between Lenin and Plekhanov over their attitudes to the establishment of class hegemony arose with the failure of the 'bourgeois' revolution of 1905 and Lenin's subsequent espousal of a class alliance with the peasantry, at the expense of the liberal capitalists. It was this that set the scene for the creation of a new phase in the struggle against Russian absolutism; it was this that also set the scene for a much wider-ranging debate over the whole strategic nature of class hegemony, both in the years prior to and *after* the 1917 revolution.

As we have already seen, Lenin's hostility to the liberal capitalists as a potential class ally for the proletariat had a long history, dating back to 1895 at the very least. Although Lenin had repressed his misgivings somewhat at the behest of Plekhanov and other Social Democratic exiles, his basic hostility to working with the liberal capitalists was never kept very far below the surface.

A fundamental turning point in Lenin's attitude to the liberals, and in his own formulation of a new strategy of hegemony, was witnessed in his 1905 pamphlet *Two Tactics of Social Democracy in the Democratic Revolution*. Convinced now that practical political events had demonstrated the revolutionary incapacity of the liberal capitalists to lead a struggle against absolutism and carry it through to the end, Lenin now began to examine the possibility of a much speedier conquering of hegemony by the proletariat:

Liberalism, of whatever kind, merits support by the Social Democrats only to the extent that it actually opposes the autocracy. It is this support of all the inconsistent (i.e. bourgeois) democrats by the only really consistent democrat (i.e. the proletariat) *that makes the idea of hegemony a reality*. Only a petty-bourgeois huckster's idea of hegemony can conceive it as a compromise, mutual recognition, a matter of worded terms. From *the proletarian point of view* hegemony in a war goes to him who fights most energetically, who never misses a chance to strike a blow at the enemy, who always suits the action to the word, who is therefore the ideological leader of the democratic forces, who criticises half-way policies of every kind.[31]

Given the inconsistency of the bourgeois democrats and their 'half-way policies', Lenin was now convinced that the interests of the working class would be much better served by recognising a potential revolutionary role for the peasantry; something utterly inconceivable, of course, for the orthodox Plekhanov.

Lenin's discovery of this potential revolutionary capacity in the peasant was by no means a simple product of the 1905 experience. It had been a discovery quite long in the making, dating back at least to 1902. In the post-1905 situation, however, it was a change of emphasis which was bound to have an enormous affect on the whole schema of hegemonic strategies.

One revolutionary figure very much against the new Leninist agenda for a worker-peasant alliance – though for very different reasons from Plekhanov – was Trotsky. As far as Trotsky was concerned, class hegemony, if it meant anything at all, was about the simple pursuit of creating, as quickly as possible – that is to say by making positive use of Russia's backwardness – the actual dictatorship of the proletariat. Having truck with political alliances with other social classes, however temporary, was only going to prolong the ultimate desired aim; and by prolonging it, one was necessarily weakening the actual possibility of its ultimate realisation.[32] Lenin's new change of direction away from the liberal capitalists to the peasantry, then, did not satisfy Trotsky at all. Ironically, however, at the moment of their greatest rift, the *seeds* had also been planted for a much greater union between Trotsky and Lenin; a union which came to fruition after April 1917.

Lenin's new strategy immediately brought into question the nature now of any post-absolutist mode of socio-economic and political development. If the liberals and capitalists were no longer to be the recipients of power after the collapse of absolutism, and if this prerogative was going to fall to the workers and peasants, what was going to happen to the liberal-capitalist phase of development? To what extent would a worker-peasant regime be *capable* of inaugurating this phase themselves? More specifically, to what extent would the worker representatives possess the sufficient *will* to enact changes of a liberal-capitalist mode?

Lenin had never hidden the fact that just as a potential alliance with the liberal-capitalists was designed to be temporary, so the alliance with the agrarian petty-bourgeoisie was also going to be temporary; the difference being, however, that in the former case it was expected that the liberals would possess power against the proletariat. What was now contended was that the proletariat themselves would have the mechanisms of power at their disposal. As Lenin remarked in his *Notes on Plekhanov's Second Draft Programme* of the party:

> ... the concept of 'dictatorship' is incompatible with *positive* recognition of outside support for the proletariat. If we really knew *positively* that the petty bourgeoisie will support the proletariat in the accomplishment of its, the proletariat's, revolution, it would be pointless to speak of a 'dictatorship', for we would then be fully guaranteed so overwhelming a majority that we could get on very well without a dictatorship ...
>
> The more 'indulgence' we show, in the practical part of our programme, towards the small producer (e.g. to the peasant), the 'more strictly' must we treat these unreliable and double-faced social elements in the *theoretical* part of the programme, without sacrificing one iota of our standpoint. Now then, we say, if you adopt this standpoint of ours you can count on 'indulgence' of every kind, but if you don't, well then don't get angry with us! Under the 'dictatorship' we shall say about you: there is no point in wasting words where the use of power is required ...[33]

Did this not already imply, in other words, a strategy of class hegemony that would have a very minimal period of transition from a bourgeois hegemony to an outright proletarian hegemony? A minimal period of transition very close to Trotsky's own key idea of permanent or uninterrupted revolution? And a minimal period that clearly implied now that the strategy of class hegemony, and the aim of the dictatorship of the proletariat, were very much synonymous in an immediate sense? It meant little, of course, that both Trotsky and Lenin were consistent advocates of the idea that such an exceptional strategy of proletarian class hegemony under these conditions would necessarily have to rely on Western revolutionary support. The all-important connection between a minimal transitional phase between absolutism and proletarian hegemony had now been made and had been put on the immediate agenda.

It was small wonder, then, that when the October revolution finally brought Lenin and the Bolsheviks to power, Plekhanov was left totally on the sidelines, criticising them for their insufficient adherence to the needs of a thoroughgoing Europeanisation of socio-economic development in Russia and accusing Lenin (and Trotsky) of donning the mantle of 'Narodniks'. Lenin's reply, of course, would have justifiably been short and to the point. Whereas Plekhanov had theorised a process of change based on his strategy of hegemony, he, Lenin, had realised it in practice. From this moment on, the history of the world would never be the same.

The Internationalisation of Hegemony

In her own account of the conceptual background of hegemony, Christine Buci-Glucksmann is convinced that in the aftermath of the revolutionary seizure of power and the victory in the Civil War, 'Lenin was led to define a relatively new relationship between hegemony [and] dictatorship of the proletariat ... .'[34] The origin of this change of emphasis, she writes, can be found during the course of the debates at the Bolshevik's Tenth Party Congress in March 1921, particularly the debates concerning the relationship between the party in its role as a state organisation and the masses of the working class itself, which in turn largely centred on the role of the trade unions. Faced, as he was, with an increasing polarisation of opinion between the likes of the Workers' Opposition, which wanted to see trade union organisations directly involved in running their own factories, and the likes of Trotsky who wanted ever-greater centralised control by the state, Lenin, it is contended, opted for a middle line which defined anew the underlying relationship between overall class hegemony and the more narrow construction of proletarian/state dictatorship.

According to Buci-Glucksmann, hegemony was now defined by Lenin in far more *expansive* terms to denote the position of the working class as a whole. 'The function of this hegemony', she continues, 'was to ensure the ideological and political leadership of the proletariat over society as a whole, including its allies.'[35] This would be achieved in the new Leninist mode by broader-based working-class organisations, like trade unions, taking on a new 'transmission belt' function, acting as an all-important link between the proletarian state and the proletarian masses and their allies.

At the same time, however, while fulfilling this task of keeping the state and the masses directly connected with each other, Lenin was not prepared to go any further than this by granting the trade unions an autonomous prerogative of exercising leadership functions. He was not prepared to forfeit the very essence of the dictatorship of the proletariat being carried out by the vanguard force that he had so scrupulously created since 1902. 'The dictatorship of the proletariat', he affirmed,

> ... cannot be exercised through an organisation embracing the whole of that class, because in all capitalist countries (and not only over here, in one of the most backward) the proletariat is still so divided, so degraded, and so corrupted in parts ... that an organisation taking in the whole proletariat cannot directly exercise proletarian dictatorship. It can be exercised only by a vanguard that has absorbed the revolutionary energy of the class.[36]

Buci-Glucksmann's conviction that Lenin's distinction between class hegemony as a whole and state dictatorship represented something 'new' in the Leninist conception of hegemony is based on the belief that for the first time since 1905 Lenin, 'in the light of the practical experience of power and the extraordinary difficulties it presented', was forced to deepen the concept of hegemony to incorporate room for much broader-based class organisations. Hegemony, she contends, was now forced for the first time to *qualify* the essence of proletarian dictatorship by expanding its whole character.[37] Consequently, in the final three years of his life, hegemony now rested on three new principal conditions for Lenin.[38] First, since the state needed the active support of a strong social base, and since this social base was itself composed of a whole range of different forces and alliances, the state would have to learn to play a mediating role over any possible contradictions within this alliance. Second, while the state must continue to 'dominate' its adversaries, its position of 'leadership' over its social allies must be of a more supportive nature. Finally, if a genuine condition of hegemony was to be sustained, the party in particular had to protect itself from the disease of bureaucratism.

Quite whether Buci-Glucksmann is right to interpret these ideas as a *new* interpretation of hegemony in an expansive capacity is open to serious doubt. The decisions of this self-same party congress to ban internal party factions; its support for the bloody repression against the Kronstadt rebellion, and the whole ambivalence of the 'transmission belt' function for social organisations like the trade unions, clearly suggest that for Lenin, class hegemony in the broadest sense of the term must be very much subsumed still to a narrow, statist interpretation of the proletarian dictatorship. Moreover, as Harding has indicated, immediately after the Tenth Congress, Lenin himself became ever more convinced that the proletariat had become 'declassed' following the exertions of the Civil War. Because of this, ever more credence had to be given to the incumbent vanguard dictatorship, which would have the extra task now of *forging* a brand new proletarian class base in Russia; if this meant temporarily exercising a proletarian dictatorship without any real proletarian hegemony in society as a whole, then so be it.[39]

If Lenin's redefinition of the dialectical relationship between hegemony and proletarian dictatorship after 1921 is not so radical as perhaps Buci-Glucksmann would have us believe, one should nevertheless not overlook some of the other significant consequences that this re-examination of the whole hegemonic framework had at this time. From a Soviet domestic point of view, for example, the concept of hegemony was now to have some considerable bearing in establishing the battle lines for the post-Leninist succession struggle. Both Stalin and Bukharin regularly utilised the Leninist concept of hegemony as a weapon in the struggle against Trotsky, citing the latter's long-standing hostility to the concept and strategy and his continued affiliation to the notion of permanent revolution as a fundamental alternative.[40] It was during this ideological struggle against Trotsky – in the era of the New Economic Policy (NEP) – that Bukharin, in particular, was now motivated to deepen his own understanding of class hegemony.

Once again, Buci-Glucksmann has perhaps overstated the issue here by referring to Bukharin's specific 'theory' of hegemony.[41] Nevertheless, his writings at this time were to represent some important landmarks in the future evolution of the concept. Two aspects of the Bukharinist conception of hegemony in particular need to be focused upon. In his *Historical Materialism,* written in 1921, Bukharin had evolved a very broad conceptual understanding of state power as the key attribute of the Marxist superstructure, which went well beyond the normal Leninist association of the state as simply a coercive apparatus. The social and political structure of society, he argued, is by no means limited to the state authority. It is composed of many varied organisations and many forms of common action, all of which are interrelated in a complex way. Class hegemony, therefore, is rooted in much more than domination of the coercive apparatus of the state and the ensuing forms of relations that are established by this. In any social system, Bukharin argued, a society is prevented from disintegrating by a whole range of social norms, such as 'morality, customs and other standards', all of which coordinate men's actions and keeps them within certain bounds.[42] Translating all of this to the Bolshevik state in the mid-1920s, Bukharin was adamant that if a genuine 'social unity' is to be maintained, and if the basis of class hegemony is to find deep roots, then the Bolshevik-controlled state must transcend the coercive apparatus at its disposal, and adopt a role as *mediator* in its relationship to its social support base as a whole:

The dictatorship of the proletariat and the state power realise a mediation between all these kinds of relationships. The power of the proletariat is based on the peasantry and leads them, and it is necessary to consolidate the worker-peasant bloc under the hegemony of the working class as the ruling and leading force in this bloc.[43]

Even its class antagonists in the existing phase of social development, however, must not be wiped out by coercive state power. 'In a certain sense, to a certain extent and for a certain time', Bukharin emphasised, 'the [proletarian state's] relationship to the new NEP bourgeoisie cannot be restricted simply to repression alone ... We have to utilise it and supersede it through its economic elimination.'[44]

Developing on from this, Bukharin was always convinced that in this new 'era of transition' represented by NEP, politics should be largely subsumed under the prevailing importance of economics. As Buci-Glucksmann has rightly commented therefore, in this sense the hegemonic base for Bukharin (unlike for Lenin and unlike for Gramsci later) was 'not first and foremost political ... but rather economic'.[45] It was the economic-based alliance between workers and peasants in an open economy that would provide socialism with its leading force, and which would forestall the post-revolutionary state from excessive coercive interference.

Aside from the domestic impact, the post-1921 debate on the fundamental essence of hegemonic strategy had a considerable impact on the wider International Communist movement as well. Nowhere was this more noticeable than at the debates witnessed at the Third and Fourth congresses of the Comintern in 1921 and 1922 respectively. One issue above all others dominated the proceedings of both these congresses – the recognition that the revolutionary tide had begun to ebb in the more advanced Western societies, and the recognition that new tactics and strategies would have to be found if class hegemony was to be won by the proletariat.

Leading the tactical renewal at both congresses (despite his debilitating illness) was Lenin himself. In several speeches to the congresses, and in conjunction with a number of articles published at this time, Lenin demonstrated an increasing awareness of just how exceptional the circumstances had been in Russia for the victorious nature of his own party's struggle. Consider, for example, his address to the Fourth Conference of Trade Unions:

The whole difficulty of the Russian Revolution is that it was much easier for the Russian revolutionary working class to start than it is for the West European classes, but it is much more difficult for us to continue.

It is more difficult to start in West European countries because there the revolutionary proletariat is opposed by the higher thinking that comes with culture, while the working class is in a state of cultural slavery.[46]

The essence of Lenin's messages at this time, then, as directed to his comrades in the West, was very clear. If class hegemony was to be secured in the more socially, economically, culturally and politically advanced countries, then a completely different strategy to the Bolshevik revolution would have to be found. It would have to be a strategy somewhat based on each respective country's own exceptional circumstances; it would have to be a strategy that was geared towards gaining the sympathy of the masses; and this, in turn, implied a strategy that would have to be somewhat more gradualist than the Bolshevik strategy had been. For Lenin, the crucial factor of this new strategy would be the securing of communist (proletarian) hegemony within a new 'United Front'; this United Front would be based on cross-class political alliances, and could incorporate other potential opponents to existing bourgeois regimes, such as Social Democrats, non-party trade unionists and religious activists.

One delegate attending the Fourth Congress of the Comintern at the end of 1922 was Antonio Gramsci, and it was precisely here, under the influence of the debates surrounding the United Front policy, that the young Italian delegate was first introduced to the Russian debates on hegemony. More importantly, it was the *negation* of the United Front strategy in the latter part of the 1920s which stimulated Gramsci to go back to a study of Lenin's concept of hegemony and to apply an updated version of hegemony to the situation then prevailing in Mussolini's fascist state. Like Lenin, and Plekhanov before him, Gramsci was primarily concerned to counter growing economistic tendencies in the communist movement, and to put forward a conception of the importance of *politics*, without which there could be no class hegemony. In short, a repoliticisation of Marxist thought which would be based on a far greater anthropological approach to human activity, aimed at politically empowering, not only the realm of the state, but even more significantly, the realm of everyday life within (civil) society itself. As he looked back on the past, particularly the recent Russian revolutionary experiences, and as he applied its lessons to the present, so Gramsci developed the foundations of a concept and strategy of hegemony which was to take on a whole new life and significance.

2 The Gramscian Legacy

A scrap of red cloth, like those the Partisans
knotted up around their necks
and, near the urn, on the waxen earth,

a different red, of two geraniums.
There you lie, banished, listed with severe
non-Catholic elegance, among the foreign
dead: The ashes of Gramsci ... Between hope
and my old distrust, I approach you,
chancing upon this thinned-out greenhouse, before

your tomb, before your spirit, still alive
down here among the free.

Pier Paolo Pasolini, *The Ashes of Gramsci*

The Forces and Realm of Hegemonic Determination

There is a passage in one of Gramsci's letters from prison which very neatly and succinctly helps to sum up the essence of his lifelong work and struggles. 'How many social worlds', he asks, 'does each individual belong to? Does not everyone strive to unify his own conception of the world, in which heterogeneous splinters of fossilised cultures are bound still to be lodged? And does there not exist a general historic process which is persistently tending to unify the entire human race?'[1] This quest for unity and the resultant desire to synthesise every particular experience that he encounters runs through the whole body of his writings. For Gramsci, of course, only Marxism has the potentiality of embodying 'all the fundamental elements needed to construct a total and integral conception of the world',[2] of being a self-sufficient whole which possesses a unique capacity to absorb 'organically' whatever was valid in all previous modes of thought. He cites, in particular, Marx's capacity to synthesise his materialist outlook with the dynamic vitality of Hegelianism, and by doing so clearly expresses his own personal desire to achieve something similar with his own formative Crocean experiences.

By far the most crucial of all Marxist assertions for Gramsci were the eleven *Theses on Feuerbach*. It was the appropriation of the ideas contained in these which ultimately governed the whole of his work in prison and which led him to ask the central question: 'in what sense could philosophy transform the world, becoming an active force in history and playing a massive educational role?'[3] Gramsci's response was that only by treating philosophy as a 'non-definitive' subject matter could one categorically resolve the question posed. Circumstances are changed, he asserted, by men; men are the ensemble of their social relationships. Truth is neither abstract nor timeless and must be proved in practice. Between subject and object, being and thought, there can be no separation; reality, in short, cannot exist independent of man, and by 'Man' what is meant is: what can man become? That is, can man dominate his own destiny, can he 'make himself', can he create his own life? Man 'is a process, and, more exactly, the process of his actions'.[4] He is to be conceived not as an individual exclusively limited to his own individuality, but in a collective sense as a series of active relationships with other men and the natural world.

From this starting point, Gramsci was now able to go on and formulate, in more precise terms, the kind of unity that he envisages existing in the social realm. Under a Notebook heading *Unity in the Constituent Elements of Marxism,* he writes:

> Unity is given by the dialectical development of the contradictions between man and matter (nature – material forces of production). In economics the unitary centre is value, alias the relationship between the worker and the industrial productive forces ... In philosophy [it is] praxis, that is, the relationship between human will (superstructure) and economic structure. In politics [it is] the relationship between the state and civil society, that is, the intervention of the state (centralised will) to educate the educator, the social environment in general.[5]

A clarification of the interrelationship Gramsci sees existing between economics (classes), philosophy (intellectual strata and popular masses), and politics (rulers and ruled) will thus provide the essential framework from which an analysis of his crucial concept of hegemony can take place.

If we take philosophy first, and the resulting relationship between the intellectual strata and the popular masses, it has already been indicated that for Gramsci this is a non-definitive subject that cannot exist outside of the realm of general human experience. Gramsci never went so far as to deny the existence of a professional class of philosophers, but he was nevertheless adamant that those who called themselves philosophers were 'much more similar to the rest of mankind than [were] other specialists'. As Adamson has shown, for Gramsci philosophy is intrinsically a social activity because it is carried on by all people in everyday life. People think, people decide and people act; actions affect others and the whole process of people thinking again starts anew. What is important here, however, is not the isolated thought, but the fact of social interaction. Indeed, even the most traditional philosopher, who believed himself to be engaged in some kind of pure and solitary contemplation, would still be intimately bound to the social order by the very mechanism of language – 'a totality of culturally produced notions'.[6] Philosophical claims about men and the world have thus always represented attempts 'by a specific class of people to change, correct or perfect the conceptions of the world that exist in any particular age and thus to change the norms of conduct that go with them; in other words, to change practical activity as a whole'.[7]

It is not just philosophy's complete and utter dependence on existing social relations, however, that marks the high point of the attempt to locate the role of philosophy in a broader, unified spectrum of social existence. Gramsci, in fact, goes much further than this by categorically stating that philosophy must become political if it is to continue to be philosophy. For Louis Althusser, this insistence on the political nature of philosophy was one of the most authentically revolutionary characteristics of Gramsci's whole theory, since it questioned for the first time philosophy's explicit role in actually *shaping* social formations.[8]

Gramsci's understanding of philosophy and its intrinsic relationship with politics was often closely associated with a much broader critique, primarily directed at two (related) types of opponents: the orthodox Marxists of the Second International as personified by the likes of Plekhanov, and the growing trend in positivism and mechanicism as personified by Bukharin. Of the two, it was his contemporary, Bukharin, who undoubtedly received the most criticism from Gramsci's deliberations in prison, particularly as regards his theory of historical materialism. Bukharin's formulation of Marxism as an objective, positive science which sought the laws of historical development erroneously presupposed for Gramsci 'an extra-historical and extra-human objectivity', which entirely overlooked 'the concepts of historical movement, of becoming, and therefore of the dialectic itself'. It was a kind of objectivity that could be likened to 'a hangover of the concept of God', transformed into a fetishism of science. The only real notion of objectivity that existed was one that took account of 'human objectivity', which in itself could therefore correspond to a notion of 'historical subjectivity', 'in other words, objective would mean universal subjective'.[9] Citing Marx's preface to the *Critique of Political Economy* to the effect that 'society does not pose for itself tasks the conditions for whose resolution do not already exist', Gramsci was nevertheless adamant that historical conditions remain the product of human creation, arising out of a process of human struggle. Of course, there may well be general laws of tendency in any historical epoch which can be empirically observed. But this was a far cry from establishing any kind of metaphysical law of causality.[10]

At the heart of Gramsci's criticism here was the way this kind of determinism reduced everything to the primacy of the economic moment. In his critique of economism Gramsci, again, was by no means denying the importance of the economic component. Far from it. But what he wanted was once more a synthesis between economics and politics which gave politics a sufficient degree of specificity and relative autonomy. The notion of *relativity* here was crucial. Gramsci was adamant that neither moment was in any way completely autonomous, something that his desire for social unity and synthesis clearly recognised. The key task of any theoretician, therefore, had to lie in ascertaining the actual nature of the dialectical or synthesised relationship between economics and politics and the social forces engaged in each realm. To achieve this, Gramsci attempted to supply an overall schema that differentiated primarily between two different kinds of social factors. The first analyses the *objective* material conditions of any historical situation. This, he writes, is:

> A relation of social forces which is closely linked to the structure, objective, independent of human will ... The level of development of the material forces of production provides a basis for the emergence of the various social classes, each one of which represents a function and has a specific position within production itself ... By studying these fundamental data it is possible to discover whether in a particular society there exist the necessary and sufficient conditions for its transformation.[11]

The second factor is the moment of the relationship between political forces, which involves 'an evaluation of the degree of homogeneity, self-awareness and organisation attained by the various social classes'. As Showstack Sassoon has demonstrated, this is the moment of *subjective* conditions in social relationships, and it is at this level of analysis that the formation of a collective political consciousness can be studied.[12] Indeed, it is this primary political moment that Gramsci sees as being the most complex, since not all social forces necessarily develop a political existence. It is a moment

> ... in which one becomes aware that one's own corporate interests, in their present and future development, transcend the corporate limits of the purely economic class, and can and must become the interests of other subordinate groups too. This is the most purely *political* phase, and marks the decisive passage from the structure to the sphere of the complex superstructures; it is the phase in which previously germinated ideologies become 'party', come into confrontation and conflict, until

only one of them, or at least a single combination of them, tends to prevail, to gain the upper hand, to propagate itself throughout society – bringing about not only a unison of economic and political aims, but also intellectual and moral unity, posing all the questions around which the struggle rages not on a corporate but on a 'universal' plane, *and thus creating the hegemony of a fundamental social group* over a series of subordinate groups.[13]

In essence, economic classes represent, what he terms elsewhere, the 'efficient cause' which prepares the stage for a struggle for hegemony in society. The actual 'determinant cause' of hegemony, however, is the political moment. If one is to analyse the realm of hegemony, therefore, one must delineate in precise terms the *political* terrain of that struggle.

Before going on to examine Gramsci's study of this terrain, it is first of all necessary to provide a broader evaluation of Gramsci's understanding of politics, which is itself a product of synthesis between Marxist and Machiavellian conceptions. From a purely Marxist perspective, Gramsci was keen to re-emphasise that the power to overcome or change society for the better does not materialise out of the air but is born from the old society itself, that is, from human activity in all its forms. That no new society ever emerges without the seeds of its development having first been planted in the old, means precisely that the old is the necessary condition without which the new cannot be realised. It also means, however, that the passage from necessity to freedom must always be a *political* act, the true unity of theory and practice (praxis).

Above and beyond this, the political struggle to create society anew is always a struggle of becoming, of potentiality, of striving to unite the 'preparatory moments' into a 'unitary moment', one that is never permanent, static or arbitrary. In this sense politics, in the Machiavellian meaning of the term, is 'the art of the possible'; it is a creative exercise which must recognise that the strategic balance of forces is constantly in flux and that ultimately, political action amounts to seizing the historical conjuncture at precisely the right moment.[14] One of the great virtues of Machiavelli, Gramsci comments, is that he wrote about politics 'neither in the form of a cold utopia nor as learned theorising, but rather [as] a creation of concrete fantasy which acts on a dispersed and shattered people to arouse and organise its collective will'.[15]

As Buci-Glucksmann has commented, Gramsci's recourse to 'the primacy of practice as the primacy of politics' in no way abolished the differential status of the other social practices he had set himself the task of synthesising. On the contrary, political practice simply represented the only possible way of unifying social reality in an entirely non-sectarian and non-dogmatic position in such fields as philosophy and economics (or history and culture).[16] It was precisely for this reason that Gramsci was so anxious to negate the orthodox determinist and economistic stance of fellow Marxist theoreticians. Any element of a class struggle which produces an economic crisis will have an effect on the dominant forces controlling the state. An economic crisis alone, however, will never *automatically* result in the transformation of society. Only the transcendence of the economic crisis into the political realm will produce the opportunities for this kind of transformation.

It was small wonder, then, that Gramsci was such an ardent Leninist during the period of the revolution and Lenin's leadership of the new Soviet state up to the time of his death. The mere fact that the revolution in Russia did not take place 'under normal conditions', as he expressed it, was a total irrelevance (for the admittedly Crocean Gramsci at this time); it simply demonstrated instead that the so-called orthodox laws of historical materialism were by no means as rigid as the likes of Plekhanov had formerly asserted, and that in practice 'fate was the excuse of men without wills'. Gramsci's revolutionary Lenin was the practical expression of a Marx described as 'not a Messiah who left a file of parables pregnant with categorical imperatives [and] absolute indisputable norms independent of time and space'. Instead, Lenin was the one leader who truly understood that the only Marxist categorical imperative was the one that stated 'Workers of the World Unite'. The Bolsheviks live Marxist thought:

> This thought sees as the dominant factor in history, not raw economic facts, but man, men in societies, men in relation to one another, reaching agreements with one another, developing through these contacts … a collective, social will; men coming to understand economic facts, judging them and adapting them to their will until this becomes the driving force of the economy and moulds objective reality …[17]

Although this excessively *idealist* interpretation of Lenin and the so-called 'Revolution Against *Capital*' was to be tempered somewhat over the years, Gramsci nevertheless consistently portrayed Lenin as the true heir to Marx's *Theses on Feuerbach,* and considered Leninism as a whole as a highly developed unitary system of thought and practical action.

There can be no doubt that for Gramsci one of Lenin's main contributions to Marxist theory was indeed his own elaboration of the concept of hegemony, and certainly in the months prior to his incarceration in prison – in articles such as *Notes on the Southern Question,* for example – Gramsci followed the Leninist definition very closely. As he began to look in more detail, however, at the nature of the political terrain that he had identified as being so crucial in comprehending the nature of any struggle for hegemony, and especially as he began to examine the terrain in his own native country, so this created the context which would lead him to modernise the Leninist roots of hegemony.

One of the main reasons for Gramsci's harsh polemic against economism, apart from its inability to formulate an accurate understanding of the dialectical links between the structure and superstructure, was the resulting over-simplistic desire to equate an immediate element of force being somehow automatically produced by the determinism of the structure. This resulted in an identification of state with government, understood as a repressive-coercive apparatus only. For Gramsci, this kind of reductionist attitude was totally inadequate. Without a proper conception of state power in all its complex juxtapositions, any prospect for future revolutionary change would be doomed from the start. The aim that he set himself, therefore, was to try to present a set of theoretical considerations which would provide a more accurate configuration of state power, ultimately applicable to any form of modern class rule.

As was usual in his efforts to expand on a given prognosis, what was formerly accepted as the norm was not to be negated in its entirety, but was to be transcended into a new type of synthesis. Gramsci did not deny that one aspect of the state, understood in a unilateral way as political society, was indeed identical with the apparatus of class dictatorship with all its coercive functions. What he wanted to show above all, however, was that there was also a *second* aspect of state power that had largely gone undefined by Marxist theoreticians of any creed. This second aspect possessed a far greater integrationist capacity, and if one was to search for its location, then one would have to concentrate much more on the terrain that was normally referred to as *civil society*.

This dichotomous approach to the state led Gramsci to come up with his well-known assertion that:

> In politics the error occurs as a result of an inaccurate understanding of what the state (in its integral meaning ...) really is ... [The] general notion of state includes elements which need to be referred back to the notion of civil society ... in the sense that one might say that state = political society + civil society, in other words hegemony protected by the armour of coercion.[18]

Clarifying this in more detail, he suggests:

What we can do, for the moment, is to fix two major superstructural 'levels': the one that can be called 'civil society', that is the ensemble of organisms commonly called 'private', and that of 'political society' or 'the state'. These two levels correspond on the one hand to the function of 'hegemony' which the dominant group exercises throughout society and on the other hand to that of 'direct domination' or command exercised through the state and 'juridical' government.[19]

What we have here, then, is a notion of an *integral state* – a term borrowed from Hegel – which acts as an equilibrium between 'the state proper *and* civil society' which encompasses 'the whole complex of practical and theoretical activities, through which [a] ruling class not only justifies and maintains its domination, but succeeds in obtaining the active consent of those over whom it rules'.[20]

Quite clearly, the significance of Gramsci's understanding of the integral state was enormous, both from a purely theoretical as well as a practical political perspective. Five points, in particular, deserve mention, many of which will be dealt with in greater detail in the remainder of this chapter. First, the traditional Marxist (and Leninist) conception of power has been radically diffused *outwards* to include a whole new set of institutions, while the task of mediating relationships of power has likewise been passed *downwards* into the much broader realm of society as a whole.

Second, apropos of Hegel, by going beyond a definition of the state as a simple repressive-coercive organisation, Gramsci was able to give it a whole set of responsibilities which were clearly *ethical* in nature. Moreover, by now giving the state a formative role in the creation (or adaptation) of a specific type of 'civilisation', it was also being given, in a very broad sense, a universal type of character, or more precisely, the *desire* to be universal.

Third, in his understanding of the importance of civil society as a mediation of all types of social relationships of power through a great variety of organisations such as churches, trade unions, parties and schools, Gramsci considerably extended the original Marxist definition of civil society. True, for some commentators – most notably, Norberto Bobbio – Gramsci's emphasis on placing civil society firmly and squarely in the ideological superstructure represented in many ways not so much an extension but a *negation* of Marxist thought, albeit for Bobbio a positive one.[21] On this point, however, I am inclined to follow Bobbio's main critic, Jacques Texier, who saw Gramsci's civil society as the ultimate embodiment of his search for a unity of social existence:

What does civil society represent for Gramsci? It is the complex of practical and ideological social relations (the whole infinitely varied social fabric, the whole human content of a given society) which is established and grows up on the base of determined relations of production. It includes the types of behaviour of *homo oeconomicus* as well as of *homo ethico-politicus*. It is therefore the *object*, the *subject* and the *locality* of the superstructural activities which are carried out in ways which differ according to the levels and moments by means of the 'hegemonic apparatuses' on the one hand and of the 'coercive apparatuses' on the other.[22]

This argument aside, it is quite clear that since it is in civil society that the fundamental task of mediation of power relationships occurs, then this is the *key* terrain of any hegemonic struggle – 'the true source and theatre of all history', to use Marx's own terminology. Certainly, Gramsci himself makes this absolutely clear when he stresses on more than one occasion that the solidity of the government apparatus (the political society) ultimately depends to a very great degree on the consistency of the civil society which serves as its basis.

Fourth, in his understanding of the nature of the integral state and the tasks to be performed by the two methodologically distinct, though spatially related, components of civil and political society, Gramsci, unlike Lenin, has provided the basis for a much clearer and stronger association between hegemony and *consent*. While Gramsci is very clear that the attainment of class hegemony has the requisite forces of coercion and domination to back it up, he is also clear that the key apparatuses of hegemony are undoubtedly to be located in the realm of civil society; the aim of such apparatuses is the creation of some form of organised acceptance of a given form of class domination, or at the very least, some kind of constructive consensus. On this point, then, Bobbio was certainly correct in his recognition that whereas for Gramsci the 'moment of force is instrumental and therefore subordinated to the moment of hegemony', for Lenin 'dictatorship and hegemony proceed together' with the moment of force being the primary and decisive one.[23]

Finally, in his understanding of this extended, integral state, it is also very clear that Gramsci is providing a description here of a very *modern*, Western state rather than the kind of pre-modern, or semi-Asiatic state that Russia had been prior to the revolution.

Hegemonic Combatants

Mention has already been made of Bobbio's assertion that as a 'theorist of the superstructures', Gramsci, in his search for a unity of social existence based on Marxist configurations, was very much in danger of perhaps giving greater credence to his idealist/Crocean background than he had ascertained to do. If we follow Texier again as our main critic of Bobbio, it is possible to assert that what 'saves' Gramsci as a definitive Marxist is his formulation of the structural (class) organisation of the main combative organisations involved in the struggle for hegemony.

Arguably the most important of the combatants discussed by Gramsci is that force which goes by the name of *historical bloc*. The term 'arguably' is used for two primary reasons. Although generally seen as a key innovation in his understanding of the complex nature of hegemony, the term itself is discussed in an explicit sense in only a few passages of his *Prison Notebooks*. Its *implicit* importance, however, certainly should not be underestimated. Secondly, Gramsci is not all that precise at times in clearly differentiating the role of the historical bloc in its struggle for hegemony from that of the revolutionary party, or what he euphemistically calls the 'Modern Prince'. It is clear, however, that for all the importance attached to the latter, the very *raison d'être* of the historical bloc is based on the transcendence of individual parties and other political organisations into a higher, synthesised unit. It is on this reckoning, therefore, that it takes pride of place in the combative arena for hegemony.

The intellectual ancestry of the term is to be located in the writings of Georges Sorel. In his debate with Labriola in the late 1890s, Sorel was convinced that a historic displacement had taken place between objective events and the actual development of a working-class, socialist consciousness. It was in his proposed formation of a new historical bloc between structure and superstructure, therefore, that Sorel saw a way of reconstituting this debilitating situation.[24] The evidence of Gramsci's affinity with Sorel here is clear-cut. In a well-known passage in the *Notebooks* Gramsci has no hesitation in maintaining that: 'Structures and superstructures form an "historical bloc". That is to say the complex, contradictory and discordant *ensemble* of the superstructures is the reflection of the *ensemble* of the social relations of production.'[25]

Although retaining the notion of 'reflection' here, the essence of his understanding of a historical bloc in this statement must be seen in conjunction with his overall search for a comprehensive unity between the economic and the political conjuncture. The central assertion is the very clear principle that a class, as it develops from a narrow economic-corporate starting point, becomes politically more powerful not simply because of its position within the economic structure, but also because it is the purveyor of certain values. These, though certainly expressions of its experience in the world of production, nevertheless are able 'to become detached as images or projections of its political outlook'.[26] Depending on the power of such images, the dominant class will be able to attract to itself other social groups (over which it exercises leadership) as mutual power-seekers, potential power-shapers and as the instigators of new cultural expressions.

It is precisely in this sense, then, that Texier (and others) would claim Gramsci as a definitive Marxist. Because it is on the terrain of ideology that people become conscious of their real position in the productive realm, the historical bloc becomes the primary organisation denoting a certain type of unity of the social whole, in which 'material forces are the content and ideologies are the form'. The historical bloc, in other words, is the practical means of joining together the economic and political levels of existence. Material forces would be totally inconceivable without some physical form, but ideologies would likewise be 'individual fancies without the material forces'.[27]

In some commentaries on the significance of the historical bloc, two (related) misconceptions are sometimes highlighted. First, it is often contended that the historical bloc amounts to nothing more than a simple form of class or political alliance. Second, it is contended that all historical blocs are hegemonic. To counteract these misconceptions, it is necessary to refer once again to Gramsci's comparative analysis of pre-modern and modern types of political organisations. In the ancient and medieval state, both politico-territorial and social centralisation were minimal – the former being a function of the latter. In a certain sense, the state was a mechanical bloc of social groups, often of different races. Under the constraint and military-political pressure that bore on them, and could at certain moments assume an acute form, the subaltern groups maintained a life of their own, with specific institutions.[28] In the era of the modern state, however, a very different process can be observed: 'The modern state substitutes for the mechanical bloc of social forces their subordination to the active hegemony of the directive and dominant group ... [It] abolishes certain autonomies, which nevertheless are reborn in other forms as parties, trade unions, cultural associations.'[29] As Buci-Glucksmann has argued, it is this transition from a mechanical bloc of social forces into other forms, capable of achieving an active form of hegemony throughout society, that is precisely the significance of the historical bloc.[30]

For Gramsci, the *real* consequence of this transition to the historical bloc is dependent on the extent to which the old mechanical way of achieving some kind of unison has been transcended by an *organic* sense of unison. A hint at what is meant here by 'organic' is given in a section of the *Notebooks* entitled *Passage From Knowing to Understanding and to Feeling*, a section quite clearly devoted to a criticism of the kind of bloc of social forces adumbrated by Bukharin in his NEP writings. One cannot make politics, Gramsci asserts, without feeling the elementary passions of the people, without understanding them, without explaining and justifying them in the particular historical situation, and without coherently connecting them to a progressive vision of the future. Without this sentimental connection, political relationships would be reduced to a purely bureaucratic and formal order. Such bureaucratic deformations, he goes on, can certainly not be classified as hegemonic. Hegemony can only be established by an 'organic cohesion' in which passions are translated into understanding and hence become knowledge, 'not mechanically but in a way that is alive'. Only then can there be a relationship of representation; only then 'can there take place an exchange of individual elements between the rulers and the ruled, leaders and led, and can the shared life be realised which alone is a social force – with the creation of the "historical bloc"'.[31] It is in the importance attached to this notion of *organic* relationships that it is possible to assert that the historical bloc amounts to considerably more than a simple form of alliance-building. Likewise, while it is clear that any successful struggle for hegemony will always emerge out of a historical bloc, this is still a far cry from asserting that all historical blocs are hegemonic.

The question which now clearly arises is: who is going to provide this vital ingredient of organic cohesion? Who is going to act as the key *articulator* of hegemony? Gramsci's answer leaves no room for doubt: it is to be the *intellectuals*. In the fourth of his *Prison Notebooks*, Gramsci maintains that as elements of organic cohesion in a bloc of forces, intellectuals are given 'the function of organising the social hegemony of a group and its state domination'. This inevitably results, he goes on, in a very great extension of the concept of the intellectual.[32]

This desire to extend our understanding of what it means to be an intellectual had long been of interest to Gramsci and was very much associated with a much broader interest in properly defining the role of culture as a whole. As early as January 1916, for example, we find him writing of the need for the proletariat to conceive of itself as having an entirely different conception of culture:

> We need to free ourselves from the habit of seeing culture as encyclopaedic knowledge … Culture is something quite different. It is organisation, discipline of one's inner self, a coming to terms with one's own personality; it is the attainment of a higher awareness, with the aid of which one succeeds in understanding one's own historical value, one's own function in life, one's own rights and obligations. But none of this can

come about through spontaneous evolution, through a series of actions and reactions which are independent of one's own will.[33]

Taking up his argument against positivism once more, and the notion that human beings were somehow nothing more than a passive force in historical development, Gramsci is absolutely adamant that 'every revolution has been preceded by an intense labour of criticism, by the diffusion of culture and the spread of ideas ... '. 'The same phenomenon', he asserts,

> ... is being repeated today in the case of socialism. It was through a critique of capitalist civilisation that the unified consciousness of the proletariat was or is still being formed, and a critique implies culture, not simply a spontaneous and naturalistic evolution ... To know oneself means to be oneself, to be master of oneself ... And we cannot be successful in this unless we also know others, their history, the successive efforts they have made to be what they are, to create the civilisation they have created and which we seek to replace with our own.[34]

As Showstack Sassoon has shown, what Gramsci lacked in these early, formative writings was a more exact linkage between the role of culture and a concrete *political* exposition.[35] It is this linkage that is provided in the *Prison Notebooks* in his broader understanding of the role and position of intellectuals. In the first of his *Notebooks*, the intellectual is defined in an entirely innovative way: 'By "intellectuals" must be understood not those strata commonly described by this term, but in general the entire social stratum which exercises an *organisational* function in the wide sense – whether in the field of production, or in that of culture, or in that of political administration.'[36] An intellectual is not just someone who blindly practices the art of eloquence in one mode or another; an intellectual is not just someone who exists above and beyond the realm of a particular economic system. An intellectual must be a product of the ensemble of a set of mediated social relations, and in this sense cannot help but play a role in other spheres of practical life as some kind of 'constructor', 'organiser' or 'permanent persuader'. Nor should one fall into the trap, Gramsci warns, of seeing intellectuals as simply scholars or men of letters. By so concentrating on their organisational capacity, he is adamant that an intellectual should be considered anyone whose social function is to serve as a transmitter of ideas either within the realm of civil society, or, more importantly, as a link between the two aspects of the integral state – political society (government) and civil society.

Going on to clarify what he means by this, Gramsci introduces a very important theoretical differentiation between two distinctive types of intellectuals: the 'organic' and the 'traditional'. The most important of the intellectuals are the organic ones since these are intrinsically linked to the essential mode of production in any given society. These are the intellectuals who provide a social class with the capacity to solidify a real sense of homogeneity and awareness, not only of their function in the narrow economic domain, but also in the broader fields of politics and social life. As for the traditional intellectuals, these can best be defined by their established existence prior to the formation of a new social system. By dint of this, they seek to convey a sense of historical permanency and frequently assert a sense of autonomy and independence from the ruling class. For Gramsci, however, such an *appearance* of neutrality needs to be categorically unmasked. While such traditional intellectuals may genuinely desire to remain 'above the fray' of a social system and a resulting struggle for hegemony within it, at the very least they will be forced to effect a compromise with that system – because of institutional pressure or financial inducements – which will totally negate their claim to neutrality.[37] Because of this, Gramsci is adamant that the position of traditional intellectuals should by no means be underestimated. The very fact that they have an appearance of neutrality can be vitally important, especially for an existing hegemonic historical bloc, in helping to secure an additional measure of consensual depth for that hegemony. For this reason, one of the most important characteristics of any *rising* class is its struggle to assimilate and conquer the traditional intellectuals in the cultural-ideological realm.

Having dealt with the theoretical differentiation between the two types of intellectuals, it is necessary to return briefly to the fundamental role of intellectuals in providing organic cohesion in a social structure. For Gramsci, the attainment of such cohesion is best understood by the notion of a *collective will*, a common conception of an existing social structure which can ultimately serve as a fundamental principle of unity. From this one can now deduce the real importance of the cultural aspect, a quest begun, as already indicated, right at the very beginning of his political career:

> Culture, at its various levels, unifies in a series of strata, to the extent that they come into contact with each other, a greater or lesser number of individuals who understand each other's mode of expression in differing degrees, etc. …
>
> An historical act can only be performed by 'collective man', and this presupposes the attainment of a 'cultural-social' unity through which a multiplicity of dispersed wills, with heterogeneous aims, are welded together with a single aim, on the basis of an equal and common conception of the world.[38]

In pre-modern times, the attainment of such a collective will geared towards a necessitated political object was perfectly capable of being fulfilled by an exceptional individual. Indeed, for Gramsci this was precisely the achievement of Machiavelli's Prince. For the working class struggling to counter the hegemony of modern capitalism, however, it is the modern form of the Prince, the political party, which has the responsibility of attaining 'the *first* cell in which there come together the germs of a collective will tending to become universal and total';[39] a modern Prince, which if it is to have any chance of success, must establish itself as a 'collective intellectual', primed and ready to help shape the necessary organic cohesion of a broader historical bloc.

On what basis, then, is a struggle for hegemony to take place? And how is an existing ruling hegemonic force to be countered? Having established an integral connection between the ethical-political terrain of civil society and the institutional arm of the state, and having established that civil society operates very much as the outer trench of hegemonic power, Gramsci is now able to come to the conclusion that the only feasible strategy available to a potential *new* hegemonic force is one of 'trench warfare' *within* civil society. This conclusion serves as the basis for the development of Gramsci's key strategic concept of a *war of position*.

In the most advanced states, 'civil society has become a very complex structure and one which is resistant to the catastrophic incursions of the immediate economic element (crises, depressions etc.)'.[40] Because of the very complexity of this structure, it follows for Gramsci that a direct assault on the state by a potential hegemonic force – a 'war of manoeuvre' – will invariably end in defeat, precisely because of the way in which an existing dominant force has institutionalised itself in so many different spheres. Instead, the requisite strategy for a bid for supremacy must be gradual, it must rely on 'exceptional qualities of patience and inventiveness', and it must involve a steady penetration and subversion of the complex and multiple mechanisms of hegemonic diffusion. It must, in other words, engage in an ideological-cultural struggle for the control of the key agencies of civil society – such as the schools, the universities, the publishing houses and the mass media. This, then, is what Gramsci effectively means by a war of position. Representing the stage in any struggle when a new hegemonic bloc is trying to cement itself, it is without doubt an extremely 'decisive moment'. Without a successful penetrative war of position in civil society, any kind of offensive aimed at overthrowing the state's institutional apparatus will come to grief precisely on the 'trenches and fortifications' of civil society. Indeed, such is its importance that Gramsci was ever keen to refer to it as 'the most important question

of political theory that the post-war period has posed, and the most difficult to solve correctly'.[41]

Is it, however, as many analysts have argued, a reflection of not only
Gramsci's, but the whole of Marxism's, pessimism and defensiveness in
the aftermath of the Russian revolution, and the steady rise of fascism in
many parts of Europe? In this, I am inclined to follow Showstack Sassoon.
On the one hand, the development of the concept did demonstrate a desire
by Gramsci to transcend the rather exceptional circumstances involved
in the revolutionary process in Russia. On the other hand, the concept
was a very *positive* way of conceptualising new methods by which state
power could be attained, as well as radically extending the notion of how
to construct a new socialist society *after* the attainment of state power.[42]

One should certainly not see Gramsci's proposed strategy, however, as a
total abandonment of the Bolshevik model, and certainly not as an illustration of a new kind of evolutionist, parliamentary strategy of the kind
associated with Bernstein. In his tactical considerations, Gramsci does not
by any means rule out an element of force in the form of a 'war of manoeuvre'. What he does say quite categorically is that the element of force is not
in itself definitive, and it must therefore be used when the tactical moment
is appropriate. That *some* element of force will have to be used, however, is
totally inevitable. No dominant order will ever simply 'wither away' without itself resorting to some kind of forceful struggle.

What is also significant in Gramsci's argument here is a very clear criticism of Trotsky and his rigid adherence to a strategy of permanent revolution,
even when the objective (and subjective) conditions in many national contexts were totally unfavourable to this kind of strategy. Indeed, after having
stated how important the question of the war of position had become and
how difficult it was to solve correctly, Trotsky is named as someone who
had categorically failed to realise this, and who had continued to espouse
a theory of frontal assault 'in a period in which it only leads to defeat'.[43]
This was in stark contrast to Lenin, who had in fact begun to adopt a similar theory of war of position towards the end of his life. However, even
Lenin, Gramsci laments, had not been able to conceive an identification
of 'the superstructures of civil society' with the kind of trench warfare
involved in a positional struggle.[44]

When it comes to the kind of basis needed for a successful war of position by a counter-hegemonic force, two primary scenarios are focused
upon. The first comprises a set of circumstances whereby huge masses pass
'suddenly from a state of political passivity to a certain activity, and put
forward demands which taken together, albeit not [yet] organically formulated, add up to a revolution'.[45] One way this situation may arise might

be due to the effectiveness of the criticism to which the ruling hegemonic force has been subjected. This could result in a process of differentiation and change in the relative weight that the component elements of the ruling bloc used to possess. What was thus previously secondary and subordinate might now desire to take on a primary function and, as a consequence, the 'old collective will dissolves into its contradictory elements [as] the subordinate ones develop socially'.[46] By means of this dissolution, the way is opened up for the counter-hegemonic force to rearticulate these elements within their own structures. The more this continues, the more the existing hegemonic force will be undermined. Alternatively, as Gramsci suggests elsewhere, historical necessity may produce an irreversible situation, such that:

> At a certain point in their historical lives, social classes become detached from their political parties. In other words, the traditional parties in that particular organisational form, with the particular men who constitute, represent and lead them, are no longer recognised by their class (or fraction of a class) as its expression.[47]

This would likewise open up possibilities for counter-hegemonic rearticulation with similar results.

The second scenario comprises a set of circumstances directly engendered by the ruling hegemonic force whereby it 'has failed in some major political undertaking for which it has requested, or forcibly extracted, the consent of the broad masses',[48] an example here being a war. Both these sets of scenarios are clearly interrelated, and certainly the ultimate result in both cases would be a crisis of authority and hegemony.

Quite clearly, on the basis of Gramsci's adherence to a philosophy of praxis and all that this entails for him, there can be no sense of *certainty* of success for an alternative hegemonic force in such a crisis situation. For Gramsci, parties come into existence and constitute themselves as organisations precisely in order to influence the situation at moments which are historically vital for their class. Nevertheless, he is certainly well aware that 'they are not always capable of adapting themselves to new tasks and to new epochs, nor of evolving *pari passu* with the overall relations of force (and hence the relative position of their class) in the country in question, or in the international field'.[49] Depending on a whole range of factors, at such moments of acute crisis a party may well find itself totally void of its social content and be 'left as though suspended in mid air'.

Hegemony and Consent

In much of what has been written so far in this chapter, an implicit relationship has already been established between hegemony and consent. It has been shown that, in its optimal form, hegemony is primarily a means for acquiring the consent of the masses through their self-organisation in a range of activities and institutions situated within civil society. Resulting from this, a national-popular will is established which binds together a historical bloc of forces which itself is capable of bridging the economic structure of society with the political superstructure. For many commentators, then, Gramsci was a theorist who 'posed the question of consent in a way new to Marxism',[50] and certainly in a way that was far in excess of anything proffered by Lenin and his own category of hegemony. To examine this relationship in more detail requires that we now approach it from two opposite perspectives: from Gramsci's studies on passive (indirect) forms of consent and on more active (direct) forms.

The notion of a 'passive revolution' is generally recognised as one of the key theoretical components of Gramsci's whole body of writings. It emerges primarily from the historical studies that Gramsci carried out on bourgeois revolutions throughout Europe (including, of course, his native Italy), though its analytical importance certainly transcends the strict confines of historical relevance. According to Gramsci, the classical pattern of bourgeois revolution was set in motion by the Jacobins in France in 1789. What the Jacobins were able to do most successfully was to make the demands of the popular masses at that time their own. Although predominantly linked with the bourgeoisie, they nevertheless transcended the narrow corporate interests of their class by appealing to the needs of all the national groups which had to be assimilated to the new dominant class, not just immediate needs, but their future needs as well. Above all, this meant the establishment of a completely new type of bond between town and country which quickly eliminated both the political and the economic basis of popular support for the old feudal forces.

Methods that were successful in France in establishing bourgeois hegemony and in creating the conditions for the further expansion of the capitalist mode of production, were rarely repeated, however, in the rest of mainland Europe. In effect, what had been a revolution from below in 1789 now became a revolution from above, nowhere more so than in Italy's own bourgeois revolution during the Risorgimento. The real stalwarts of the transition at this time were the Piedmontese monarchy, army, bureaucracy and a few prominent intellectuals. At no time in the struggle for power, however, was there ever a genuine attempt to establish a much broader historical bloc of forces – incorporating the peasants, for example – which could in turn be cemented by a clearly defined collective will. For Gramsci, therefore, the result of the Risorgimento was largely negative. The bourgeoisie 'said that they were aiming at the creation of a modern state in Italy, and they in fact produced a bastard'.[51]

From these historical illustrations, Gramsci is now able to draw a number of general theoretical principles of such passive-type revolutions. First, the notion is a means by which one can understand the passive manner of a change in political and social power relationships at the top, occurring *in conjunction with* radical changes in the means and relationships of economic production in the base of society. Second, it helps to explain the means by which changes in relationships of power occur within the realm of the state with the aim of preserving state control by the minority elite over the masses. And third, it is a means by which a dominant class is able to maintain its power more because of a weakness on the part of an adversary, rather than because of its own positive attributes of hegemony.

Having given an analysis of how the bourgeoisie (in one national context) was able to acquire hegemony in this passive consensual way, Gramsci is concerned to demonstrate, in much broader terms, various ways in which this kind of hegemony can likewise be *maintained* in an equally passive manner. Whenever Gramsci writes about the maintenance of hegemony under the bourgeoisie and capitalist mode of production, he understands a notion of consent as signifying 'some degree of *conscious attachment to,* or *agreement with,* certain core elements of the society'.[52] As Femia notes, therefore, it is largely a *psychological* interpretation of consent, rather than a moral or prescriptive interpretation.[53] Or, as Tamburrano puts it, it is an expression 'of intellectual and moral direction through which the masses feel permanently tied to the ideology and political leadership of the state as the expression of their beliefs and aspirations'.[54]

At the heart of Gramsci's writings here is his study of linguistics and the role of language as an important component of hegemony. In his concept of *translatability,* for example, Gramsci was able to provide a cognitive method of linguistics that was firmly linked to his desire to formulate an organic unity of the constituent parts of the philosophy of praxis:

> Translatability presupposes that a given phase of civilisation has a fundamentally identical cultural expression, even though the language is historically different, determined by the particular tradition of any national culture and any philosophical system, from the predominance of an intellectual or practical activity.[55]

They are reciprocal and translatable because each individual language, from a materialist perspective, is 'adherent to reality'; because each language is adherent to reality, they ultimately represent organic cultural expressions of a given set of social and political forces.[56]

Cognitive, theoretical methods aside, what interested Gramsci most was the way in which language served a practical hegemonic function. In the section of the *Prison Notebooks* where he ascertained that a historical act can only be performed by collective man on the basis of a cultural-social unity, this is then followed up with the conclusion that 'since this is the way things happen, great importance is assumed by the general question of language, that is, the question of collectively attaining a single cultural climate'.[57] Because language is the mechanism of attaining an integrative social consciousness, it follows that this inevitably gives it a political importance of great magnitude. For as long as concepts like 'freedom' and 'democracy' are given a linguistic connotation which helps to preserve a cultural unity for a dominant class formation, then it will clearly make it very difficult indeed for alternative interpretations and definitions to be widely propagated, let alone accepted. Even if groups are dissatisfied by a given social system, they have an immense hurdle to cross in being able to *define* that dissatisfaction, before going on to find ways of remedying it.

Another element very much associated with the role of language for Gramsci is the phenomenon he calls *common sense* – 'the folklore of philosophy'. In essence, common sense refers to the whole realm of human sentiments, human myths and human superstitions. It is Gramsci's way of trying to understand some of the *uncritical* and *unconscious* ways in which all human beings try to make sense not only of their own lives, but of the world around them. In particular, it is an attempt to understand the manner in which people absorb long-established historical ideas and aim to fit them in a contemporary setting to provide some element or some desire for stability. Gramsci makes it plain that common sense is by no means equivalent with, or reducible to, a ruling-class ideology. It is instead 'an infinity of traces without an inventory'. Nevertheless, as a means of perpetuating fragmentary and superstitious attitudes, it is equally made plain that a ruling class will inevitably be tempted to harness such sentiments for its own ends. And certainly, language – understood again as 'a totality of determined notions and concepts and not just of words grammatically devoid of content'[58] – is one of the tools for reinforcing certain 'desirable' commonsensical values.

If one is to free oneself from the restrictions of common sense, and if one is to look at the world from the perspective of a *senso buono* (good sense) – one that is able to define the *real* needs and interests of the masses of ordinary people – then it is almost certainly incumbent to learn a *new* language so as to attack all the old encrustations embedded deeply in the existing form of language. Overcoming the deficiencies of common sense and viewing the world with good sense, however, is no easy matter, as Gramsci himself admits. Even if the basis of the existing form of common sense begins to break down, there is still the phenomenon of *contradictory consciousness* to be overcome. What Gramsci is alluding to here is the dichotomy that often exists between thought and action, 'between one's intellectual affirmation and one's mode of conduct'. The latter may well produce a set of circumstances which might represent an objective denial of the existing form of hegemony. But if this practical situation is not complemented by a subjective, conscious comprehension of such circumstances, then the practical counter-hegemonic moment is lost.

It is precisely through such *passive* notions as common sense and contradictory consciousness, backed up by a requisite set of linguistic definitions, that capitalism is able to preserve itself on a largely consensual basis. Capitalism is not maintained by a mass popular affirmation or affection for what the system objectively produces for society as a whole; it is maintained by the way it has hitherto marginalised alternatives against it, a 'better the devil you know' kind of common-sense attitude, which in turn promotes a notion of apathy and disinterestedness in the very possibility of change. Many social groups, meanwhile, who derive little material benefit from such a socio-economic system often lack the conceptual and linguistic tools to understand their position in this system, let alone do anything about it. After all, Gramsci argues, nearly all the key institutions of civil society which are encountered by the individual or group exist to perpetuate the given conventions of a capitalist society, and therefore operate as an effective barrier to the promotion of radical alternatives.

Of course, not all conflicts and expressions of disaffection are stifled or eradicated on the terrain of civil society. Nevertheless, Gramsci is likewise adamant that the room for manoeuvre is often limited by the way in which not only values and desires, but *expectations* as well, are moulded by the institutions loyal to the ruling forces. As for those elements, meanwhile, that do actively support the socio-economic system for the material gains it offers, it must be remembered that they are perfectly capable of mystifying any sense of inequality that is produced.

How, then, does Gramsci suggest that all these passive mechanisms of consent can be transformed into *active* mechanisms under a viable communist-based hegemony? On the level of consciousness, he is adamant that his development of the concept of hegemony as a critique of bourgeois systems 'represents a great philosophical advance, as well as a politico-practical one, [because] it necessarily supposes an intellectual unity and an ethic in conformity with a conception of reality that has gone beyond common sense and has become, if only within narrow limits, a *critical* conception'.[59] This process of supersedure is often described by Gramsci as a catharsis, a process which takes an individual out of the realm of necessity, viewed as 'an external force which crushes man, assimilates him to itself and makes him passive', and takes him into the realm of freedom.[60] Here, the power of man's rationality is developed by an ability to comprehend objective interests and needs at any given stage and to develop a course of action that suitably corresponds to these needs. By this means as well, contradictory consciousness can slowly be transcended by a more *authentic* type of consciousness whereby man's perceptions and evaluations of his own practical social existence become more consistent and less superficial. Gramsci emphasises, however, that this is not an authenticity that is passively created outside of an individual's own experience capabilities. An authentic consciousness does not exist in opposition to the spontaneous feelings of the masses; if there is a difference between the two, it is one of quantitative difference of degree, not one of quality. As Femia has rightly noted, Gramsci's desire to formulate an authentic consciousness of the masses 'does not go beyond drawing out the theoretical implications of what they are *in fact* doing and saying'.[61] And as Gramsci himself goes on to note, it is a matter of 'rendering practice more homogenous, more coherent [and] more efficient in all its elements, and thus ... developing its potential to the maximum'.[62] Summing up the task of trying to instigate a more active form of conscious awareness the following, purely rhetorical, question is thus posed:

> [Is] it better to 'think' without having a critical awareness, in a disjointed and episodic way? ... Or, on the other hand, is it better to work out consciously and critically one's own conception of the world and thus, in connection with the labours of one's own brain, choose one's sphere of activity, take an active part in the creation of the history of the world, be one's own guide, refusing to accept passively and supinely from outside the moulding of one's own personality?[63]

Away from the realm of consciousness, on the level of active consentient practices, Gramsci is clear in his desire to give new life to that central tenet of classical democracy – popular forms of participation. In a rare passage in which he looks forward to the new society based on council democracy, he argues categorically that consent should not be considered reducible to one fleeting moment of casting a vote. Rather, it should be 'permanently active'.[64]

Of course, no amount of fine words and theorising about the *a priori* benefits of an active critical consciousness and the self-determining, self-governing advantages of greater participation could have much of an effect if not backed up and demonstrated in a practical form. As has already been demonstrated so often, all concepts and ideas possessed validity for Gramsci only in so far as they were able to be demonstrated in practice. It was not practice of any kind, however, that Gramsci was interested in. The clear deficiencies of bourgeois passive practices would have to be addressed head on by a counter-hegemonic force fully prepared to give widespread credence to *anti*-passive practices; this could only be achieved if such counter-hegemonic forces represented an embodiment of active consentient ideals in their own internal structures, and in the kind of practical relationships that existed between leaders and led within these structures. In other words, a counter-hegemonic force must attempt to portray itself, in all ways possible, as a future *state in miniature*.

From the perspective of the party organisation, this meant, in particular, the development of a highly *expansive* form of consent, which would exclude all forms of bureaucratism, corporatism and any reduction of democratic principles to their formal or legal aspects only. Instead, the expansive nature of the party must promote the active participation of all members even at the risk of provoking an appearance of break-up and tumult. A collective consciousness is a living organism which is not formed except after multiplicity has been unified through the friction of the individual members. One thing that will help maintain the unity of any party is discipline. But here again, from the perspective of encouraging an expansive form of consent for the actions of a party, discipline should never be imposed in a formal manner, which might result in a passive and servile acceptance of orders or as a mechanical execution of a command. Finally, and perhaps most significantly of all, the expansive nature of the party must produce a situation in which any activity it undertakes is constantly compatible with the actual experience of its members and supporters in their everyday social existence. The optimal result must be the establishment of a reciprocal relationship in which 'every teacher is always a pupil and every pupil a teacher'.[65] The day-to-day reality of social life, in other words, must be 'translated' into the language of theory and not vice versa. After all, it is experience itself which provides the ultimate validity of ideas.

From the perspective of the broader counter-hegemonic historical bloc, meanwhile, Gramsci insists that an active form of consent can only exist here if there is a genuine process of interest *articulation*, rather than – as occurred in the Risorgimento – a process of interest absorption and neutralisation (transformism). Whereas the latter aims simply to prevent subordinate interests from ever being in a position to perhaps challenge the interests of the dominant class within a bloc of forces, the former, expansive type of articulation aims to promote the full development of *all* interests within the bloc, and aims to resolve any contradictions of interest and demands so as to produce a greater synthesis of unity. This synthesis of unity will make the society as a whole advance, rather than one component part.

As most commentators point out, the vast bulk of Gramsci's writings on the need for an active, expansive type of party and historical bloc represented an explicit attack on the ideas and practices of his fellow communist activist in Italy, Amadeo Bordiga. A more intriguing question, however, is to what extent they also represented an implicit criticism of the Russian revolutionary experience. After all, Gramsci's ideas on the internal mechanisms of the party did seem to suggest a distinctly different set of relationships than those that were observable in the Bolshevik party, while the stress on articulation rather than absorption or assimilation of subordinate interests likewise appeared to be distinctly non-Bolshevik. It is to questions of this kind, and Gramsci's own – albeit often surreptitious – analysis of the Russian revolutionary experience in his later, more reflective prison writings, which will now be taken up in the remainder of this chapter.

Gramsci's East–West Dichotomy

Of the many motifs contained in the *Prison Notebooks,* the East–West motif is undoubtedly one of the most important. It is to be found in Gramsci's understanding of the significance of the relationship between state and civil society and in the contrast between pre-modern and modern conditions; in his debt to Lenin in his own formulation of the logic and scope of the conceptual remit of hegemony; in the contrasting role of revolutionary strategy, between manoeuvre and attrition, movement and position; in the general lessons to be learned from revolutionary success following the Bolshevik victory in October 1917, and in a whole host of other areas as well.

Before going on to assess some of the pivotal implications of this series of motifs, let us be clear about one thing right from the outset. No one celebrated and glorified the achievement and experience of the Bolshevik revolution more than Gramsci. From some of his very first writings as a young journalist to his very last writings in prison, he determinedly adhered to the line that the events of October 1917 represented the most decisive turning-point in the whole of human history. But what also characterised the continuity of his understanding of the revolution was its fundamental *exceptional* nature. Exceptional in the sense that the revolution clearly did not conform to the accepted paradigm of a socialist transcendence of a well-developed capitalist foundation, in the sense of Lenin's unique qualities as an inspired revolutionary leader, and in the sense that what occurred in Russia was unrepeatable in a Western context in precisely the same form.

In Gramsci's view, one of Lenin's main legacies was his own recognition of the uniqueness of the Russian situation. As he puts it in the *Prison Notebooks:*

> ... Ilitch understood that a change was necessary from the war of manoeuvre applied victoriously in the East in 1917, to a war of position which was the only form possible in the West ... This is what the formula of the 'United Front' seems to me to mean ... Ilitch, however, did not have time to expand his formula – though it should be borne in mind that he could only have expanded it theoretically ...[66]

The use of the word *theoretically* here is very significant. As Gramsci goes on to note, given the fact that the fundamental task of the revolutionary is to be acutely aware of the specificities of the national context in which the struggle is being waged, Lenin's contribution could have only been that of an outsider, even if a committed and engaged one. It is also significant because it allows us to question just how successful Gramsci himself was in developing a broader theoretical basis for his own ideas on the East–West dichotomy.

According to Perry Anderson, what really sets Gramsci apart from his contemporaries is not so much the persistent advocacy of the belief that the Russian revolutionary experience could not simply be repeated in the West, but his attempt to understand *why* this was so. It was here that Gramsci was entering largely uncharted territory for a socialist thinker of this particular era.[67] The essence of Gramsci's conception of this 'why' can be found immediately after the aforementioned comments on Lenin, in a passage which is arguably one of the most celebrated ones of the entire prison writings:

> In the East, the state was everything, civil society was primordial and gelatinous; in the West, there was a proper relationship between state and civil society, and when the state trembled a sturdy structure of civil society was at once revealed. The state was only an outer ditch, behind which there was a powerful system of fortresses and earthworks: more or less numerous from one state to the next, it goes without saying – but this precisely necessitated an accurate reconnaissance of each individual country.[68]

The importance of a 'proper relationship between state and civil society' in the West has already been extensively dealt with. But what precisely did Gramsci mean by his reference to a primordial and gelatinous civil society in the East and what significances stemmed from this? Certainly one thing he meant by it was the way in which state power in the East was more explicit, more visible, and far less reliant on the kind of *voluntary,* albeit largely passive, forms of consent that exist in the West. Precisely because state power was not camouflaged behind the plethora of rights ensconced in civil society – rights such as universal suffrage or freedom of the press – then it clearly meant that a full-scale assault on the state was the only real alternative open to an opposition force which desired to be in power. For all its explicit show of strength and domination, therefore, the Russian state was far more susceptible to a rival force (than a Western state) because of its *lack* of popular consent. This, then, is Gramsci's basic reason for continuing to justify the Bolshevik war of manoeuvre strategy in 1917, without wanting it to be considered as the most viable strategy of opposition in the different conditions in the West.

The question is, however, is this a sufficient basis in itself to construct a theory on the dichotomies distinguishing East from West? In the view of Anderson, the answer is no. Indeed, not to mince words, Anderson is adamant that Gramsci ultimately failed in the task which he had apparently set himself. While he undoubtedly had a deep intuition about the significance of the difference between East and West and the fact that this would mark a fundamental differentiation of Marxist theoretical and political approaches, and while these deep intuitions contained a great deal of historical truth, he was never really able to comprehend the underlying reasons for this. A Marxist – or, more accurately speaking, a 'scientific' – account of the distinction between East and West always eluded him. To use Anderson's own phrase: 'The image from the compass itself proved, in the end, a snare.'[69]

Gramsci's dichotomy, continues Anderson, was ultimately nothing more than geographical in character which therefore assumed 'an unproblematic comparability' of the terms East and West. In social terms, this assumption was that East and West 'exist in the *same temporality,* and can therefore be read off against each other as variations of a common category'. This was nowhere more apparent than in Gramsci's view of the state. His 'natural assumption' was that the state in the East and the West was the same *'type of object'* in both. Little did Gramsci realise, laments Anderson, that it was precisely this assumption which needed to be questioned. By preserving such a simultaneity of terms, such a *'paralogism',* Gramsci was blocking off the one approach which could have given him access to a far more genuine theoretical understanding of the East–West dichotomy, an understanding which had to be underpinned by an appreciation of the differentiated historical time which the two realms inhabited. Only by this means would socialist militants come to see the enormous gulf between the Russian autocracy and the capitalist states with which they were confronted in the West (and whose theoretical conception had to be constructed *separately*).[70]

Moreover, just to rub salt into Gramsci's already profuse wounds, Anderson goes on to argue that where Gramsci failed to formulate the true nature of the distinction between East and West, it was his great antagonist at this time, Amadeo Bordiga, who *did* succeed; although not even Bordiga was able to utilise this truth and theorise it 'into any cogent political practice'. The claim to Bordiga's superiority here lay precisely in the fact that he unambiguously recognised the true nature of the dichotomy as one pitting a feudal autocracy against a bourgeois democracy. Because of the accuracy of this formulation, it 'allowed him to grasp the essential twin character of the capitalist state'. Not only was it stronger than the Tsarist state because it rested on a more advanced basis of mass consent. More significantly, it was also a superior repressive apparatus. What Bordiga thus recognised, and Gramsci did not, was that the 'keys' to the power of the capitalist state in the West lay in this *conjoined* superiority.[71]

Given the crucial importance of the East–West dichotomy in Gramsci's writings, there can be no doubt that if Anderson's critique is valid, it would seriously undermine not just many of the key theoretical contributions made by Gramsci at this time, but it would also undermine much of his whole strategic approach, an approach which still continues to have enormous contemporary salience. What defence, then, can be made of Gramsci in this crucial domain? Three things, it seems to me, are important to stress. First, while it is undoubtedly true that Gramsci never achieved a 'scientific' basis for his understanding of the East–West dichotomy, it must be recognised that it was never his intention to do so – at least not in the terms of 'science' denoted by Anderson. Indeed, Gramsci was always rather suspicious of the term 'scientific', believing it to be a methodology supposedly general and universal in scope, but which in reality only gave rise to a logic which consisted 'solely in being in conformity with the end'.[72]

Second, Anderson himself openly acknowledges that when he charges Gramsci with the 'crimes' of paralogism and terminological simultaneity, these are in effect based upon no stronger forms of evidence than 'unspoken presuppositions'[73] which lie behind the central texts of the *Prison Notebooks*. And third, the 'deep intuitions' possessed by Gramsci, which in themselves contain a great deal of 'historical truth', are far more substantively accounted for in a theoretical manner than Anderson gives him credit for; what is more, they are accounted for in ways which do not assume, naturally or otherwise, paralogistic commonality or terminological simultaneity.

The stress on civil society and its relationship with the state is, of course, most crucial here. Gramsci's writings do not just capture the strategic differences between Russia and the West and the kind of revolutionary politics that will be determined by these differences. They also capture very adequately the *theoretical* specificities underpinning the divergence of political, social and economic conditions in Eastern and Western societies. Moreover, in understanding and theorising the relative position of the domain of civil society, this cannot do otherwise than differentiate the role and status of the state in the two locations. Because of the difference in the nature of the two civil societies, Gramsci is well aware that the state is *not* the same type of object in both; it cannot possibly be the same, and if there is any natural assumption at work here, it is this.

As for Gramsci's supposed assumption that East and West inhabit the same temporal realm, which therefore gives rise to an 'unproblematic comparability', most of the textual evidence very much contradicts this viewpoint. Gramsci has an acutely keen awareness of many different forms of temporal disparities, not least as they specifically affect the geopolitical dichotomy between East and West. Indeed, as Fabio Frosini has pointed out, the themes of 'specificity', 'difference', 'stratification' and the 'inelegant incoherence of real history' are the most consistent ones permeating the whole of Gramsci's political theory, both in and out of prison.[74] Moreover, far from being 'unproblematic', Gramsci is more than acutely aware of their intractability. If there is a task he sets himself in this domain, however, it is to try to find ways to overcome some of these ingrained problems. Take, for example, his writings on the notion of translatability. As we have already seen, Gramsci's main premise here is that two fundamentally similar socio-economic structures will have 'equivalent' superstructures that are mutually translatable, irrespective of particular national languages. If his argument was limited to this, Anderson's critique would undoubtedly have some validity. Gramsci, however, does not limit his analysis to this, but goes one step further. Where the real problem is to be found is in the nature of the reciprocity and translatability of two civilisations where each one has attained a different level of historical development. Gramsci's answer to this problem is to suggest that by means of the 'philosophy of praxis' it might be possible to resolve this problem by an extension of the logic of translatability in one of two possible ways. What needs to be seen, he writes, is

… whether one can [still] translate between expressions of different stages of civilisation, in so far as each of these stages is a moment of the development of another, one thus mutually integrating the other, or whether a given expression may be translated using the terms of a previous stage of the same civilisation, a previous stage which however is more comprehensible than the given language, etc.[75]

This is the real problem, then, that needs to be resolved. But it is a problem clearly founded on the strongest possible recognition of historical-temporal disparity, and it is a problem, the resolution of which, cannot possibly ignore the fundamental basis of that disparity. Moreover, it is a problem of immense contemporaneous significance for as Gramsci's introduction to his writings on translatability pointed out, it was none other than Lenin himself who admitted that, from the Russian Bolshevik perspective, 'we have not been able to "translate" our language into those of Europe'.[76]

Last, but not least, when it comes to crediting Bordiga with a greater appreciation of the 'conjoined superiority' of the Western capitalist state, and the supplementary claim that Gramsci overestimated the consensual basis of this superiority while underestimating its superior repressive abilities, such a claim appears to be very wide off the mark (as a detailed reading of Notebook 13 in particular demonstrates). The stress on the consensual mechanisms of Western capitalist power and the associated need for a revolutionary war of position to undermine this consent was, of course, absolutely crucial for Gramsci. But at no time did he regard this as sufficient in itself to obtain power for the working class in its fight with the bourgeoisie. The war of position was consistently seen as a vital prelude to the ultimate requirement of a full-scale war of manoeuvre; Gramsci was the last person to underestimate the repressive power of the state which would be used when this moment arrived. What Gramsci most wanted to avoid by his stress on the war of position was immature, artificial and ultimately lethal forms of adventurism, as witnessed for example in Germany in the spring of 1921 (and which was also a form of self-criticism of his own actions for much of the period prior to his arrest). But this was not in any sense of the term some kind of apologia for reformism, neither in intention, nor in consequence. Nor was it a sign, to use another formula of Anderson's, that this weakness in strategy was 'symmetrical with that of his sociology'.[77]

Apart from the kind of disputes outlined above in the debate with Anderson, Gramsci's writings on the East–West dichotomy have frequently given rise to a whole series of fundamental disagreements on numerous other crucial issues as well; as a matter of policy, one can certainly say that any commentator entering this 'minefield' of debate must do so with extreme care and caution. For example, although there is undoubtedly a near-universal recognition that the ideas of Gramsci represented a major contribution to the foundation of a very specific form of *Western* Marxism, which clearly delineated the very different kind of terrain which revolutionary socialists had to work in, such a distinction should most definitely not carry a simple or easy qualitative assessment concerning some kind of intrinsic superiority of the West over the East. In the aftermath of the 1917 revolution, particularly at a time of great optimism about its possible and potential developmental capacity, Gramsci was one of the first to recognise the West's new-found inferiority to Russia. Nor, perhaps more importantly, should Gramsci's East–West dichotomy be understood as a desire to impose a process of Westernisation upon Russia. He most certainly did not want to 'occidentalise' the Bolsheviks after 1917.

Likewise, one should avoid the over-reductionist trap of equating a simple correlation between an East–West dichotomy with that of a dictatorship–hegemony dichotomy. The potential for a more expansive type of consensual hegemony as envisaged by Gramsci was not in some way *naturally* inconsistent with Russian patterns of development. Nor was Gramsci averse to supporting the use of dictatorial methods (by the Bolsheviks or any other group) if the situation or the circumstances warranted it for the good of the socialist cause.[78]

Perhaps the biggest bone of contention in the East–West domain, however, relates to the nature of the relationships between Gramsci and Lenin on the one hand, and with Stalin on the other. On the first of these relationships, much has already been written and does not merit repetition. On the specific issue of the concept of hegemony, I think that there can be little doubt that while Gramsci was always oriented towards a Leninist line (referring to Lenin's theorisation and realisation of hegemony in one instance as one of the 'great metaphysical events') and always defended Lenin's strategic use of hegemony in the Russian national context in 1917, he nevertheless went on to evolve a conceptual form of hegemony of his own which was far richer than anything Lenin was able to achieve. In the view of Giuseppe Tamburrano, by the time of the *Prison Notebooks,* any Leninist attributes which Gramsci had previously given credence to were now definitively overcome.[79] This, it seems to me, is taking matters much too far, and too easily paves the way for a false, incongruous social-democratisation of Gramsci. It also overlooks the fact that Gramsci was always adamant that his own ultimate measurement of revolutionary success would be the achievement of a result 'identical' to that attained by the Bolsheviks. A more accurate comparison, then, is surely that given by Carl Boggs: 'while Gramsci had the same revolutionary impatience as Lenin, his outlook contained a democratic sensibility and cultural breadth that was absent from Leninism'.[80]

More problematical, of course, is the extent to which Gramsci's writings are able to supply us with a running commentary on how he viewed developments taking place in Soviet Russia under the leadership of Stalin. 'Problematical' not so much because there are strong disagreements as to whether he had any real residual sympathies for Stalinist methods and policies – there can be almost no doubt that he did not – but because from the confines of his prison cell, such developments as he got to hear about were so sketchy and partial that one is left with little more than oblique references to his views. Such problems aside, however, the art of hidden detection and deduction does at least provide us with some scope for serious analysis.

Without doubt, the foundation of any implicit criticism of Stalin can first of all be located in the last exchange of letters Gramsci had with Togliatti in Moscow and in his (in)famous letter of 14 October 1926 to the Central Committee of the Soviet Communist Party itself. Written very much as an unsolicited response (and against Togliatti's own wishes) to the leadership struggle that was being waged between the majority Stalin-Bukharin faction and the minority Trotsky-Zinoviev-Kamenev faction, these letters were to have enormous repercussions in Soviet–Italian Communist Party relations for many years to come, and an even longer impact on internal relations inside the Italian Communist Party.[81]

Ostensibly supportive of the Stalinist majority faction, Gramsci's letter not only made his own party's support highly conditional, he also lamented the potentially excessive price at which Stalin's victory, particularly in his struggle with Trotsky, had been gained. The conditionality of the support was evident in a number of ways, ranging from the need for the majority to be magnanimous in its victory and to recognise the legitimate rights of the opposition, to the even wider claim that the supremacy of the Soviet Communist Party in the broader international communist movement would continue to be recognised only for as long as it fully appreciated its real internationalist duties on the 'general perspective of socialism'. As for the costs incurred, Gramsci was most concerned here precisely with the effect it would have on the Bolshevik's hegemonic capacity. Summing up some of his misgivings, Gramsci writes in his very last letter to Togliatti:

> Today, at nine years distance from October 1917, it is no longer *the fact of the seizure of power* by the Bolsheviks which can revolutionize the ... masses, because this has already been allowed for and has produced its

effects. What is active today, ideologically and politically, is the conviction (if it exists) that the proletariat, once power has been taken, *can construct socialism*.[82]

The distinction between capturing state power and being in a position to construct a viable form of socialism which is genuinely hegemonic in an active, consensual, democratic, participatory way was from now on to be the centrepiece of Gramsci's political writings, and the motivation for this distinction in the practical experience of the Bolsheviks is, of course, extremely incisive.

As already mentioned, in the *Prison Notebooks* themselves, direct and explicit references to developmental processes in the USSR are extremely sparse and sporadic. Nevertheless, in light of his concerns expressed in his final pre-prison letters, there can be little doubt that inserted within his reflections on other issues and matters is a continuing worry about the future of the Soviet experiment under Stalin's direction.

Let us return, for example, to Gramsci's writings on the nature of the state–civil society relationship. The consequences of a lack of a fully functioning civil society in the East have already been alluded to. What Gramsci now begins to do is to look at the kind of problems implicitly associated with a capture of power by means of a direct assault on the state in conditions where a civil society is negligible or non-existent. One of the intrinsic problems of such a scenario is the way in which a degenerate form of statisation, or what Gramsci terms *statolatry*, may well become endemically entrenched. That is to say, having not been able to rely on a mass popular initiative for the capture of power, the process of transition afterwards may also come to rely primarily on the state as the key protagonist of change rather than on a more expansive base of support. Should this occur, what you are faced with is essentially another form of a very passive type of revolution, based on a totally passive form of consent, in which politics becomes identified purely with the statist and instrumental domain of domination, characterised by such things as bureaucratic centralism, authoritarian paternalism, state fanaticism and totalitarianism. The inevitable result of all this is what Gramsci calls a *dictatorship without hegemony*, a phenomenon very well summarised by Buci-Glucksmann:

In the event that the state becomes a partisan-state (or even a party-state), hegemony is restricted not only in its mass basis, but also within the class itself: 'the hegemony will be exercised by a *part* of the social group over the entire group, and not by the latter over other forces in order to

give power to the movement.' ... Thereupon, the hegemonic apparatuses ... become ideological state apparatuses.[83]

The precise contextual location of Gramsci's discussion of the phenomenon of dictatorship without hegemony is explicitly set in Italy, forming
part of the broader analysis of why the Risorgimento led to a 'bastard' kind
of state. It clearly does not stretch the imagination too much, however, to
see that Gramsci was equally motivated here by an obvious concern that
a genuine capacity for hegemony – as he understood it and not as Lenin
understood it – might also fail to materialise in post-revolutionary Russia,
particularly in light of the fact that these notes were written at exactly the
time in which Stalin was trumpeting the very notion of a 'perpetual statolatry'.[84]

From his analysis of the Risorgimento, however, Gramsci does at least
implicitly offer one piece of advice to his Russian comrades from his
prison cell. If an expansive class is to avoid being replaced by a narrow
dictatorial state, it must gain hegemony both before *and* after the seizure
of power. Now we know that Gramsci fully understood that the Bolsheviks had no chance to create a hegemonic base *prior* to the seizure of power
in October 1917 because of the primordial and gelatinous nature of Russia's civil society and its all-encompassing state. But Gramsci's stress here
on the need to gain hegemony *after* the seizure of power is very instruc-
tive. What he seems to be exhorting Stalin and the rest of the Soviet
leadership at this time to do, is to construct for themselves a fully functioning civil society with a full range of non-institutional apparatuses,
which would in turn encourage a dynamic and positive sense of adhe-
sion to the new socialist project through the 'socialisation of politics'.
Gramsci fully recognises that: 'For some social groups, which before their
ascent to autonomous state life have not had a long independent period
of cultural and moral development on their own ... a period of statolatry
is necessary and indeed opportune.' However, 'this kind of statolatry must
not be abandoned to itself, must not, especially, become theoretical fanaticism or be conceived of as perpetual'.[85] Instead, the capturing of state
power must represent a

> ... movement to create a new civilisation, a new type of man and of
> citizen, *[it] must serve to determine the will to construct within the husk of
> political society a complex and well-articulated civil society,* in which the
> individual can govern himself without his self-government thereby
> entering into conflict with political society – but rather becoming its
> normal continuation, its organic complement.[86]

As things turned out, of course, Stalin did not take up Gramsci's advice and instead implemented a revolution from above, whose only links with the base of society were the social 'transmission belts' firmly under the control of the dictatorial state apparatus; in other words, instead of the new state giving birth to civil society, it smothered it. For all his references to the Communist Party's leading role in society, the Stalinist process of development clearly resulted in a triumph of 'domination' over 'leadership' from a Gramscian perspective. Bureaucratic centralism, authoritarian paternalism and totalitarianism were indeed the results of this 'fanatical state domination', this dictatorship without hegemony. There can be little doubt that, even from the confines of his prison cell, Gramsci was sufficiently well informed of the visible signs of degeneration permeating Stalin's Russia. His warnings about the dangers of the party relying on bureaucratic, rather than democratic forms of centralism, for example, is an obvious case in point. Bureaucratic centralism might well be the appropriate organisational mechanism for a church, but a political party aspiring to create the nucleus of a new expansive type of hegemony must be able to go beyond the use of such regressive methods. The consequences for the party if it cannot achieve this are clear: it will stagnate and ossify under illusions of unity and immutability.

In his own analysis of the importance of Gramsci's writings on passive revolution and their direct association with Stalinist developments in the USSR, Giuseppe Vacca has gone even further in his critical appraisal. Concentrating in particular on the economic consequences of Stalinist policies after the introduction of the First Five Year Plan, he is adamant that Gramsci's constant references to an 'economic-corporatist phase of the state' are directly inspired by his very negative views on Soviet developments. The model of centralised planning ultimately adopted by Stalin is seen as extremely poverty-stricken, based as it was on a misdirected reading of the schema of economic reproduction outlined in the second volume of Marx's *Capital*.[87]

Of particular concern to Gramsci is the course of economic development outlined in the first official Stalinist manual on Soviet economic policy *(Politicheskaya ekonomika),* written by Lapidus and Ostrovitianov and published in 1928.[88] In subsequent notes written over a three-year period from 1932 to 1935, Gramsci not only gives testimony to the deficiencies of the type of centralised planning mechanisms which were being envisaged, and which were later put into practice, but also to the fact that if this was now an 'official' manual on economic policy, it signified already just how dogmatic and ossified intellectual activity in the Soviet Union had become. On such a crucial issue as this, which required maximum intellectual abilities, mental freshness and scientific inventiveness, the result had been nothing more than wretched 'mumbo-jumbo' of the worst mystificatory kind. As Vacca thus goes on to point out, on the basis of his reflections of intellectual life in the Soviet Union and what he went on to define as the resulting 'scarcity of superstructural elements', Gramsci was acutely aware of Stalin's growing incapacity 'to elaborate any kind of hegemony'.[89] Moreover, negative criticisms applied by Gramsci to the industrial side of Stalinist economic activity after 1928/29 were reflected even more critically in his underlying references to agricultural collectivisation – a policy Gramsci found most abhorrent, Francesco Benvenuti and Silvio Pons imply, given its effect of destroying the old alliance between the working class and the peasantry which had been the very backbone of the uniquely positive side of Leninist hegemony.[90]

In answer to the question, then, as to whether Gramsci considered Stalinism a progressive or regressive form of 'Caesarism', there can be little doubt that it was the latter. As Vacca notes, the real regressive features of Stalinist Caesarism lay precisely in the fact that the Stalinist state could not provide the motive force for a 'universal' progression and expansion in a development of all the national energies. The dominant economic-corporate interests embodied in Stalin's state did not address itself to the task of finding a stable equilibrium with those subordinate forces it was supposed to lead. Its mode was not one of equilibrium, but of outright destruction.[91] In its specific ideological form, it amounted to nothing more than polemicism rather than a genuine canon of historical interpretation. As some of his fellow prison inmates later testified, there were times – particularly as regards the notion of 'social fascism' – when Gramsci openly alluded to Stalinist ideological orientations as acts of 'political suicide' carried out by an old-fashioned 'despot'.[92]

Indeed, on occasion, Gramsci's criticism of Stalinist policies even penetrated the barriers of implicitness, as witnessed, for example, by his stinging critique of the artistic policy of socialist realism. For Gramsci, 'art is art and not "willed" political propaganda', and any simplistic or mechanical attempt to harness the intrinsic aesthetic qualities of art to political control will make it fictitious and dull.[93]

The ultimate conclusion of Gramsci's analysis of the dichotomy between East and West, then, is this. Gramsci remained a Leninist in so far as he fully supported and justified the revolutionary onslaught against the Russian state in the unique conditions which prevailed in October 1917 as a historically necessary and progressive act. He was also adamant that the foundation of Leninist hegemony was the maintenance of the alliance between workers and peasants. He was not a Leninist, however, if this implied (as it frequently did), a reduction of hegemony to a form of proletarian dictatorship exercised primarily within and through the institutional realm of state power. And he certainly was not an advocate of the Stalinist process of state-dominated developments after 1929, but instead criticised it, as we have seen, for its closed, dogmatic, rigid, uncritical and elitist methods across the whole policy domain. The struggle for hegemony in Russia in the years after the revolution necessarily had to be fought on a different terrain than that waged in 1917 itself, or in the Civil War years. It was a struggle, however, that was ultimately lost. As Giuseppe Vacca has rightly asserted, in Gramsci's eyes the dichotomy separating East and West was not only not resolved by Stalin, it became ever more crystallised.[94]

As time went by, the light which had once burned bright from the East and which had so powerfully illuminated the aged Western world in 1917 had begun to lose at least some of its resplendence for Gramsci by the end of his prison confinement. What had started out as such a promising new civilisation, culture, and way of life had become frustrated. Writing many years later, Régis Debray recommended that: 'The Gramscian task for us today is to seek out the reasons, the modalities and the consequences of that frustration.'[95] To engage in that task is not only to employ Gramsci's methodology of analysis, or even the basis of his own hopes and aspirations. It is to engage in his own first-hand account of the frustrations which he himself bore witness to even from the confines of his fascist incarceration.

3 From Monologue to Dialogue: Gramsci's Reception in Soviet Russia

> I know the force of words, I know their clarion call.
> They aren't the words applauded in the stalls,
> Such words rouse coffins from the grave
> And bring them striding on oaken legs!
> Rejected sometimes, unpublished and unread,
> But still the word hurtles on, tightening its saddle girths
> Ringing through the ages; and trains crawl up
> To lick the calloused hands of verse.
>
> Vladimir Mayakovsky, Unfinished poem

Gramsci the 'Dissident'

As we have already seen, many of Gramsci's criticisms concerning developments that were taking place in Soviet Russia throughout the 1920s and early 1930s were necessarily of an implied form. That the interpretation of these implications should engender negative forms, however, is backed up by Gramsci's youngest son, Giuliano. Born and brought up in Moscow (where he has subsequently spent his whole life), Giuliano Gramsci has no doubts that his father's concerns for the fate of socialism in Soviet Russia at this time were very genuine and very deep-seated: 'My father knew the situation very well in the USSR. He had learned the language and was closely following what was happening. He saw and he knew many things that caused him considerable anxiety.'[1]

For Giuliano Gramsci, as for many others, the evidence of this concern really commences with the last letters written by his father prior to his arrest in November 1926, all of which closely addressed the situation inside the Soviet Union and, in particular, the Communist Party. As was mentioned in the last chapter, pre-dating some of the major themes of his later prison writings, Gramsci makes it clear in these letters that the attainment of hegemony (in its broadest possible form) is not only a matter of importance prior to the conquest of political power, but should also be the major objective of a new ruling force *after* it has acquired the levers of state control. Indeed, such is the significance of this criticism that Giuliano Gramsci is not averse to describing his father as a Stalinist-era 'dissident'.[2]

Given the nature of such criticisms, along with those that appeared in the *Prison Notebooks*, it is perhaps not surprising that this strongly affected the official Soviet interpretation of Gramsci's legacy over many years. This is immediately noticeable on the occasion of Gramsci's death in April 1937. Although the announcement was treated with the solemnity due to a communist leader who had died a miserable death as a result of his incarceration in a fascist jail, the news nevertheless warranted nothing more than a rather short, overly stiff obituary, signed by members of the Comintern, tucked away on an inside page of *Pravda*.[3] Gramsci was honoured, it is true, with being one of the leading campaigners for the liberation of humanity from the capitalist exploitative yoke, and was referred to as 'a true fighter for liberty and peace and for the socialist cause'. The main bulk of the obituary, however, was much more concerned with canonising Gramsci as a 'great Bolshevik' who had been 'raised and educated in the ranks of the Communist International', and as someone who had undoubtedly applied the 'great teachings of Marx, Engels, Lenin and Stalin' in the proper spirit of the times.

In terms of intellectual interpretations, the first noted Soviet scholar on Gramsci was Emanuil Egerman, who came to prominence almost a decade after Gramsci's death. A lecturer at the Moscow Institute of Linguistics and a recognised authority on the history of Italian literature, Egerman was responsible for publishing an anthology of Italian literature in 1947 which included, for the first time, a brief selection of some of Gramsci's prison letters. This was followed two years later by a further selection of letters, which, according to Giuliano Gramsci (who maintained close contacts with Egerman), were not very well received at all.

Following the first publication of the *Prison Notebooks* in Italy at the end of the 1940s, Egerman himself now started to publish more widely on Gramsci's ideas, and indeed became something of a pioneer in the evolution of a specific form of 'Gramscianism'. Although most of his publications were on issues relating to the narrow sphere of literature, linguistics and culture in general – and notwithstanding the fact that there were the obligatory references to 'Gramsci, the trusted ally of Lenin *and* Stalin' – it was nevertheless discernible from his writings that Gramsci was already being used as a potential intellectual critic of Stalinism.[4] Not surprisingly, the reaction that this caused amongst the authorities was extremely severe, the more so as Egerman was frequently to be found delivering lectures on Gramsci in the factory workplace, in army barracks, in universities and wherever he was invited. Increasingly attacked by the Soviet authorities for his work on Gramsci, his house and office were frequently searched and raided for 'subversive' material – especially in the last months of Stalin's explicitly anti-Semitic purges – and eventually considerable restrictions were placed on him.

Recalling this particular period of Egerman's harassment, Giuliano Gramsci is in no doubt why the authorities took such a hostile line. Egerman was 'presenting Gramsci as being far superior to Stalin'. The system at that time had its own irrepressible theoretical hierarchy. In the great socialist pantheon there was Marx, Engels, Lenin and Stalin. Gramsci, therefore, clearly had to be 'less' than these: 'Just as St. Peter cannot possibly be superior to Jesus Christ, so Gramsci could not be allowed greater theoretical significance than Stalin and Lenin. I myself was often asked to affirm that my father was Lenin's pupil and my answer always used to be: "pardon me, he was Croce's pupil!"'

What was particularly galling to the authorities was precisely the fact that Egerman's publications on Gramsci were creating some degree of interest: 'I remember that I used to receive letters from scholars from a variety of towns across the USSR who wanted to know more and who wanted to study and prepare theses on Gramsci.' Indeed, it was precisely this fear of an uncontrolled reading of Gramsci's writings, particularly those undertaken in prison, that so worried a great many other 'loyalist' communist leaders during this period. Take, for example, Togliatti's own expression of these fears in a letter he wrote to Georgii Dimitrov, the leader of the Comintern, as early as April 1941: 'The notebooks of Gramsci, which I have almost finished studying, contain material which could be utilised only after a proper processing. Without such treatment the material cannot be utilised and, in some parts, if the contents were found in their unexpurgated form, it would not be in the party's best interest.'[5]

In the aftermath of the Communist Party congresses in 1956 and 1961 and the de-Stalinisation campaigns which followed, the quantity (though not always the quality) of publications on Gramsci noticeably increased. In 1957, the first volume of *Selected Writings* appeared in print (covering the *Ordine Nuovo* period). This was followed by a second volume of prison letters, and a third volume (published in 1959) which consisted for the first time of extracts from the *Prison Notebooks*.[6] In 1963, meanwhile, Boris Lopukhov came out with the first officially sanctioned biography of Gramsci.[7] The (unofficial) reviews, however, were far from favourable. In a later, scathing attack, for example, Evgenii Ambartsumov openly criticised it for its mistakes, inaccuracies and sometimes blatant misportrayal of Gramsci's approach on many key issues.[8] It is true that some of these 'inaccuracies' were later corrected in a new, lengthier, and far more substantial biography by Aleksandr Golemba in 1968.[9] What is perhaps most noticeable, however, is that Giuseppe Fiori's esteemed 1966 biography was never translated into Russian, clearly being considered 'too risky'.[10]

What can be witnessed from this period, then, is the extent to which a fierce intellectual struggle was clearly taking place now, often in full public view, concerning the interpretation of Gramsci's ideas and the importance of those ideas in the context of both internal (Soviet) developments and external events. And once again, it did not take too long before the question of Gramsci's intellectual legacy and his version of creative Marxism was regarded in some quarters as a potentially dangerous destabilising force.

Amongst those who had an enormous amount of respect and sympathy for Gramsci's ideas, and who clearly saw them as having considerable relevance in a Soviet context, was Aleksandr Lebedev. Like Egerman before him, Lebedev's primary interest lay in Gramsci's notions of art and culture and their ultimate significance in the struggle for hegemony. What was different about Lebedev, however, was the manner in which he strove to apply a Gramscian *methodology* in all other areas of his work, applying it, for example, in studies that he performed on nineteenth-century writers and political figures such as Herzen, Chernyshevsky and Nechaev. Nor was he alone in this endeavour. Throughout the 1960s, it was widely recognised that a discernible Gramscian approach was being applied by a number of scholars across a whole range of disciplines from philosophy and sociology to historiography, literature and aesthetics.[11] Lebedev saw enormous creative possibilities in his understanding of Gramsci; however, there were many others, in stark contrast, who refused to countenance such approaches and who rigidly treated Gramsci according to the strict norms of (neo) Stalinist conformism.[12]

One of the undoubted high points of the debates in the 1960s on Gramsci's theoretical legacy and contemporary significance was witnessed in the first-ever international conference on Gramsci to have been held in Moscow, which took place in April 1967 on the thirtieth anniversary of his death.[13] Organised by the Institute of the Workers International Movement, the conference attracted considerable academic and media interest from across Europe and Latin America. Of those participating from the host country itself, a number of issues dominated the proceedings. One of the most important themes concerned the nature of the relationship between Gramsci and Lenin, in particular, the extent to which the notion of hegemony was synonymous with the traditional Leninist understanding of the dictatorship of the proletariat. In the event, all of the Soviet participants firmly adhered to the line that there was no fundamental difference in the two approaches, and strongly refuted the countervailing opinion which had just been formulated by Norberto Bobbio.

Another significant debate at the conference revolved around Gramsci's formulation of the relationship between base and superstructure. In the presentation made by Kirill Kholodkovskii, considerable support was given to Gramsci's formulation of civil society as the primary realm guaranteeing the widest possible form of hegemony. It was always emphasised, needless to say, that he was speaking of the situation in capitalist countries and not of his own experience under Soviet socialism, which had no need of a bourgeois-style civil society. Nevertheless, such references (and further nuances) were again a clear testimony to the serious nature of the debates that were taking place at this time.

For German Diligenskii, the key concern was Gramsci's interpretation of class consciousness, not least because this also raised serious questions concerning the role of ideology, as well as issues like bureaucratism, the cult of personality, and the degeneration of theoretical and cultural creativity into a 'subaltern religion'. The question of ideological dogmatism was likewise a key aspect of Aleksandr Lebedev's address. He reminded the audience that Marx himself had repudiated the tendency to dogmatise many of his own assertions into some form of rigid, scientific communism, when he stated at the end of the 1870s that in such instances he himself could not countenance being a 'Marxist'. Gramsci's real importance, therefore, lay in the fact that he had done more than most to unburden Marxist thought from the tendency towards dogmatisation and had provided Marxist theory with a unique sense of creativity and inventiveness.

The role of intellectuals in contemporary society was the main theme of the address given by Merab Mamardashvili. Although primarily concentrating on the situation in the West, he nevertheless touched on issues which also had enormous salience in his own society at this time, and elaborated in particular on Gramsci's writings concerning the problems of intellectual alienation from the rest of society, and the need to combat all forms of 'standardisation'. All in all, then, given the essence of the presentations from the Soviet delegates, Evgenii Ambartsumov was certainly correct when he commented that, for most of the participants, Gramsci's ideas were still very much alive and clearly addressed a contemporary audience on both sides of the East–West divide.[14]

For a short time after the conference, the critical momentum of the Soviet intellectual debate on Gramsci's ideas was sustained. Indeed, in one instance, it perhaps even reached new heights. In an article in *Novyi mir* at the beginning of 1968, Grigorii Vodolazov touched on a number of themes which had long since been 'out of bounds' for serious intellectual debate. Asked to review a new edition of Gramsci's writings on literature and art (which included an introduction by Aleksandr Lebedev), Vodolazov wasted no time in drawing the readers' attention to the explicitly *political* implications of Gramsci's writings. Quoting directly from Gramsci, the article asserted that 'a revolution cannot be acknowledged (in an obligatory manner) as proletarian and communist simply because it sets itself the task and realises the overthrow of a bourgeois-controlled state'. It likewise 'cannot be acknowledged as a proletarian and communist revolution even if the people who accede to power call themselves communists (no matter how sincerely)'. A revolution can be called proletarian and communist 'only when and if it demonstrates a genuine capacity in practice to help further the interests of the workers and other social groups it represents, and if it genuinely creates the conditions in which a new social order can be created'.[15]

Gramsci, as with Marx, it was argued, was highly critical of those who sought to impose their will in a situation that was not objectively ripe. Indeed, this was the whole basis of his struggle against the so-called 'vulgar communists'. A proletarian state simply cannot be created on the basis of 'waving a magic wand'. It is a process which demands time and fundamental preparation. If the workers are not ready for the revolutionary transition, no amount of 'enthusiasm' from certain political quarters can act as compensation for this deficiency. Moreover, on the basis of such an attempt, 'ever greater sacrifices will be required to ensure the consolidation of a proletarian state'. As for the 'fundamental preparation' which is required, this is first and foremost a problem of culture and civilisation. A 'new culture' must be engendered which prepares the ground for a new political structure, and this new culture cannot be imposed but must be organically and creatively fostered. Needless to say, Lenin is spared direct criticism in Vodolazov's – and, of course, Gramsci's – view, because he was fully cognisant of the cultural deficit which needed to be overcome in the immediate aftermath of the revolution. Nevertheless, the degree of implicit criticism in Vodolazov's article, both of Lenin, and more significantly of his successors, is clear for all to see.

This, however, was to be the last of the truly innovative Soviet intellectual commentaries on Gramsci for almost two decades. There had already been indications that many editors were closely monitoring the material that was being published and were increasingly censoring, if not publications about Gramsci, then at least direct quotations that could be 'decoded' in certain specific ways.[16] With the invasion of Czechoslovakia in August 1968, the official tolerance towards a creative application of Gramsci's ideas dried up completely. Not for the first time, Gramsci's legacy was to be paraded before the public primarily on anniversary celebrations where he could be sufficiently eulogised in a ritualised and sterilised form.

Any articles that did reach their way to publication once again trumpeted the notion that Gramsci was an unalloyed Leninist in everything he did and in everything he wrote. The Russian revolutionary experience had completely shaped his whole outlook and had given him a whole new perspective on the objective laws of development. Similarly, virtually all references to the notion of hegemony in Soviet literature throughout the 1970s and early 1980s was nearly always propagated as an exclusively Leninist conception.[17] As for the rare manuscript that was in any sense creative in scope – such as Irina Grigor'eva's 1978 study of Gramsci's understanding of history as an organic system – the ultimate effect of this was minimised by a ridiculously low print run; in Grigor'eva's case, 1,740 copies.[18] At a time when interest in, and critical debates about, Gramsci was reaching an avalanche in the West, in the Soviet Union published materials were thus both sparse and highly distorted. Similarly, every attempt was made to withhold even the most basic kind of information on the developing debates which were taking place. In a Soviet bibliography of Gramsci which came out in 1981, for example, reference was made to no more than 370 works, when in reality more than 1,200 works were already in print.[19]

Given the atmosphere which existed in official circles at this time, the one forum which remained to keep any interest in Gramsci alive was that of dissidence. In the view of Boris Kagarlitsky, it was the critical debates of the 1960s which sharply defined the parameters of the dissident-era debates, and one question more than most was at the heart of that debate: 'how did it happen that, under the slogan of emancipation of labour and amid the talk about "socialist construction", we arrived at totalitarianism?'[20] For the left-wing critical opposition, Gramsci remained a key figure in this debate, and a number of *samizdat* journals now began referring to the guiding influence that his ideas were having.[21]

With the onset of *perestroika,* of course, the intellectual scenery was once again drastically altered. Under the guidance of the officially sanctioned policy of *glasnost*, the level of interest in Gramsci in a whole range of different forums after 1985 began to reach new heights, and a considerably broader appraisal of his theoretical legacy was now embarked upon. His writings on the intelligentsia, the notion of consciousness, questions of political determinism and historicism, the notion of praxis, the significance of the historical bloc, and the interdependence of politics, culture and ideology were just some of the many Gramscian themes which were now discussed in great detail. The concept of Caesarism and its relationship to Stalinism also received an official airing; even the old taboo of the significance of his pre-prison letters in October 1926 was now finally broken in official publications. In April 1987, meanwhile, the Institute of Marxism-Leninism and the Gramsci Institute in Rome collaborated in the organisation of a new conference devoted to the theoretical and practical legacy of Gramsci; this was followed by a regular series of symposia and television documentaries. Last, but not least, in his first official visit to Rome, Gorbachev himself promised the leadership of the Italian Communist Party that all the 'blank pages' of Gramsci's most important writings would now be filled in, a promise which was partially fulfilled with the publication of a revised edition of the *Prison Notebooks* and a new two-volume edition of *Selected Writings,* many of which had not previously been available in Russian translation.[22]

Looking in general at this new-found interest in Gramsci after 1985, it is possible to discern at least three very different approaches. First, there is a clear sense in which Gramsci was used as an 'agent' of the new reform-minded authorities to articulate and to provide legitimacy for the underlying aspects of the whole *perestroika* process. Having officially 'served' Stalin in the 1940s and early 1950s, Khrushchev after 1956, and Brezhnev after 1968, Gramsci was now called upon to be a loyal servant of Gorbachev in his own hour of need. This was particularly noticeable in the period after January 1987, which witnessed both the radicalisation of the reforms and the open emergence of stronger forms of internal party opposition to the new Gorbachev line.

In his opening address to the April 1987 conference on Gramsci, for example, the director of the Marxist-Leninist Institute, Georgii Smirnov, left none of the participants in any doubt that from now on Gramsci was officially to be considered a key theoretical forefather of *perestroika*. Nowhere was this more so than in the realm of propagating the significance of the so-called 'human factor', which at that time was one of the key planks of the reforms. 'Today, the ideas of Gramsci have a particular resonance for us', Smirnov informed the assembled delegates, 'particularly as regards his original and bold elaboration of the problem concerning the active participation of the masses in all realms of social life', as well as in the way that this affects the traditional notion of 'the party as a political vanguard of the workers movement'.[23] This was a theme subsequently taken up by many other pro-reform commentators.[24]

Elsewhere, in an article by Leonid Popov and Genrikh Smirnov in the official party journal *Kommunist,* Gramsci's ideas were now used to support the notion that the world-wide anti-capitalist alliance needed to be broadened to incorporate the activities of the new progressive social interest groups. This was especially important, it was argued, if a nuclear catastrophe with all its tragic, final consequences, was to be overcome. Again, then, this was a key plank at this time in Gorbachev's desire to win over the support of all manner of Western interest groups, as well as in his broader notion of global interdependency.[25]

Yet another illustration of this official usage can be seen in a number of works which explicitly drew on Gramsci's ideas to buttress the notion that the previous Brezhnev era was indeed a period of 'stagnation', and that one of the main causes of this was the self-defining role of intellectuals in this period and their total estrangement from the fundamental needs of other social groups in society.[26]

A second aspect of the increased interest was the manner in which Gramsci was similarly put to use by the radical opposition to 'official' *perestroika* from the emerging *neformaly* (informal) groups on the radical left; that is to say, as a means of highlighting the inadequacies, ineffectiveness and inconsistencies of the official approach to reform, and the self-definition of these reforms as supposedly a process of 'socialist renaissance' and 'democratic innovation'. Boris Kagarlitsky, for example, is one amongst many left opposition activists who has frequently referred to the pivotal importance of Gramsci in determining the emergence of a 'New Left' in Soviet and later Russian political life.[27]

It was arguably the third form of renewed interest in Gramsci, however, that was perhaps the most interesting. Beginning in the early 1990s – and the date here is very significant – there emerged, really for the first time, a much broader intellectual interest in Gramsci. This interest stemmed not so much from the perspective of his parochial allegiance to Marxism (although this could never be ignored, of course), but rather from the perspective that here was a vital theorist of *transitional epochs* who could shed considerable light on the nature of events taking place in the Soviet Union at that time, and who therefore deserved to be studied in a manner that transcended officially authorised propagandistic purposes. A good example of this kind of new (or in a Soviet context *original*) perspective on Gramsci was Milii Gretskii's *Antonio Gramsci: Politician and Philosopher*.

A close associate of Irina Grigor'eva, Gretskii was no newcomer to Gramsci, having previously contributed a number of articles in Soviet journals, including traditional-type eulogies on the anniversaries of his death. What was different about this particular study, however, was precisely the non-propagandistic tone of the book and the fact that he was able to make use of previously inaccessible material, both in relation to Gramsci's own writings as well as a much greater degree of Western intellectual commentaries and analyses. For Gretskii, the key concern now was the manner in which Gramsci's notion of hegemony encompassed the central problem of the 'contemporary transitional epoch' – the problem of 'the fundamental transformation of society'. What was most apparent now, he argued, was that the original process of *perestroika* had been transformed into a full-scale *revolutionary* situation, not strictly equivalent to a classical revolution, but nevertheless one in which all the traditional features of the Soviet social, economic, cultural and political structure were experiencing a definitive type of change.[28] In particular, a new type of civil society was slowly beginning to take shape and this was having a profound effect on the old-style interrelationship between the realms of political society and economic society.

In short, brand new historical blocs were in the process of being formed and only a new application of Gramscian criteria could throw light on the nature of these new blocs.[29] If Gramsci, however, was to be of any applied methodological use, then Soviet intellectuals themselves had to reorientate their fundamental approach. In particular, they had to reassess their traditional understanding of the relationship between Gramsci's and Lenin's ideas on hegemony, as well as on the nature of the relationship between Western Marxism and Leninism. Even more significantly, if Soviet intellectuals were to fully appreciate the contemporary significance of Gramsci's ideas, then they had to gain a new awareness of the 'unorthodox' nature of many of those ideas, as well as an awareness of the debt that Gramsci owed not only to non-Leninist, but also non-Marxist influences.[30] Only then would Gramsci finally become accessible to Soviet theorists, and only then would they be able to gain a much fuller understanding of the nature of the changes that were happening all around them.

Gretskii was by no means alone in his conclusion that a totally different type of intellectual approach to Gramsci was now needed – this was likewise made very clear in a round table organised by the Academy of Social Sciences in January 1991. As one participant cogently expressed it:

> Of course, Gramsci's main interest is in the destiny of the working class, the peasants ('the subordinate classes') and their corresponding political party. Nevertheless, based on his analysis of common forms of questions concerning the overall correlation of forces, hegemony, power, the state and civil society etc., he also appeals to, and is certainly taken notice of by, other classes and different social groups and is therefore an acknowledged purveyor of common historical laws of development.[31]

It is clear, then, that what started out largely as a monologue in Soviet Russia concerning the nature of the legacy of Gramsci ultimately became a genuine, multifaceted dialogue, a search for a deeper, richer legacy and one which could assist not only political actors of one kind or another in the official and unofficial realms, but a new enquiring intellectual class desirous of applying new methodologies and criteria to the changing environment around them.

Gramscian Affinities with Bakhtin

Before moving on to concentrate on the post-Gramscian debates on hegemony in the West, which for obvious reasons of intellectual autonomy have been recognisably more substantial and theoretically innovative over the years, it is nevertheless important to stress that at the same time that Gramsci was increasing in popularity in the Soviet Union in the 1960s and after 1985, becoming in some senses a popular cultural icon, so too was another theorist – Mikhail Bakhtin. That the fortunes of these two thinkers should be linked in this manner is of no great surprise to those who are familiar with their respective ideas. Notwithstanding his very different worldview – based as it was on Husserlian phenomenology, neo-Kantianism and strong religious influences – if any Russian theorist can be said to have elaborated creative ideas somewhat similar in shape and design (though not *scope*) to Gramsci's ideas on hegemony, then it was Bakhtin and his philosophy of culture (or what later Soviet theorists called 'culturology').[32]

In his prison writings, Gramsci had drawn attention to the fact that in state authoritarian conditions all forms of residual sociopolitical struggle were invariably shifted to the sphere of culture. With their mutual experience of authoritarian conditions from the mid-to-late 1920s onwards, it is perhaps not surprising that the common terrain of the two thinkers is the realm of culture in general, and the realm of linguistics, in particular. As Craig Brandist has remarked, a comparison provides the researcher with arguably

> … a more widespread and deeper meeting of Marxism and idealist philosophies of language than has hitherto been acknowledged. Out of the respective critiques of positivist-dominated social science and romantic aesthetics emerges a strikingly similar pragmatist recasting of the Marxist theory of ideology which anticipates many of the themes of contemporary post-structuralism while embedding the realm of ideas firmly in the social practice of different social groups.[33]

For Gramsci, one of the main motivations defining his interest in linguistics was the need to engage critically with the existing dominant ideas of Croce and his adherence to a form of 'individualistic subjectivism', an idealist theory of language which stressed the paramountcy of individual speech acts as an unceasing process of creation, and which likewise denied that there were any pre-existing, deterministic norms. An overzealous, reactionary adoption of this line had resulted, he argued, in a continual failure to establish a universally utilised *national* language; for as long as this was the case – that is, for as long as regional dialects predominated – then there was little chance of a new united opposition coming into force which could engage in a serious counter-hegemonic campaign.

For Bakhtin, on the other hand, the motivation was somewhat different. Although large elements of Croce's work had been translated into Russian in the early 1920s and had attracted a not insubstantial following amongst theorists of the Russian Symbolist movement, it was nevertheless a polar opposite school of thought which had gained supremacy in the aftermath of the revolution. This school of thought was 'abstract objectivism' and was most closely associated with the ideas of the Swiss theorist, Ferdinand de Saussure, whose *Course in General Linguistics* had been interpreted and widely articulated in the writings of the leading theorist, Sergei Kartsevskii.

At the heart of Saussure's notion of abstract objectivism was the essential belief that language was nothing more than a pure system of laws that confronted individual speakers as inviolable norms over which they had no control whatsoever. In other words, there could be no meaningful creativity on the individual's part. Individuals are merely prisoners of a rigidly prescribed set of formal rules and criteria over which they could exert no kind of impact. This was also the approach taken by many classical Marxist materialists in Russia at this time, particularly Plekhanov, and in its own overzealous, reactionary interpretation was to provide much of the theoretical underpinning for the later dogmas of Socialist Realism.

Coming as they did, then, from different starting points and motivations, it was their capacity to formulate a distinctive *synthesised* approach of the two polar extremes that makes a fundamental correlation of Gramsci and Bakhtin possible. For both theorists, the social determinants of culture and language are ineluctably accepted and demonstrable. At the same time, however, both are equally convinced of the capacity for language and culture to exert a creative, transformative function on the social environment in which they operate. In other words, language in its own right is an ideological battleground with decisive consequences: 'Each word … is a little arena for the clash and criss-crossing of differently oriented social accents. A word in the mouth of a particular individual person is a product of the living interaction of social forces.'[34]

The all-pervading feature of Bakhtin's work from the early 1920s onwards was his theory of dialogue (or dialogism), and it is here that we can extrapolate or correlate the most important parallels with Gramsci's concept of hegemony. In Bakhtin's lifelong critical engagement with Saussure's theory of abstract objectivism, there is one fundamental assertion which is accepted root and branch: namely, Saussure's innovative account of the way in which all aspects of language are ultimately rooted in *social experience*. The shift that Saussure enacted, of treating linguistics as a sociological phenomenon and not simply as a historical-grammatical phenomenon, had enormous significance for Bakhtin and all his close associates. In his own enquiries, however – as well as in those of Valentin Voloshinov – Bakhtin's main task is to move on from this sociological foundation stone. And this he does by posing an entirely different kind of research agenda. For Bakhtin, the real point of linguistics from now on is to study the actual manner in which language is used; this should be done not just by concentrating on the product of language (that is, the words actually used), but by concentrating also on the *speaker* of those words. It is here, then, that the real significance of the theory of dialogue comes into force.

Underpinning much of Bakhtin's approach is the way in which he 'uses the literary genre of the novel as an allegory for representing existence as the condition of authoring'.[35] Human existence is understood as a cover of a book whose text is filled in on the basis of the communication entered into by the author. By having the capacity of being authors of our own life book, Bakhtin is adamant that the individual self is never entirely given, but can always create him or herself. Indeed, as he often expressed it, 'we are all authors'; a phrase remarkably similar in scope to Gramsci's notion that 'we are all philosophers'.

What, however, is the essence of our 'authorship'? For Bakhtin, there are ultimately two essential forms: monologue or dialogue. By dialogue, Bakhtin is essentially referring to a process which is perpetually open, ungiven and inventive, the experience of which leads to an enhancement of creative consciousness. It is also a process perpetually in motion which integrates into a unique whole, not only the participants engaged in the process of dialogic communication, but also the 'outcome' of that process. Expressing it in strictly cultural terms, there is an inseparable, integral relationship between the artistic creator, the artistic observer and the artistic product; each time an observer engages in dialogue with the creator over the significance of the product a potentially unique set of relationships is thereby engendered. This set of integral connections cannot be fractured to find absolute meaning and significance in one element as against another. Any attempt to do this would thereby transform the creative and unique process of a dialogue into its opposite – a standardised, reactionary form of monologue. Monologic authorship, in stark contrast, can only ever be compatible with uniformity and compulsion. Moreover, as Michael Holquist has noted, when monologue becomes the basis of 'official discourse', a pathological condition is engendered in which everyone is forced to speak exactly the same language. It is almost like 'a collective version of the mysterious disability called autism, victims of which cannot communicate with others because they (apparently) are not aware of them'. Official discourse which is monologic is thus 'autism for the masses';[36] a condition not unlike Gramsci's understanding of bureaucratic centralism.

There can be little doubt that in his writings on monologue, Bakhtin is inviting a correlation with the onset of Stalinist authoritarianism and cultural homogenisation, what later followers of Bakhtin would call *monophilia* – a belief that everything can be reduced to a very simplistic, indivisible and atemporal form.[37] Small wonder, therefore, that following the publication of his study of Dostoevsky in 1929, where he vehemently argues against the 'hegemony of absolute authorial control',[38] he should find himself the subject of suspicion (and ultimately arrest) by the political authorities.

For Bakhtin, all human history is a perpetual struggle between monologue and dialogue. No monologue is ever permanent, no matter how strong the illusion, and all dialogue is by nature constantly in flux and ever-changing. As the final words of his very last article make emphatically clear:

> There is neither a first word, nor a last word. The contexts of dialogue are without limit. They extend into the deepest past and the most distant future. Even meanings born in dialogues of the remotest past will never be finally grasped once and for all, for they will always be renewed in later dialogue. At any present moment of the dialogue there are great masses of forgotten meanings, but these will be recalled again at a given moment in the dialogue's later course when it will be given new life. For nothing is absolutely dead: every meaning will someday have its homecoming festival.[39]

As we shall see later, such a vision of a perpetual, ever-changing struggle is very close to conceptual ideas of hegemony as formulated by Raymond Williams. As for the condition which makes the dialogic process possible, Bakhtin has no doubts that it is the freedom to shape meaning constantly anew. In his *Discourse in the Novel,* having highlighted the essential nature of official discourse, Bakhtin then goes on to contrast this with the notion of 'internally persuasive discourse', which is described as an affirmation through assimilation. This, he states, is the fundamental basis of an individual's interactive process. Our whole ideological development

> ... is just such an intense struggle within us for hegemony amongst various available verbal and ideological points of view, approaches,

directions and values. The semantic structure of an internally persuasive discourse is *not finite,* it is *open;* in each of the new contexts
that dialogize it, this discourse is able to reveal ever newer *ways to
mean.*[40]

Where official discourse binds an individual to accept phenomena without recourse to other possible perspectives on offer, internally persuasive
discourse is clearly the expression of a much more progressive 'hegemonic principle'. In Gramscian terms, we are close here to the notion of
contradictory consciousness and passive consent. In contrast to official
discourse, which makes an individual a passive recipient of conceptual
forms, internally persuasive discourse at least opens up the possibility of a
new type of 'critical understanding of self', which is in turn the first precondition for the possible emergence of a 'new conception of reality'.

Concluding his own study of the two theorists, Craig Brandist is certain
that 'Bakhtin's novelist and Gramsci's "modern prince" both structure and
maximize dialogism so as to intensify representational adequacy; ... they
both served to enrich historical materialism, but to do so they had to completely dismember the methodology of those theories'.[41] This is undeniably
correct. He also makes two other conclusions, however, which are more
subject to disputation. First, he argues that 'Bakhtin, at his best, supplies a
welcome corrective to some aspects of Gramsci's work which led the latter into a partial accommodation with Stalinism ... .'[42] Precisely what the
nature of this 'accommodation' is, either as regards Gramsci's conception
of linguistics or any other aspect of his theories, is nowhere detailed and
is therefore an accusation totally devoid of substance. Second, and from a
very different perspective, he argues that:

> While Gramsci's anti-realist epistemology allowed him to break with then
> dominant 'false consciousness' Marxist theories of ideology, facilitat-
> ing the development of an account of ideology as something continually
> reorganized in the face of the struggle between classes, it often led him
> to reduce the social to the subject's consciousness of it.

This, continues Brandist, was a reduction always avoided by Bakhtin. More
significantly, it was also a reduction that paved the way for the later post-
Marxist school of thought – as represented by the likes of Ernesto Laclau –
which was able to propagate the damaging conception (that is, damaging
to Marxism), that 'there is *no* correlation *at all* between discursive meaning and the economic organization of society'. In other words, 'meaning
is solely the unstable effect of shifting relations of difference'.[43]

That Bakhtin should be considered a more 'classical' Marxist than Gramsci seems to ignore a great many factors, not the least of which was the pressure placed on Bakhtin to conform to at least some of the most basic ideological canons of Soviet ideology if he gave any value at all to his life. As for the theoretical legitimacy or succour provided by Gramsci to the contemporary post-Marxists, this is an issue which encompasses the broader domain of Western post-Gramscian debates on the concept of hegemony, and will therefore be discussed in greater detail in the following chapter.

4 Post-Gramscian Debates on Hegemony in the West

> Ah, when one studies thus, a prisoned creature,
> That scarce the world on holidays can see, –
> Scarce through a glass, by rare occasion,
> How shall one lead it by persuasion?
>
> Johann Wolfgang von Goethe, *Faust, Part I*

There can be no doubt that Gramsci's development of hegemony – both as political strategy and as analytical theory – has had enormous influence amongst a whole range of Western theorists in the second half of the twentieth century. In assessing this influence, the purpose in this chapter is to dissect the Gramscian understanding of hegemony into what are considered to be three of its most important constituent parts.

Hegemony and Civil Society

We have seen in Chapter 2 that Gramsci's revaluation of civil society had a number of implications for the development of his theory of hegemony. First, there is his emphasis on the moment of consent rather than force predominating in the realm of civil society. Second, Gramsci invokes a sense of multi-dimensional, rather than one-dimensional, representations to the operation of civil society, which leads him to understand the phenomenon of struggle as being reliant on a diverse range of *articulatory* processes. And third, in his understanding of the workings of a complex modern society, he is adamant that civil society represents more than an illusory front, which therefore further implies a movement away from the notion that the state is *essential* in a totalising sense.[1]

For the last thirty years or more, the academic debates about the meaning and significance of Gramsci's interpretation of civil society have raged far and wide, certainly too far and too wide to take stock of them all. If one had to give pride of place to the most crucial of these debates, however, then two of them would certainly stand out above the rest. Taking them chronologically, the first concerns the debate which arose in 1968 between Norberto Bobbio and Jacques Texier; it was a debate, as was briefly indicated in Chapter 2, which was largely to do with the Marxist credentials of Gramsci.

Bobbio's line of argument, broadly delineated, is as follows.[2] Civil society is the key concept of Gramsci's whole political thought and represents something novel in the history of the usage of that concept. In essence, Gramsci is really the first Marxist who uses the concept of civil society with a direct and positive textual reference to Hegel, and it was precisely because of this that he was able to come up with a new innovation in the Marxist tradition. According to Bobbio: 'Civil society in Gramsci does not belong to the structural moment, but to the superstructural one.'[3] That is to say, it does not just include 'the whole of material relations', but 'the whole of ideological-cultural relations' as well; not 'the whole of commercial and industrial life', but 'the whole of spiritual and intellectual life'. As a consequence of this, Gramsci has effectively shifted 'the real home and the theatre of all history'.[4]

It is further contended, apropos of Marx, that Gramsci sees civil society, not the state, as the active and positive moment of historical development. But unlike Marx, this active and positive moment is ideological, cultural and spiritual in nature, not economic. 'In short', Bobbio goes on,

> ... the civil society which Gramsci has in mind, when he refers to Hegel, is not the one of the initial moment, that is of the explosion of contradictions which the state will have to dominate, but it is that of the final moment, when the organisation and regulation of the various interests ... provide the basis for the transition towards the state.[5]

This apparent inversion of the structure–superstructure dichotomy is followed by a second inversion between 'the moment of civil society and the moment of the state'. Of these two terms, the first is always the positive moment and the second is always the negative. Furthermore, it logically follows that there must be a corresponding inversion between institutions and ideologies, whereby ideologies become the primary moment of history and the institutions the secondary one:

> Once the moment of civil society is considered as the moment in which the transition from necessity to freedom takes place, the ideologies, which have their historical roots in civil society, are no longer seen just as a posthumous justification of a power which has been formed historically by material conditions, but are seen as forces capable of creating a new history and of collaborating in the formation of a new power, rather than to justify a power which has already been established.[6]

Finally, Bobbio contrasts the hoped-for result of Gramsci's and Marx's ideas. In Marx and Engels, he writes, the hoped-for transition is structural in nature, encompassing a transition from 'society *with* classes' to 'society *without* classes'. In Gramsci, meanwhile, the hoped-for transition is superstructural in nature, encompassing a transition from 'civil society *with* political society' to 'civil society *without* political society'.[7] Put in another way, civil society moves from being 'a mediating element between the structure and the negative moment of the superstructure' to a situation in which civil society becomes so 'enlarged', or indeed, so 'universal', that it eliminates all the space which was formerly occupied by political society. This process, concludes Bobbio, is not one of supersession (in the manner of Marx), but *reabsorption*.

Texier's response to Bobbio – a response which influenced the account of Gramsci's ideas given in the earlier chapter – is to place Gramsci's understanding of civil society firmly within the totality of his political/philosophical framework, rather than to isolate it as Bobbio does.[8] 'The theory of superstructures', he argues, 'is also a theory of the relations between infrastructure and superstructures, the theory of their unity and of the "historical bloc" which they comprise.'[9] Just as Gramsci would have found it nonsensical to separate quality from quantity, so the same applies to the idea that liberty can be separated from necessity and ideology from economy. Bobbio's attempt to isolate civil society only upsets what Gramsci would have regarded as 'the unity of the real process of history'. Bobbio's methodology, therefore, leads to a 'de-realisation' of the superstructures. Ideologies would in fact be nothing more than 'appearances' or 'individual whims' if their economic and social content did not give them the 'organicity' which forms the basis of their 'historical rationality' and consequently their efficacy.

A second mistake made by Bobbio is to designate a whole range of superstructural phenomena as polar opposites: coercion and persuasion, force and consensus, domination and leadership, dictatorship and hegemony, political society and civil society. While it may be analytically useful to do this, such distinctions can only operate at certain levels. Quoting Gramsci to support his case, Texier argues that a methodological distinction of this kind should not be confused with an organic distinction: 'The distinction between the moment of force (political society) and of consensus (civil society) is a practical canon of research, an instrument permitting a better analysis of an organic reality in which it is radically impossible to separate these two moments.'[10] Gramsci's very use of the term *integral* to denote the combination of the civil and political societal realms indicates that in the real world, as distinct from the purely methodological world, there is an inseparable bond between them. It equally follows that Gramsci was well aware of the same kind of intrinsic bond existing between all the other opposites which Bobbio mentioned.

Finally, Texier goes on to counter Bobbio's assertion that Gramsci inverted the classical Marxist relationship between structure (active and primary) and superstructure (passive and secondary). Here Bobbio has provided 'a reading of the marxism of Marx which is nothing but a reduction of Marx to economism and mechanicism'.[11] Croce did exactly the same and Gramsci explicitly criticised him for doing so. Gramsci recognised that Marx himself regarded the superstructures in an active and positive way and his task was therefore to provide further clarification of the operational nature of the superstructures *in conjunction with* the economic base. As he himself wrote: 'Material forces are the content and ideologies the form, though this distinction between form and content has purely "didactic" value, since the material forces would be inconceivable historically without form and the ideologies would be individual fancies without the material forces.' In other words, the economic structure was not something immovable and absolute, but it was something in constant motion. At the same time, however, human beings were constantly having an active reaction on this structure in motion, confirming once again the essential unity of the reality of social existence.

Underlying Texier's criticism is the excessive degree to which Bobbio interprets Gramsci culturally. As will be shown below, a cultural perspective on Gramsci is more than legitimate, providing it does not associate hegemony exclusively with cultural phenomena. Likewise, it is very apparent that one of the primary motives of Bobbio's analysis was to pave the way for an appropriation of Gramsci into a broader *liberal* school of thought, something regarded by Texier and many others as demeaning not only to the philosophical ideas of Gramsci, but to his practical political engagement throughout his life.

For the second of the landmark debates, it is necessary to turn to the publication of Perry Anderson's 'The Antinomies of Antonio Gramsci' in the special centenary edition of *New Left Review*.[12] There can be no doubt that Anderson's essay represented, to use his own words, an unparalleled 'depth of enquiry' into the work of Gramsci. Recognising that Gramsci had been forced by the requirements of prison censorship to make use of 'contradictions, disorders, allusions [and] repetitions' to portray his ideas, Anderson wanted to overcome 'this uniquely adverse process of composition' in order to discover the unadulterated, uncontaminated train of Gramsci's thought processes. The result, as was inevitably going to be the case, was a mixture of genuine enlightenment and disappointment. While some terms and concepts (including hegemony itself) were given greater historical context and provided clarification of Gramsci's precise meaning, others remained embedded in the quagmire of arbitrariness and constant oscillation of meaning and interpretation. More to the point, argued Anderson, for those concepts which found themselves subject to oscillation, there was an irrevocable conclusion that Gramsci precisely meant this to be the case.

One of the central concepts which Gramsci was unable, or deliberately did not seek, to clarify was civil society. In terms of the relationship which exists between civil society and the state, Anderson argues that Gramsci oscillated between at least three different positions. First, the state 'is in a balanced relationship with civil society'. Second, the state 'is only an outer surface of civil society'. And third, the state is the 'massive structure' which cancels the autonomy of civil society. To make matters worse, Anderson goes on, these oscillations concern only the relationship *between* the terms 'state' and 'civil society'. It does not take account of the fact that the '*terms themselves* ... are subject to the same sudden shifts of boundary and position'. In one instance, the state is to be strictly contrasted with civil society. In another, the state encompasses civil society. And in a third, the state is seen to be identical with civil society.[13]

As a result of all these uncertainties, it is likewise contended that there is not one, but three different models in Gramscian thought. The essence of the first model is the notion that a modern class system (that is, a capitalist system) is almost exclusively hegemonic by means of societal consent rather than state coercion and should be combated exclusively by ideological methods of power demystification rather than more direct methods, a position supposedly adopted by Gramsci and which Anderson finds 'illusory'.[14]

Gramsci's second model offers a more balanced symmetry between civil society and the state, whereby hegemony is now distributed evenly between the two spheres, 'while itself being redefined to *combine* coercion and consent'. Though this represents an improvement on the first model, Anderson however is still not happy with the definition. While congratulating Gramsci for recognising that ideological controls stem from the state itself as well as civil society, he does not accept that the tool of repression is likewise equally present in both spheres. What Gramsci fails to recognise is that there 'is always a *structural asymmetry* in the distribution of the consensual and coercive functions of this power. Ideology is shared between civil society and the state: violence pertains to the state alone. In other words, the state enters twice over into any equation between the two.'[15]

The third model is one which completely denies the very institutional and functional independence of civil society. Here there is a complete *fusion* of political and civil society. Civil society now disappears as a distinct entity and becomes not only a part of the state, but 'indeed is the state itself'. This model, however, also has its problems for Anderson. If the very distinction between state and civil society is effectively denied, then one is virtually consigning all modern states to the realm of totalitarianism. Gramsci's difference between a pre-modern and a modern state, in other words, is not a qualitative, but merely a quantitative difference concerning the greater capacity and effectiveness of state power.[16]

As thoroughgoing as Anderson's critique appears to be, can one really say that his three-model interpretation of Gramsci is accurate? Is Gramsci's analysis as badly framed, confused and misleading as it is made out to be? The simple answer is no. While there are undoubtedly points of confusion and omissions in Gramsci's analysis, the essence of his position is quite clear. Anderson's first model is very narrowly focused and is by no means a true reflection of Gramsci's understanding of the civil society–state, consent–coercion dichotomy. In similar fashion to Bobbio, it overemphasises Gramsci's motivation for at times *isolating* the component parts of the dichotomy and gives too much weight to this methodological approach at the expense of Gramsci's organic approach.

The second model is undoubtedly closest to Gramsci's understanding of the optimal, desired relationship between civil society and state in a modern capitalist society. As for Anderson's criticism of Gramsci for locating coercion in both spheres rather than exclusively in the state, it has to be said that there are perfectly good reasons for this. In many instances there is indeed an organic structural *symmetry* as regards the distribution of consensual and coercive functions of power across the realms of civil society and state. As Ellen Meiksins Wood has argued, for example, in the context of the role of the market in the domain of civil society, coercive practices should not be seen as some kind of 'disorder', but as one of civil society's 'constitutive principles'.[17]

As for Anderson's third model, Gramsci here is quite clearly alluding to the fact that if the optimal, balanced, organic establishment of hegemony within civil society and the state begins to break down, then the state will secure its position by limiting the importance of the institutional sphere of civil society. This is indeed the essence of his understanding of dictatorship and fascism and he rightly believes that a modern-day version of absolute state power represents a negation of the *qualitative* differences with pre-modern forms of absolutism, that qualitative difference being precisely the diffusion of power downwards into the realm of civil society and the greater reliance on predominantly consensual mechanisms to buttress and sustain that power. In other words, this is not an *alternative* model being put forward by Gramsci, but the same model applied in a set of circumstances which threatens the optimal operation of modern class hegemony.

Up until now the concentration has focused on the largely academic-inspired debates arising out of Gramsci's understanding of civil society. When it comes to an analysis of other key Marxist theoreticians who have directly or indirectly engaged in a debate with Gramsci as regards his interpretation of the relationship between hegemony and civil society, two thinkers inevitably come to mind for particular attention: Louis Althusser and Nicos Poulantzas.

Althusser's appreciation of Gramsci is well known and clearly stated in many of his works. It is Gramsci, he emphasises, who has touched on all the basic problems not only of Italian, but the whole of European, history. In his writings on the superstructures, Gramsci's arguments are not only original, but 'genial insights'. As for the concept of hegemony, it is very much to be lamented that no one has really taken up and followed through this 'remarkable example of a theoretical solution in outline to the problems of the interpenetration of the economic and the political'. Such praise notwithstanding, it is by no means an exclusively uncritical form of gratitude.[18] Indeed, as regards Althusser's conception of civil society, the debt of gratitude to Gramsci is of an inverse proportion. Holding firmly to the belief that for all his radical innovations, Gramsci was still at heart 'a theoretical leftist' (even if in a 'commendable political direction'), Althusser was particularly keen to 'de-negate' the whole Gramscian interpretation of civil society and the function it supposedly performed in modern societies. Regarding it first and foremost as an unwanted phantom of Hegelian influence on Marx – a phantom, moreover, which Marx himself 'abandoned' in his transition to historical materialism – Althusser insists that there is no such thing as civil society, if by that one infers a distinct or autonomous site of social relations and actions.[19] Instead, Althusser seeks – rather like Anderson misleadingly portrayed Gramsci of seeking to do in his third model – to expand the nature and the role of the state to such an extent that it becomes fundamentally coterminous with *all* aspects of social relations. What for Gramsci is the specific realm of civil society, becomes for Althusser 'ideological state apparatuses', which would include, amongst other things, churches, parties, trade unions, families, schools, and all forms of culture and media. 'It is unimportant', he declares, 'whether the institutions in which they [i.e. ideologies] are realised are "public" or "private"' – for these all indifferently form sectors of a single controlling state which is 'the precondition for any distinction between public and private'.[20]

The real purpose behind the Althusserian conception of ideological state apparatuses – which exist alongside the other apparatuses of the state more narrowly defined as repressive – is essentially to explain the manner in which a given set of productive relations are *reproduced* in society. As Gregory Elliott has shown, Althusser's conception of ideology amounted to three main principles.[21] First, there was his belief that 'ideology represents the imaginary relationship of individuals to their real conditions of existence.' An individual's condition of existence is not made known to him through experience alone, as many Marxist humanists and Gramscian historicists had previously contended. The task of ideology, however, was not to provide an awareness of the real nature of man's condition of existence, but instead was meant to foster an imaginary understanding.

Second, Althusser put forward the proposition concerning 'the materiality of ideology'. An ideology is not simply a set of ideas, but is something firmly located in the material terrain of social life. It is endowed with a physical existence compounded of a whole gamut of actions and practices. An individual's ideas 'are his material actions inserted into the material practices governed by material rituals which are themselves defined by the material ideological apparatus from which derive the ideas of that subject'.[22]

Thirdly, and perhaps most significantly of all, there is Althusser's contention that ideology has the task of transforming individuals into subjects, who accept the imaginary relationship with their real conditions of existence 'as if they were determinant of them – as if they were *constitutive,* rather than *constituted,* subjects. In other words, ideology constitutes individuals as conscious *subjects* of society ... so as to enforce their *subjection* to the social order and its demands on them.'[23] It is on this understanding of the nature of ideology and the functions of ideological state apparatuses that Althusser understands the manner in which a modern class system is perpetuated and reproduced. It is also on this basis that he makes the claim that 'no class can hold state power over a long period without at the same time exercising its hegemony over and in the State Ideological Apparatuses'.[24]

At one stage in the mid-1960s, when structuralism was considered by many to represent the highest stage of Marxism, it looked as if Althusser was well on the way to outstripping Gramsci's own growing influence on the left with respect to his conception of hegemony *within* civil society. Such supremacy, however, remained short-lived, not least because of the theoretical and strategic weaknesses of many of Althusser's ideas. Althusser himself had always vehemently claimed that a primary motivation of his theories was the construction of an anti-Stalinist critique from a left-wing perspective. Ironically, however, the more he developed his position, the more he brought on himself the charge of developing a *new* form of Stalinism. For many, this was the logical outcome of his de-negation of civil society. Without giving any credence to this realm of social existence,

Althusser was inevitably embodying his understanding of hegemony in an exclusively statist manner; something which was bound to appear totalitarian in nature, which it had not been in Gramsci. For E.P. Thompson, in particular, there seemed hardly sufficient vitriolic words in the English language with which to indict Althusser and his ideological state apparatuses. With the Soviet invasions of Hungary and Czechoslovakia no doubt still weighing on his own political conscience, Thompson asserted that one had to look no further than the Soviet Union itself for a perfect illustration of Althusserianism in practice: 'The Soviet repressive and ideological state apparatuses, in inhibiting any open argument about values, have not only denied to "individuals" the right of "self expression", they have denied to Soviet society the means to express, and to examine, itself.'[25] For Thompson, therefore, Althusser was not a critic of Stalinism, he was its theoretical justification.

Away from Thompson's emotive – and one would have to say very unfair – criticisms, John Keane has criticised Althusser's notion of ideological state apparatuses as an overstatement of the capacity of all ideologies 'to mobilise public support, to ensure consensus and to silence alternative forms of life'.[26] The logicality of a 'real existing' realm of civil society in modern states cannot be spirited or theorised away so simply. Gramsci at least had the merit of trying to understand its existence and its complex relationship with the state, and sought for an opposition-based strategy which could utilise its democratic potential.

On a somewhat similar basis, Terry Eagleton has criticised Althusser's replacement of civil society with ideological state apparatuses on the basis of functionalist reductionism. Amongst other examples which he cites, he argues that it is difficult to see how schools and families are structures exclusively oriented towards an ideological legitimisation of state power. Not to mention the fact that it 'would come as a pleasant surprise to His Holiness the Pope to learn that the church in Latin America was nothing more than a support of imperial power'.[27] Eagleton's point is that institutions such as these are *internally contradictory* and should not be seen 'as a fixed realm of institutions which operate in an invariable way'. Rather than representing an advance on Gramsci, Althusser had simply found a new way of reincarnating the pre-Gramscian emphasis on economism by arguing that such institutions should be seen as mono-functional ones in relation to society's economic base.

Another prominent criticism of Althusser, which has Gramsci very much in mind, is the way in which the inherent structure of the ideological state apparatuses would almost deem it futile to engage in most forms of political struggle and conflict. If, as Althusser maintained, the class struggle is in essence 'a struggle in ideology', then one would have to agree with Elliott that the cards will always be 'stacked in favour of the ruling class because its particular interests coincide with the universal functional requirements of social reproduction'.[28] Hegemony here would be seen as permanent since there would be no space whatsoever in which an oppositional ideology could genuinely evolve. Ted Benton, too, has made a similar criticism. If Althusser's account is really accurate, then there would simply be no room even for a discourse, let alone the practice, of an ideology which could resist or oppose the incumbent ideological social reproduction.[29]

For the many followers of Althusser, the rejection of any basis of civil society was often seen as a *sine qua non*. And certainly this was the case for a long while for Nicos Poulantzas. Based on Althusser's main works in the mid-1960s, Poulantzas was convinced that the notion of a separate entity of civil society was nothing more than an invention of eighteenth-century political theory and, in its continued usage by Gramsci, he had ended up 'contaminating' his broader concept of hegemony with the virus of historicism.[30] Nor was this all. Gramsci's use of civil society obscured the distinctive and specific operational methods of the economic, political and ideological institutions in capitalism.[31] Perhaps most importantly of all, Gramsci was wrong to conjecture that by capturing this so-called realm of civil society, the working class could thereby acquire hegemony *prior* to the conquest of the state. Recognising that this was one of the most disputed points in Gramscian debates, Poulantzas was for most of his life convinced that the actions of Gramsci's civil society were in reality *determined* by the actions of the state repressive apparatus: '[The] destruction of the ideological apparatus [must have] *its precondition* in the destruction of the state repressive apparatus which maintains it.'[32] To fail to recognise this would inevitably lead one into the liberal realm of believing that the state was nothing more than a neutral mediator in the class struggle.

In place of the civil society–state dichotomy based around the antagonistic interests of the egoistic 'homo economicus', Poulantzas preferred to talk of the atomisation of civil society and the antagonism of individual interests, brought about by what he termed the 'isolation effect':

> ... the real problems posed bear no relation to any separation of the capitalist state from civil society, which is held to have been atomised as a result of the dissolution of mixed or organic feudal relations. The real problems are concerned with the specific autonomy of the instances of the [capitalist mode of production], with the effect of isolation in the socio-economic relations of this mode, and the way in which the state

and the political practices of the dominant classes are related to this isolation.[33]

As Bob Jessop, an undoubted admirer of Poulantzas, has written, it was within this (Althusserian) framework that Poulantzas had hoped to go on to develop a more substantial concept of hegemony.[34] It was an ambition, however, which never entirely manifested itself, partly because, unlike Gramsci, Poulantzas was only ever really able to apply his concept of hegemony to the political practices of the dominant classes. It therefore became synonymous with similar dominant ideology theories at this time, whereas Gramsci's concept was much more all-encompassing.[35] Indeed, even Jessop readily admits that Poulantzas's search for a new approach to hegemony too readily conflated it with domination. In addition, Poulantzas's remained a 'seriously underdeveloped' concept which could not demonstrate how it secured and reproduced itself; it remained at the level of being 'descriptive, impressionistic and intuitive' rather than becoming a 'clear theoretical category'; it was frequently inconsistent, and it failed to develop the notion of oppositional strategy and tactics beyond those laid down by Gramsci (along with Lenin and Mao).[36] Jessop was also critical of Poulantzas for too long denying the actual existence of civil society, for neglecting its complexities and for replacing it with the Althusserian ideological state apparatuses.

This criticism was somewhat offset, however, by a very dramatic intellectual shift towards the end of Poulantzas's life. What Poulantzas begins to do now is to subject his whole Althusserian background to considerable critical scrutiny. In particular, he begins to argue that the notion of the relative autonomy of the state, which considered social reality in terms of instances or levels, 'was a conception which did not succeed in exactly situating the specificity of the state', nor did it succeed 'in grasping the relations between state, society [and] economy in a sufficiently precise fashion'. Thus, instead of considering the state (with its ideological apparatuses) as the almost exclusive site of the institutions of power, he now begins to argue that 'there are a whole series of other power centres which are extremely important in society'.[37] Focusing, in particular, on the way in which a transition to a greater democratic society should be conceptualised, he begins to argue that the state should be transformed in such a way that 'the extension and deepening of political freedoms and the institutions of representative democracy ... are combined with the unfurling of forms of direct democracy and the mushrooming of self-management bodies'.[38] The existence of new types of social, as distinct from strictly political, movements must be recognised and these must be given their own social space to develop their particular projects. Indeed, for this to happen, they must *not* be appropriated by the traditional type of political party and these parties themselves must now 'develop new forms of presence *within* civil society'.[39]

What is also noticeable in these last writings is the way in which Poulantzas's criticism of Gramsci likewise undergoes a dramatic shift. Gramsci is now criticised, along with Lenin, for his statist attitude. He did not show sufficient appreciation for such things as representative democracy, party pluralism and the rule of law. His view of civil society is now described as being too political; while his conception of the 'Modern Prince', coordinating all forms of social relations through its own organisational mechanisms, is seen as too monopolistic. In short, such are the nature of the problems left outstanding by Gramsci that nothing less than a 'Copernican revolution' in socialist political thought is needed.[40]

Poulantzas's suicide shortly after this apparent conversion can only make one conjecture as to how he himself would have gone on to contribute to this ongoing debate in socialist political theory. To what extent did he now accept the importance of an autonomous realm of civil society? And to what extent might he even have made a contribution to the development of a specifically *socialist* form of civil society? This latter question, in particular, has begun to feature quite regularly in socialist debates over the past decade or so. In its very nature, of course, it is a highly contradictory phenomenon, which must carefully steer a course between the Scylla of capitalist appropriation and the Charybdis of orthodox Marxist transcendence of the concept. Nevertheless, attempts have been made to conceptualise its basic form and content, and irrespective of Poulantzas's latter-day criticisms of Gramsci, many of the attempts to locate this socialist civil society have drawn at least inspiration, if not something more, from Gramsci's influence.

To a large extent it was the evolution of a highly critical intellectual debate, directed against the incumbent authoritarian regimes in Eastern Europe during the 1970s and 1980s, which did most to stimulate an interest in this complex issue. That Gramsci's writings became very popular and influential in this critical attack on the all-pervading state in Eastern Europe was in many ways easy to predict.[41] His understanding of the realm of civil society as a site of evolutionary popular struggle made it a very attractive campaigning stance for all the opposition forces, socialist and anti-socialist alike; the fact that they could all utilise a Marxist-oriented theorist against a self-proclaimed Marxist-oriented state was an opportunity too good to pass up for most of the intellectual dissidents.

Perhaps the most prominent of the neo-Gramscian, socialist intellectuals at this time was Ivan Szelenyi. According to Szelenyi, the most central issue facing the whole of modern socialist theory is indeed the question of civil society. Writing in 1979, he formulated this issue in the following simple way: 'Is "civil society" identical with capitalism, or is it a broader concept? What is the substance of socialist transformation: is it just a negation of capitalism, or does socialism necessarily also transcend "civil society"? In other words, is a "socialist civil society" possible at all?'[42]

Szelenyi's answer was a convinced yes. Arguing that what was necessary in Eastern Europe was a comprehensive socialist critique of vanguardism, he identified three main problems which needed to be tackled. First, on the economic front, the workers needed to be emancipated from their old chains, not by a change in the existing legal form of ownership, but by changing the nature of governmental institutions which expropriated production surplus and which thereby denied any genuine degree of enterprise self-management. Second, there had to be a fundamental overview of the operations of democratic centralism and the introduction of new substantive democratic rights. Finally, the whole question of bureaucratic domination had to be addressed. It was precisely by this means of a critique of vanguardism and the way in which the state had become too embedded in society that demonstrated for Szelenyi that 'without the institutional guarantees of civil society, self-management, political self-determination, workers' control, participatory planning and decision making are turned into empty slogans, caricatures of democracy'. This was by no means, however, a plea to return to a capitalist civil society based on its system of inherited wealth and privileges and its reproduction of ascribed differential statuses. For Szelenyi, this was nothing but a 'deformed' version of the potential offered by civil society, a potential that could only be achieved by a fully democratic socialism.

That Szelenyi's criticisms of Eastern European socialism were very much associated with a specific interpretation of Gramsci's heritage cannot be questioned. It was an interpretation of Gramsci which claimed that his ideas amounted to much more than an attempt to instrumentalise civil society for no other purpose than the eventual aim of abolishing it once the socialist-dominated political society had been achieved. This latter, highly reductionist and extremely one-dimensional interpretation of Gramsci has become the hallmark of writers such as Jean Cohen and Andrew Arato, whose analysis is so littered with 'totalitarian', 'authoritarian' and 'apologetic Stalinist' expletives that one wonders whether they have been reading a North Korean version of the *Prison Notebooks*.[43] Instead, what one needs to understand is that there were two different civil societies in the Gramscian framework. In the bourgeois-controlled state, there was a realm of civil society which had to be won over to socialism's cause as a means of undermining the effective reproductive power of the state. In the socialist-controlled state, meanwhile, a realm of civil society had to continue to exist to ensure the active, consensual, hegemonic potential of socialism, and to ensure that this form of hegemony was not subsumed under an all-pervading form of state domination. In short, this dual approach to civil society can be understood in the following simple formula: in a bourgeois state, the realm of civil society is characterised as a site of antagonistic struggle; in a socialist state, the realm of civil society is characterised as a site of full and effective *participation*. As for the line of demarcation between the two types of civil society, this is by no means absolute (in the way that Cohen and Arato, for example, portray it). Counter-hegemonic institutions and processes created in the former can subsequently be developed and expanded in the latter. The logic at work here, in other words, is not one of absolute destruction followed by a desire for reconstruction, a desire for reconstruction which will inevitably fail (according to Cohen and Arato) because of the state's total control over the very process of destruction. Instead, the process of construction should be a continuous one which runs parallel with, and then supersedes, the process of destruction. What Gramsci is really striving for (in the context of the modern West at least) is a situation whereby as the old begins to die, the new is *already* being born. In this sense, the institutions of civil society can perfectly well be conceived as both an instrumental means and a normative end in their own right.

Such a distinction, it should be noted, likewise became a dominant theme in the last writings of Georg Lukács, whose affinities with Gramsci were nowhere more apparent than in his own attempts to re-politicise Marxism, and to lay the foundations for his own conception of a socialist civil society. Particularly in his essay, *The Process of Democratization* [44] – written in direct response to the Soviet invasion of Czechoslovakia in 1968 – Lukács expresses his concern that '[the] economic as an individual science, as the sole causal determinant of social evolution, had lost its organic connection with the historical destiny of the human species'.[45] Where Marx and Gramsci had seen the economic as one factor of social evolution, and as organically interconnected with other social causal determinants, Soviet praxis – at least in the post-Leninist period – had 'individualised' the domain of the economy and had removed its interdependent connections with other causal agents for reasons of mere tactical exigency. The ultimate aim of any Marxist-oriented politics, however, must be the empowerment of civil society; the investment of political power is not in the narrow domain of the state, but in the institutions of civil society, strong enough to hold and wield that power in trusteeship, for it is precisely these institutions which are closest to the 'species needs' of humankind and which are therefore best able to reflect such needs. Only in this way can 'the protocols necessary for the democratic governance of a socialist society' be established.[46]

Hegemony and Culture

Turning now to the domain of culture, there can be little doubt that Gramsci's writings here are as significant for his concept of hegemony as anything strictly political or economic. Once again, along with Lukács, Gramsci did much to foster a growing interest in cultural studies in general and a new form of cultural Marxism in particular. What now emerges is an area of study which focuses much more on the institutionalisation of values, beliefs and attitudes and their conscious and unconscious effect on social interaction. It is also one which attempts to analyse the manner in which normative standards of society appropriate and universalise a conception of truth and reality and how this is then internalised as a constituent part of the individual.

A list of those writers and theorists who Gramsci has influenced, stimulated, anticipated, or provoked a response from within the cultural studies domain would be far too excessive for a study of this kind. A few of the more prominent ones, however, can be briefly mentioned. In his writings, for example, on the emerging 'culture industry' of his day – concerning the way in which needs and desires can be fabricated and manipulated and can preserve a given status quo – there is a clear correlation here with the Frankfurt School theorists, most notably Herbert Marcuse and Theodor Adorno. In some of his discussions on 'perspectivism' in relation to a theory of truth, we are also given a foretaste of some of the writings of Max Horkheimer.[47]

In his understanding of the hegemony of the Occidental world *vis-à-vis* the Orient, and the *necessity* the former has to relate to the other as an inferior culture, there are indications of a critical theory of anthropology, now primarily associated with Edward Said. In the realm of linguistics – particularly the relationship between language and the structure of social existence in general, and social values in particular, mediated by supporters of the hegemonic bloc – Gramsci anticipates many aspects of the critical theories of present-day writers such as Pierre Bourdieu and Noam Chomsky. There are also undoubted affinities, in this general field of study, with the semiological approach of Roland Barthes and Maurice Merleau-Ponty's phenomenological theory of perception.

Finally, in his understanding that power is ubiquitous and is something that is produced and reproduced in the practices of everyday life (subject to the disciplined control of the mind), Gramsci certainly anticipates a number of later writers, most notably Henri Lefebvre and Michel Foucault. The latter, in particular, shares many points of contact with Gramsci: similar ideas, for example, on the way in which the dominated *consent* to their domination, on the production of that consent, as well as on the effect of domination. Foucault was certainly far in advance of Gramsci in his understanding of the way in which gender and sexuality was an important component category of hegemony, though his reluctance to search for the comprehensive reasons as to *why* power exists and his lesser capacity to appreciate the hierarchical structure of power relations make his ideas on hegemony somewhat weaker than Gramsci's.[48]

One should also note the differences between the two thinkers as regards their understanding of the role and importance of intellectuals. While Foucault's distinction between a 'universal' and a 'specific' intellectual shares some affinity with Gramsci's traditional and organic, he is nevertheless far less desirous in wishing to preserve any kind of 'leading role' for the intellectual. For Foucault, modern societies are so pervaded by technical-scientific structures that it is virtually impossible for an intellectual now to possess anything other than a specific or localised form of knowledge and understanding. Consequently, intellectuals of a radical disposition against an incumbent system of power must accept a more diminished and limited role for themselves. Instead of playing a full-scale emancipatory role, they must operate at the level of seeking to detach a given construction of truth or reality 'from the forms of hegemony, social, economic and cultural, within which it operates at the present time'.[49]

All of these writers, then, have certainly contributed greatly to our conceptual understanding of contemporary modes of hegemony. It has to be said, however, that very few of them have been apt to draw as clear a distinction between hegemony and domination, or between passive and active forms of consent, as Gramsci. This has consequently given the concept much more of a statutory *negative* connotation than Gramsci perhaps implied, something which can especially be seen in Pierre Bourdieu's sociological re-categorisation of Gramsci's hegemony as 'symbolic violence'.[50]

Of all the cultural theorists, however, who have taken on board ideas located in Gramsci and who have sought to extend our understanding of those ideas, one writer certainly deserves a special mention – Raymond Williams. Four primary reasons can be cited in choosing Williams above all others. First, Gramsci's *direct* influence on Williams is perhaps more clear-cut than in most other cases indicated above. It is certainly true, as Eagleton has noted, that 'Williams was not only deeply suspicious of orthodoxies, but rarely even quoted another thinker or paused to note an influence.'[51]

Gramsci, however, was a frequent exception. Second, there is an intellectual evolution in Williams – from his 'structure of feeling' to 'cultural materialism', and from works such as *Culture and Society* to *Marxism and Literature* – which could be said to follow Gramsci's own evolution from his early Crocean idealism to his mature prison writings. Third, there can be no doubt whatsoever of Williams' primary responsibility in developing and popularising the academic discipline of cultural studies, and in the process, popularising Gramsci's writings throughout the English-speaking world. And finally, and perhaps most important of all, few readers of Williams would deny, as Renate Holub has so rightly pointed out, that he has 'written some of the most beautiful pages on hegemony'.[52]

It is often pointed out that Williams' discovery of Gramsci only occurred in the second half of his intellectual life. While this is strictly true, I am nevertheless inclined to follow Fernando Ferrara and argue that part and parcel of the discovery that Williams made at this time was a recognition that he had essentially been working along Gramscian lines, albeit unconsciously, in the *early* part of his intellectual career as well.[53] Certainly, his understanding of a modern-day transition to socialism by means of 'a long revolution' which was capable of permeating the 'lived experience' of individuals in society, their everyday values and feelings, and which was capable of embodying the most important structures of the national culture bore many recognised affinities with Gramsci's own emphasis on the importance of gaining hegemony in the cultural domain.

One of the key concepts to have emerged in these early works – most notably in *The Long Revolution* – was that of 'structure of feeling'; something, he writes, which corresponds to 'the culture of a period', which is 'as firm and definite as "structure" suggests, yet … operates in the most delicate and least tangible parts of our activity …: the particular living result of all the elements in the general organisation'.[54] Such a structure of feeling is not learned in any formal sense. Elements of a structure of feeling can certainly be passed down and transmitted from one generation to the next, but each generation will develop its own unique kind of structure of feeling, which to all intents and purposes will not appear to come from anywhere. This inability to comprehend its derivation, however, is deliberately misleading. Every dominant culture is purposively selective in what it chooses to take on board at any given time, in what it chooses from history and in what it chooses to reject; this process of selection is not something that an abstraction like time performs. On the contrary, it 'will be governed by many kinds of special interest, including class interests'.[55] Thus, 'the traditional culture of a society will always tend to correspond to its *contemporary* system of interests and values, for it is not an absolute body of work but a continual selection … '.[56] And what is just as underestimated, it is a continual process of *interpretation*. The task at hand, therefore, is to demonstrate more actively the selectivity and biased nature of values which have been classed as historically given, and to demystify the real relationship between values and narrow group interests.

In his later collected interviews, Williams recalls the hostility and invective which greeted *The Long Revolution*.[57] That it came from the political right and from the established press did not surprise him at all. What did take him by surprise, somewhat, was the extent of the criticism which was levelled at him from the left, where his ideas were generally considered to be too much of an abstract generalisation, too evolutionary as regards his understanding of culture, and too lacking in determinacy.[58] His drift towards a more direct Gramscian-Marxist approach in the 1970s and 1980s precisely addressed these issues and undoubtedly provided his later writings with far greater conceptual depth.

What seems to concern Williams most in these later writings is the question of determination. Taking issue with the notion of a differential base and superstructure – whereby the latter is seen in simplistic and mechanical terms as a 'reflex', an 'echo', a 'phantom' or a 'sublimate' of the former – the relative novelty of the task which he sets himself is not so much to highlight the autonomy of the cultural sphere of existence, so much as its primary *materiality* and its subsequent importance in delineating real social relations. What he attempts to demonstrate, and what in the most part he achieves in demonstrating, is the way in which cultural activities are themselves material forces of production. Re-addressing an old debate in Marx's *Grundrisse,* for example, he argues that, if for Marx only a piano-maker was strictly to be considered as a productive force, then the same denotion should apply (if not exactly in equal measure on a causal hierarchical scale) to the pianist as well. That is to say music, or any other form of culture and art, should be grasped for what it is: a real practice and an element of 'a whole material social process', full of specific conditions and intentions within a variable framework of productive practices. To fail to see this:

> … is not only to lose contact with the actuality of these practices, as has repeatedly occurred in forms of analysis derived from the terms of this specialised (industrial) materialism. It is to begin the whole difficult process of discovering and describing relations between all these practices, and between them and the other practices which have been isolated as 'production', as 'the base', or as the 'self-subsistent world', in an extremely awkward and disabling position. It is indeed to begin this most difficult

kind of work head down and standing on one foot. Such feats of agility are not impossible, and have indeed been performed. But it would be more reasonable to get back on both feet again, and to look at our actual productive activities without assuming in advance that only some of them are material.[59]

Above all, the productive materiality of cultural phenomenon is expressed in the operations of language: 'Language is not a medium; it is a constitutive element of material social practice.'[60] It is not something through which the reality of different experiences can flow. One cannot say that there is material social life first 'and *then,* at some temporal or spatial distance, consciousness and "its" products'.[61] '[Language] is a socially shared and reciprocal activity, already embedded in active relationships, within which every move is an activation of what is already shared and reciprocal or may become so.'[62] Sentences are like tools in economic production and words are equivalent to 'condensed social practices, sites of historical struggle, repositories of political wisdom or domination'.[63] Little wonder then, that, in the words of one of his articles, the central theoretical problem of Marxism, or any radical social and political theory in the late twentieth century, is not so much the ownership of the means of production as the ownership of the means of communication.

Having developed this form of *cultural materialism,* Williams' earlier understanding of structure of feeling is now substantially revised. In *Marxism and Literature,* for example, it is defined as a set of 'social experiences *in solution,* as distinct from other social semantic formations which have been *precipitated* and are more evidently and more immediately available'.[64] The limits of the term are also more clearly defined in his later works; most important of all, structures of feeling are now subsumed as one component part, along with 'traditions', 'institutions', and 'formations' under an explicitly Gramscian type of hegemony. What the concept of hegemony can offer, that structures of feeling never quite could, is a constitutive understanding of power and a sense of determinacy defined as the setting of limits and the exertion of pressures. As such, it is not only a more comprehensive, but a more *dynamic* concept. Gramsci's great contribution, Williams writes, is to have understood the complexity of hegemony 'at a depth which is, I think, rare'. 'Hegemony', he continues,

> … supposes the existence of something which is truly total, which is not merely secondary or superstructural, like the weak sense of ideology, but which is lived at such a depth, which saturates the society to such an extent, and which, as Gramsci put it, even constitutes the substance

and limit of common sense for most people under its sway, that it corresponds to the reality of social experience very much more clearly than any notions derived from the formula of base and superstructure.[65]

For Williams, then, hegemony goes beyond ideology in its *wholeness* and in its capacity to relate a lived social process as one that is 'practically organised by specific and dominant meanings and values'.[66] It also goes beyond any narrow definition of culture because it can likewise relate this whole social process to a specific distribution of power and influence and can identify specific forms of dominance and subordination.

Two primary advantages are attained by our conceptual understanding of hegemony. First, our capacity to comprehend different forms of domination and subordination is a closer reflection of the reality of social existence and social organisation in modern-day societies, and is thereby able to transcend earlier simplistic, somewhat trivial, explanations of outright manipulatory forms of control. As a result, our comprehension of systems of class rule and possible forms of opposition to it, in spheres which are not directly political or economic, is also transformed in hugely beneficial ways. Second, the very nature of hegemony has an enormous effect on the whole approach to cultural practices and cultural theory. And here, of course, Williams is able to connect his new-found interest in hegemony with his emerging ideas on cultural materialism. Because of the depth at which any cultural hegemony is lived, cultural practices cannot possibly be seen as simple reflections or even mediations of an established social and economic structure. Rather, they should be seen as 'among the basic processes of the formation itself' and as 'active experiences and practices' in their own right, which cover 'a much wider area of reality than the abstractions of "social" and "economic" experience'.[67]

Because of the wholeness, the depth and the saturation which a true form of hegemony can achieve, Williams recognises that any attempt at a fundamental social transition is always prone to immense difficulties. Notwithstanding this, however, he is equally convinced – just like Gramsci (and Bakhtin) were convinced – that the basis for a potentially successful *counter*-hegemony will always exist. Because of the very complexity of hegemony, and because 'hegemony can never be singular' and static, the social forces which seek to sustain it are constantly having to search for ways to renew, recreate, modify and defend it; it is here that the opportunities for social alternatives arise. No mode of production, no dominant society or order of society, and no dominant culture, 'in reality exhausts the full range of human practice, human energy [and] human intention'.[68] There will always be spheres which an incumbent hegemony will not be fully able to adapt or conquer, and interests which it will not be fully able to incorporate. Taking on board some of his ideas referred to in *The Long Revolution*, he writes that the dominant mode is always subject to a conscious process of selection and organisation. It will always aim to incorporate a ruling definition of the social, but there will always be sources of actual human practice which it perforce will have to neglect, exclude, or will not be able to recognise as significant at every immediate moment. These are what he calls *residual* and *emergent* forms of consciousness.[69]

One of the most important components of any hegemony for Williams is tradition. Tradition should not be understood as 'an inert historicised segment … [but] as the most powerful practical means of [hegemonic] incorporation'.[70] What tradition is able to offer the hegemonic forces is the capacity to promote an intentionally selective version of the past and relate this with a 'pre-shaped present' – or, what he later terms a *predisposed continuity*. Its powerful capacity stems from the kind of continuities it embodies – families, places, institutions and language, in other words, the most direct forms of lived experience in ordinary people's lives. More interestingly, perhaps, is the way in which Williams recognises tradition as equally the most *vulnerable* part of hegemony and as the key domain for any potential counter-hegemonic force. By striving to recover discarded elements of the past and by seeking to redress all manner of selective and reductive interpretations of a society's tradition, a counter-hegemonic force can skilfully undermine the accepted version of the past and can attempt to demonstrate alternative forms of future continuity.

What, then, does Williams add to our understanding of hegemony? First, he not only emphasises that any analysis of hegemony must seek to comprehend its active and formative mechanisms, but he also underlines its *transformational* activities. The significance of this, as Eagleton has pointed out, is the almost inseparable relationship between hegemonic and counter-hegemonic processes, such that the latter will invariably prove to be *partly constitutive* of the former.[71] Second, Williams re-emphasises – in contrast, for example, to Foucault and Althusser – the imminent counter-hegemonic potentialities which are inherent in any form of historical configuration. There will always be hegemonic constraints on power, in the form of contradictions and unresolved conflicts, and all oppositions must maintain sufficient 'resources of hope' to turn these to their own advantage.[72] Finally, in his very style of analysis and description – which is often 'nearer to Wordsworth than to Marx'[73] – Williams brings a tremendous sense of personal experience to our understanding of hegemony, something that Gramsci, for obvious reasons, was perhaps less able to do in his prison writings:

I learned the reality of hegemony, I learned the saturating power of the structures of feeling of a given society, as much from my own mind and my own experience as from observing the lives of others. All through our lives, if we make the effort, we uncover layers of this kind of alien formation in ourselves, and deep in ourselves. So then the recognition of it is a recognition of large elements in *our own* experience, which have to be – shall we say it? – defeated. But to defeat something like that in yourself, in your families, in your neighbours, in your friends, to defeat it involves something very different, it seems to me, from most traditional political strategies.[74]

Hegemony and Class

How essential is the relationship between hegemony and class? This is one of the crucial questions posed by Ernesto Laclau and Chantal Mouffe in their post-Marxist, post-structuralist *Hegemony and Socialist Strategy: Towards a Radical Democratic Politics*. The work represents one of the most comprehensive attempts to provide the concept of hegemony with an up-to-date setting in modern (or postmodern) political societies. In its efforts to deny an intrinsic compatibility between hegemony and some of the most basic categories of traditional Marxist theory, however, it also makes it one of the biggest challenges to certain crucial aspects of the Gramscian legacy.

One of the primary tasks of Laclau's and Mouffe's study is to produce some kind of dialectical synthesis out of what they see are some fundamental contradictions in Gramsci's theory of hegemony. They want to 'recover the basic concepts of Gramscian analysis' so as to 'radicalise them in a direction that leads us beyond Gramsci'.[75] This, it is argued elsewhere, encompasses the very essence of the general task of post-Marxism.[76] Influenced very much by the ideas of Jacques Derrida, it is an attempt to undermine (or deconstruct) the old unities and 'closures' found in classical Marxism so as to re-create not only the original meaning of the categories located within the tradition, but also to relocate the vast array of theoretical alternatives which were formerly dismissed by the universalisation of the limited range of options taken on board by Marxism.

What they accept from Gramsci's analysis of hegemony is first and foremost his 'logic of articulation', his acceptance that social complexity is the very condition of political struggle which 'sets the basis for a democratic practice of politics, compatible with a plurality of historical subjects'.[77] That is to say, these subjects must in some sense be socially constructed. Following on from this, they also accept some of the primary elements of Gramsci's strategic concept of a war of position, especially his notion that individual civilisations are always prone to progressive disaggregation, whereby the identity of the opponents are never entirely fixed on a rigid continuum, but constantly move about during the process of disaggregation. As they themselves put it: 'Only the presence of a vast area of floating elements and the possibility of their articulation to opposite camps – which implies a constant redefinition of the latter – is what constitutes the terrain permitting us to define a practice as hegemonic.'[78]

Having gone so far with Gramsci's analysis, however, they have now reached the decisive point at which they can go no further. Although Gramsci has accepted a certain 'fluidity' in the process of articulation and has accepted the notion that diverse social elements have a distinctive specificity of their own, his mistake now, as Laclau and Mouffe see it, is to continue to place a fundamental restriction on the nature of this fluidity by arguing that 'there must always be a *single* unifying principle in every hegemonic formation'. For Gramsci, of course, this single unifying principle is to be found in the *class* structure of society; it is class which is the ultimate determining core of a hegemonic force and it is this that Laclau and Mouffe cannot accept. 'Gramsci's thought', they argue,

> ... appears suspended around a basic ambiguity concerning the status of the working class which finally leads it to a contradictory position. On the one hand, the political centrality of the working class has a historical, contingent character: it requires the class to come out of itself, to transform its own identity by articulating to it a plurality of struggles and democratic demands. On the other hand, it would seem that this articulatory role is assigned to it by the economic base – hence, that the centrality has a necessary character. One cannot avoid the feeling that the transition from [an] ... essentialist conception ... to a radical historicist one has not been coherently accomplished.[79]

Indeed, not only is the reductionist principle of class as *the* determining logic of hegemonic articulation 'incoherent', it is also variously described as 'vain' and 'illegitimate'. In their conception of hegemonic struggle, the class nature of that struggle might well be an effect of a process of hegemonic articulation, but it is by no means an *a priori* condition. So, for example, they would both argue that there is nothing intrinsically antagonistic in the wage labour-capital relationship. It is only when, and if, an individual worker resists the form which this relationship takes – that is, extraction of his/her surplus value – that it then becomes antagonistic. But this process of resistance is only constituted by something *outside* the relations of production itself; it is constituted by the nature of the *discourse* which provides a sense of *meaning* to that particular relationship. Consequently, as both authors have affirmed elsewhere: ' … interests never exist prior to the discourses in which they are articulated and constituted; they cannot be the expression of already existing positions on the economic level'.[80] And 'the hegemonic act will not be the *realisation* of a rationality preceding it, but an act of radical *construction* … '.[81] In other words, it is the practice of discourse which fixes a meaning to an event, not something indigenous to that event, such as its given class logic. This denial on their part of any kind of privileged class status in the social struggle for hegemony becomes the point 'where the Gramscian view becomes unacceptable' to them.[82]

Having abandoned this 'essentialist apriorism' in Gramsci's analysis of hegemony, Laclau and Mouffe go on to consider two further issues. The first relates to the notion that any potential articulating force will itself never remain static or unchanged by the hegemonic process. They say this was never an issue for Gramsci, an observation which is clearly erroneous. And the second issue, which is the one that I want to concentrate on, takes the abandonment of class as an ultimate core of a hegemonic force even further by stating that the very idea of *any* single, central location of hegemony is misconceived. The former abandonment of class, then, is now couched in universalist terms. In a given social formation, there can be a whole range of hegemonic 'nodal points' (as they call them), so many, in fact, that there is an *irreducible plurality* of the social sphere of hegemony. This abandonment of any single, central location of hegemony clearly has very important significance in Laclau and Mouffe's conception of political struggle: it serves as the basis for their attempt to achieve, what they see is, a radicalisation of pluralism and democracy and an ultimate defence mechanism against any possible encroachment of totalitarianism. It is also the basis – and here again the reference is to Gramsci and Marx – that they go on to negate even the very essence of society:

> In order to place ourselves within the field of articulation, we must begin by renouncing the conception of 'society' as founding totality of its partial processes. We must, therefore, consider the openness of the social as the constitutive ground or 'negative essence' of the existing, and the diverse 'social orders' as precarious and ultimately failed attempts to domesticate the field of differences.[83]

Not surprisingly, the sweeping nature of their post-Marxist claims and their criticisms of Gramsci's 'non-democratic', because class-oriented, understanding of hegemony have met with a considerable amount of hostility and subsequent defence of Gramsci's original positions. Before looking at the case for the defence, let us just be clear what the main tenets of Laclau and Mouffe's ideas on hegemony amount to. First, they are not saying that class interests cannot be a factor in a project of hegemony; only, they cannot be the central, unitary, unifying, essential factor. Second, nor can anything else hold a position of essential centrality. One form of interest is as important and significant as any other in the project of hegemony. And third, when they talk of interests as components of a project of hegemony, they mean by this a set of aspirations and desires which have been created by a form of discourse. There can be no such thing as interests which exist independently, autonomously or objectively beyond the realm of creative discourse. The question of why an individual may possess a given set of interests has nothing to do with their particular location in the social conjuncture. The process of discourse, in other words, is not a reflection of reality, but is itself *constitutive* of reality, and as a result individual identities and interests are seen as entirely malleable and are shaped by the kind of discourse (and attractiveness of that discourse) which is encountered. Until the encounter with discourse, social interests and social elements are intrinsically neutral.

If we thus take this last point first, the central criticism which can be levelled at Laclau and Mouffe (and indeed all discourse theorists) relates to the fact that they can never adequately answer the question as to where or how social interests based solely and exclusively upon a process of discourse originate. As Terry Eagleton has very dryly commented: 'Where interests derive from ... is as opaque a matter for post-Marxism as where babies come from is for the small infant.'[84] It is impossible for the post-Marxist to say where they derive from: 'they simply drop from the skies, like any other transcendental signifier'.[85] The issue is not helped by the frequent assertion of Laclau and Mouffe that no real importance should be attached to the question of *who* the agent of hegemony is. What is important is the question of *how* an individual becomes a subject through the process of hegemonic articulation. The contention is made, in other words, that 'hegemony supposes the construction of the very identity of [the] social agents [being hegemonised]'.[86] This, however, is pure vacuousness and tautological nonsense. Again, in the words of Eagleton, this would amount to the statement 'that there are no social agents at all until the process of political hegemony creates them, in which case hegemony is a circular, self-referential affair, which like a work of literary fiction secretly fashions the reality it claims to be at work upon'.[87] Alternatively, of course, it might also mean that the *subject* of hegemony here is someone or something which has a unique, special ability to fashion a new form of collective alliance out of a previously indeterminate mass for purposes it has somehow autonomously created. If this is the case, however, the sinister connotations of this kind of hegemonic project should be very clearly noted.[88]

The flames of mystical confusion are stoked up even more by a later statement by Laclau which clearly owes its influence to Georges Sorel. Not content with denying that there is an intrinsic form of social interest beyond the realm of creative discourse, Laclau goes on to argue that even the links between discourse and *any* kind of social reality are very tenuous indeed. Both the project of hegemony and the aspiration for a radical form of democracy, it seems, 'can ... only live and assert itself through the constant production of social *myths*'.[89] What we have here, then, is an opportunist's fantasy paradise and one cannot help but concur with Ellen Meiksins Wood's comment that: 'In the beginning (and the end) was the Word, and the Word was with God, and the Word was God, the ultimate Subject made incarnate in ... Laclau and Mouffe.'[90] Indeed, is it any wonder that both authors often conflate the notion of hegemony with nothing more than a 'game'?

Being more charitable to Laclau and Mouffe – than, for example, Norman Geras, who describes their *Hegemony and Socialist Strategy,* amongst other things, as 'a product of the very advanced stage of an intellectual malady'[91] – one can admit that *within strict limits,* post-Marxist discourse theory has the capacity to clarify, and in some instances, even deepen certain elements of our existing Gramscian understanding of the logic of hegemonic practice. They have, for example, adequately demonstrated that there is no automatic relationship between one's location in the economic structure and one's political or ideological tastes. A process of social construction and articulation, as Gramsci himself so clearly recognised, is not only required, but is absolutely crucial. And they have very cogently demonstrated that the very process of social construction, articulation and discourse is itself an active process. The process is not a passive reflection of a determined social environment; it can play a significant role in shaping and modifying that environment. But these positive reaffirmations (and ultimately this is all they are) are a far cry from their much bolder assertion that there is no connection whatsoever between social location and a given set of social interests. At the very least, an individual's position within the social sphere will provide a necessary reference point for the kind of interests he/she will be most amenable to. The underlying reasons for these interests, in other words, will exist *prior* to any discourse which comes to articulate them. An individual's amenability to a particular form of discourse cannot be otherwise shaped to some considerable extent by a reference back to *real,* not mythical, interests in the social realm.

Ellen Meiksins Wood has made this point very forcibly. To assume otherwise would imply that within the framework of a capitalist system workers are no more affected by the operations of that system than anybody else; their disadvantages are equal to everyone else's disadvantages, including supposedly, capitalists themselves. It would also equally suppose that there are no fundamental social and political consequences stemming from the relationship between capital and labour. But, then, if this is the case, we are left advocating the totally absurd position that there is no real reason why all monopoly capitalists should not suddenly become committed revolutionary communists tomorrow, provided an attractive enough form of discourse can be formulated. Or, alternatively, there is no real reason to refute the claim that 'a caveman is as likely to become a socialist as is a proletarian – provided only that he comes within hailing distance of the appropriate discourse'.[92] Expressed in another way, we can say that all phenomena have inherent properties attached to them that cannot be altered by the kind of discourse which is used to classify them. For example, at a sublime level, we might decide that from tomorrow all chairs will henceforth be called 'nomags'. The process of discourse has thus effected a change in the identity of a given phenomenon. But irrespective of how we label that phenomenon, 'chair' or 'nomag', the properties essential to it remain the same. The same principle also applies to the more serious example of capitalist productive relations. We can apply all sorts of discourse – what many would call 'verbal conjuring tricks' – to identify the appearance of that relationship, even to the extent of glorifying its benevolence. But what our discourse cannot do is affect the inherent properties of that relation, namely, the property of surplus value extraction.

Granted that social interests have a *pre*-discursive reality, what about the other two main specific criticisms of Gramsci by Laclau and Mouffe: namely, his retention of class interests as an *a priori* privileged phenomenon in the process of hegemony and the ability of class to unify and give real alignment to a range of diverse social interests? Another severe limitation of Laclau and Mouffe's spiriting away of pre-discursive social interests is their total inability to comprehend how social formations are constituted, reproduced and transformed.[93] As we have seen, such is their excessive fear of essentialist, teleologically-oriented system theories, that Laclau and Mouffe are left with little or no other option but to support the most excessive kind of anti-essentialist theory, one which is totally system-blind and one which also analyses all kinds of practices in a total institutional vacuum. As many commentators have noted, theirs is a habit of consistently viewing things in the most simplistic black/white, either/or terms. Gramsci's conceptual and theoretical advantage is the exact reverse of this and this leaves his concept of hegemony, if somewhat more complex than Laclau and Mouffe's, certainly richer. Gramsci's starting point is his attempt to locate, what Esteve Morera has termed, the key 'generative mechanisms whose concurrence produces social phenomena' in a given social system.[94] This inevitably requires that he must engage himself on the nexus of *ascertainable causes* and *ascertainable effects* and must be prepared as well to attach differential weight and significance to all manner of phenomena. Since a social system operates on the basis of its ability to produce and re-produce the inherent properties of its own existence, it follows that a required form of social relations and social agents are a necessary, essential part of this reproduction. Without these social relations and social agents the essential logic of the system would fall apart. Since these fundamental relations are discursively identified as *class* relations, without going into the arguments as to what exactly constitutes a specific type of class, it does seem difficult to counter the basic logic which thus claims that relations of class and agents of class do indeed have an *a priori,* privileged role in the process of re-producing (or in some historical instances, *not* re-producing) a given social system.

Certainly, for Erik Olin Wright, the basic logic justifying the centrality of class is a simple one. 'It is sufficient to argue', he writes, 'that the class structure constitutes the central mechanism by which various sorts of resources are appropriated and distributed, therefore determining the underlying capacities to act of various social actors. Class structures [therefore] are the central determinant of social power.'[95] Likewise, since the class structure 'distributes the basic access to the resources which determine human capacities to act', it also follows for Wright that this must constitute a line of 'demarcation in trajectories of social change' as well as providing an ultimate 'limit' within which non-class mechanisms can effectively operate.[96] To repeat, all of this can be logically deduced outside of the realm of debate positing the specific make-up of a particular class in a particular social system. Quite simply, if this view of the privileged position of the class structure is not acceptable to the likes of Laclau and Mouffe and other post-Marxist, post-structuralist theorists, then they should at least be able to give some explanation as to what other kind of social relation and social interest could play such a comparable fundamental and basic role in the operational logistics of social existence. This, however, is precisely what their adherence to discourse theory will not allow them to do.

If we accept that the class structure is the key ascertainable cause of a social system's reproduction, can we also locate any key ascertainable effects which stem from a particular set of class relations and interests within that structure? The answer here depends on the nature of the class relations and the class interests we are dealing with. If it can be demonstrated that class relations and interests are intrinsically harmonious, then clearly a different kind of effect will be ascertained than if those relations and interests can be demonstrated to be intrinsically antagonistic. For Gramsci, of course (as for all Marxists), a demonstrable case can be made to show that within the confines of a capitalist system, class relations are indeed intrinsically antagonistic ones. It therefore follows that one of the key ascertainable effects of an antagonistic class system is the perpetual need of the dominant class, assuming it wants to guarantee a continued reproduction of the system, to retain control of the primary levers of coercion available to society; that is to say, control of the state by the dominant forces must be considered a *necessary, essential* ascertainable effect.

For Gramsci, this is the logical bottom line of essentialism. Above and beyond the recognition that the class structure of society, and the relations which stem from that structure, represents the most important element in a system's reproduction; above and beyond the assertion that a dominant class will always have need of the coercive powers of the state, Gramsci was, as we know, far from being an 'essentialist'. As has already been demonstrated, Gramsci is well aware that the relationship between the class structure and such things as an *effective* class formation, an *effective* class consciousness and an *effective* class struggle is one that depends on a necessary process of active social construction. Without this social construction, there is only a potential linkage between a class-in-itself and a class-for-itself. Similarly, he does not deny a strong degree of autonomy to such practices as politics and culture; nor does he deny the importance and the *specificity* of social groups who emerge in the realm of civil society and whose attachment to, and identity with, strict class interests is purely *contingent*. After all, this is the reason why he attaches so much importance to the process of hegemony, the task of which is precisely that of unifying these heterogeneous and dispersed social interests within civil society and converting them into an organic, coherent bloc.

But Gramsci is equally adamant that one should not forget that the ultimate aim and effect of the hegemonic process is necessarily bounded within the framework of a given system's essential constitution and reproduction. The task of creating a more unified civil society ultimately serves the purpose of accommodating it to the society's structural class relations. Nor should one be taken in by the fact that in modern societies a ruling force has considerably extended its ability to cloak its allegiance to the dominant class interest. This it can do in various ways such as giving itself the appearance of universality, as well as by making it appear that the state–civil society relationship is more significant than the strict state-class structure relationship. Finally, one should also remember that while a dominant class will always be prepared to make concessions to social interests within the complex arena of civil society, the extent of such concessions will again always be limited by its need to preserve the essential structure of the social system so that its basic interests will continue to be satisfied.

For Ellen Meiksins Wood, what Laclau and Mouffe have effectively done with their post-Marxist, post-Gramscian interpretation of a postmodern route to 'socialist' hegemony is to have played right into the hands of the dominant capitalist classes.[97] By arguing that class interests are nothing more than one other form of 'personal identity', discursively equal with such identities as gender and race, and thereby no longer privileged by its historic constitutive centrality, they have conceptualised away the inherent property of exploitation which is part and parcel of the capitalist system's make-up. In effect, they have accepted capitalism's permanent hegemonic status. They have made 'the totalising logic and the coercive power of capitalism become invisible'; they have denied its ability to provide an over-arching power structure in society. They have denied its ability to provide society with a 'totalising unity' based around the system's logic of accumulation, its commodification of all social life, its creation of the market as a necessity and its compulsive desire for self-sustaining growth – all of which act as primary determinative forces in all aspects of social existence and social relations.[98] The oppression which exists from one's class position in capitalist society must therefore be considered as more than another form of identity, equal with such things as gender and race. While all oppressions may have equal *moral* claims, 'class exploitation has a different *historical* status, a more strategic location at the heart of capitalism'.[99] And for this reason 'class struggle may have a more *universal* reach, a greater potential for advancing not only class emancipation but other emancipatory struggles too'.[100] It is a lesson which Gramsci himself never failed to teach, and rightly so.

5 Does Hegemony Have a Postmodern Future?

... The grand words
of the times in which events were still visible,
are no longer for us.
Who speaks of victory?
To resist today is everything.

Rainer Maria Rilke

Spectral Counter-Hegemony

Whatever the weaknesses and deficiencies of Laclau and Mouffe's hostility to a sense of class essentialism in any hegemonic context, there is, how can one put it, at least an 'imaginative' attempt on their part to constitute a positive social alternative in their advocacy of a new 'radical democratic politics'. This is a project, they claim, which is infinitely more ambitious and radically more libertarian in its objectives than that of the classical left. It is also one – and this is crucial to bear in mind – that retains the ambition of *transcending* the existing capitalist hegemonic order. If this was not the case then there can be little doubt that one would want to engage with their ideas in a different way. Indeed, many on the left would no doubt feel free to ignore them completely. So, how exactly 'radical', 'democratic' and 'political' is the project of Laclau and Mouffe? The answer in many ways is that it is none of these things at all.

Take, for example, the notion of 'radical'. What exactly is being signified by this term? An answer, unfortunately, is never categorically given, although one assumes it is being used in its positive connotation to denote vigorous and fundamental change by having an effect on the foundation of things. But this is precisely what Laclau and Mouffe do not achieve. How can they have an effect on the foundations of capitalism, for example, when they perpetually insist that in reality there is no such thing as capitalism? Instead, there is simply a system of power that has certain discursive features which we readily identify as constituting a capitalist order.

As for other possible justifications of the 'radical' label, one would similarly have to conclude that, if anything, the exact opposite notion of 'conservative' appears all too often to have far greater salience. They are defenders, for example, of a very classical bourgeois notion of individualism. They are negative libertarians. And they not only want to 'consolidate' the existing liberal state; even more disconcertingly they conceive this state in almost exclusively *ethical* terms, to the point where they are convinced that even the anti-capitalist struggle itself can succeed by a defence and consolidation of the liberal state.

Turning to the 'democratic' conception of their project, it will be remembered that for Laclau and Mouffe, the true essence of democracy consists in 'the recognition of the multiplicity of social logics along with the necessity of their articulation'.[1] This articulation, however, is never static. It is constantly being renegotiated and re-created and there will be no final point at which any kind of balance will be achieved definitively. As for the hoped-for 'extension of democracy' which is envisaged, this stems from their claim that social agents can at last assert their legitimacy on their own definable terms.

A number of questions immediately spring to mind here. What kind of legitimacy is it, for example, that is actually being asserted? For what ends and for what purposes are different social organisations asserting their legitimacy today? Is this act of autonomous assertion an intrinsic 'democratic' virtue in its own right? In answer to some of these questions, both authors are always very (arguably *too*) keen to stress that the essential logic of articulation is not in the least incompatible with certain kinds of conservative, even authoritarian, forms of discourse. This, it is dismissively claimed, 'merely means that the democratic articulation of [such authoritarian] demands is the result of a hegemonic struggle like everything else'.[2] But is not the insertion of 'merely' here, as well as the retention of 'democratic' in this context, rather unnerving, to say the least?

As for some of the potential *theoretical* inconsistencies and contradictions of their approach, some of these, it has to be said, are at least openly alluded to by both authors. For example, they make no attempt to disguise the fact that there might be a deep-seated 'incompatibility between the proliferation of political spaces proper to a radical democracy and the construction of collective identities on the basis of the logic of equivalence'.[3] To counter this potential incompatibility, they go on to stress that the strengthening of specific democratic struggles will always require 'the expansion of chains of equivalence which extend to other struggles. The equivalential articulation between anti-racism, anti-sexism and anti-capitalism, for example, requires a hegemonic construction which, in certain circumstances, may be the condition for the consolidation of each one of these struggles.' They also recognise that the

> ... logic of equivalence ... taken to its ultimate consequences, would imply the dissolution of the autonomy of the spaces in which each one

of these struggles is constituted; not necessarily because any of them become subordinated to others, but because they have all become, strictly speaking, equivalent symbols of a unique and indivisible struggle.[4]

But as we have already seen, once there is this 'indivisible' sense of struggle created, some of them will inevitably (and properly) become *subordinated* to others.

This incompatibility is recognised by Laclau and Mouffe, but is then immediately dismissed on the grounds that the ultimate moment of this incompatibility would somehow never arrive because the logic of autonomy would always take precedence over the logic of equivalence. The different nature of the demands of the autonomous groups would always set up barriers between them. But if this is the case, Laclau and Mouffe are getting themselves into deeper water. If there can be no ultimate equivalence between different groups with different specific agendas, then what would be the basis of any (counter) hegemonic process? Since each group would have no choice but to suppress some subjectivity of another group, this would therefore dissolve any notion of real equivalence between them. On numerous occasions, Laclau and Mouffe state categorically that they do not want to create a new 'essentialism of the elements'. Nevertheless, this is undoubtedly what they go on to create. The notion of a unified and homogeneous subject has been effectively replaced by a fragmented multiplicity in which each of the fragments does indeed retain a closed identity.

Another serious criticism of their conception of democracy, and in particular their acceptance of democracy in its purely *liberal* form, is their seemingly complete failure to understand that all democratic discourse is itself very much constituted by the process of antagonistic social (class) conflict. This has been very well brought out in the numerous writings of Ellen Meiksins Wood. No matter how much subordinate classes may have appropriated the language of liberal democratic discourse, there can be no escaping the fact that this form of democracy does undoubtedly serve the class interests of capital 'by denying the relations of subordination on which capitalist power rests, and by delimiting the sphere in which popular power may operate'. This is a far cry, of course, from the original conception of democracy which 'reflected the interests of the *demos* as against those of the propertied classes in Greece'.[5] Any genuine attempt to transcend capitalism, therefore, must intrinsically seek to transcend the particular conception of democracy which underpins it. The relationship between the two is much more than a contingent or a conjunctural relationship; any theory which reduces the relationship to this basis cannot help but give succour to the mystifying forces that so help to sustain the hegemony of capitalism.

If Laclau and Mouffe's project is not quite so radical or democratic as they would have us believe, what about the 'political' aspect? Is it indeed a political project at all? A number of things are perhaps most striking here. Notwithstanding all their own claims about the supremacy of politics, their concerns that due to the 'destruction of the symbolic framework' of modern societies this has led to the unravelling of the social fabric which is synonymous with 'a disappearance of the political', and their oft-repeated desire to bring about a 'return of the political', the first thing that strikes any reader of Laclau and Mouffe's work is their unadulterated hostility to any kind of party, or even a broader 'movement', which might be established to act in the capacity of an actual political agent of change. Consequently, a sense of real *commitment* to this project is almost totally unimaginable. There is little or no conception of an actual *process* of transformation, just a vague idea about a utopian vision of a transformed reality which is so malleable in form as to give it little or no concrete shape whatsoever.

Second, and picking up on points made earlier, the kind of 'politics' envisaged by Laclau and Mouffe is nothing more than 'neo-tribal' in nature. The new social agents are far too heterogeneous to create anything other than a very loose, very temporary 'alliance', which will then immediately dissolve into fragments following any parochial success. Moreover, where Laclau and Mouffe see a virtue in *fragmentation,* believing this to be a sign of a growth in demands against the existing system which will be all the harder to manipulate and disregard, the exact opposite would surely be the result. The multiplication of social spaces will nearly always end up weakening and totally diluting the actual political capacity for sustained opposition. Laclau and Mouffe, in other words, are too easily taken in by quantitative rather than qualitative features of politics and hegemonic struggle.

Third, despite all the claims of a tremendous extension of the politicisation of social agents, this is not really a political phenomenon at all, so much as a *cultural* phenomenon. What Laclau and Mouffe have done is to conceptualise a 'counter-culture ... in an enclave of the capitalist wilderness'.[6] They have given credence and prominence to a set of 'alternative spaces' within capitalism – with the operative words here being 'alternative' (rather than antagonistic) and *within* capitalism (rather than outside of its constitutive norms and *raison d'être*). After all, let us not forget that the myriad (cultural) life-styles and options that are now available are themselves totally subject to the capitalist laws of commodification; they are fashionable items to be packaged, marketed and sold in the ever-broader consumer-friendly market place. The subcultures do not represent a threat to capitalist hegemony; they buttress and sustain it and give it the appearance of adaptability and progress. Either that, or many of today's subcultures are opt-out ones, which again implies no intrinsic threat to the existing capitalist structure.

Finally, for a theory that relies so much on the power of discourse in the hegemonic struggle, there is virtually no attention given to the practical problem of precisely how an opposition discourse can be articulated to wide sectors of society. The fundamental problem of the ownership of the means of communication – which so came to preoccupy Raymond Williams – is simply ignored by Laclau and Mouffe.

In developing the theoretical basis of their ideas, Laclau and Mouffe have clearly drawn inspiration from a number of intellectual trends, with the three that instantly come to mind being phenomenology, post-analytical philosophy and post-structuralism. In terms of individual thinkers, meanwhile, undoubtedly their greatest intellectual debt is owed to Jacques Derrida. Indeed, in many ways, one of the underlying purposes of Laclau and Mouffe's project for a new radical democracy was to give a whole new *political* meaning to Derrida's anti-metaphysical and anti-essentialist conception of deconstruction, which had hitherto nearly always been assessed, rightly or wrongly – Derrida himself would insist wrongly – in largely *apolitical* terms.

In the spring of 1993, in a series of lectures at the University of California, Derrida himself finally made his own long-awaited and long-anticipated (re)entry into the world of explicit political gestures. Entitled *Specters of Marx: The State of the Debt, the Work of Mourning and the New International*, the lectures, while focusing primarily on key aspects of Marx's theoretical writings, nevertheless were broad enough in scope to offer a whole new political dimension to the notion of deconstruction. Indeed, in places, there were even clear signs of a *programmatic* engagement, suggesting that the politics of deconstruction*ism* was not only the logical heir to a specific theoretical, *radicalised* interpretation of Marx, but was also the strongest potential challenge to the incumbent hegemony of the liberal capitalist order.

Given the sense of pessimism and conservatism, if not outright negativity, that pervades the real, effective counter-hegemonic potential of Laclau and Mouffe's project for a new radical democracy, is there anything more positive and more optimistic that one can derive from Derrida's more committed politicisation of deconstructionism? Does he go anywhere nearer to satisfying Laclau and Mouffe's own stated intentions of formulating not just a 'strategy of opposition', but an actual 'strategy of construction of a new order', a strategy of construction which would not be reduced or condemned to marginality because of its predominance of negation, but which would truly seek to offer a positive *re*construction of the existing social order? Does he, at least, fulfil his own pledge to utilise the tools of deconstruction in order to affirm that the experience of the impossible must always be understood as 'a radical experience of the *perhaps*'?[7] Unfortunately, any answer to these questions would again have to be a definite 'no'. Indeed, if anything, the aforementioned doubts and misgivings of Laclau and Mouffe's project are even more accentuated in Derrida's political offering.

Throughout the *Specters of Marx* there is, to be sure, a very powerful, incisive critique of present-day liberal capitalist hegemony. Its political and economic dysfunctions, its violence, its exclusion and its oppression are all explored in deeply heartfelt ways. Likewise, there is arguably no writer better equipped and capable than Derrida in conjuring up evocative images of the 'manic, jubilatory and incantatory' forms of the current period of capitalist hegemony; how its incantations repeat and ritualise themselves, clinging to formulas 'like any animistic magic'.[8] And who better than Derrida, when deconstructing the reality of this hegemony, to highlight the ways in which the present capitalist order, seemingly at its most triumphant height of power, is nevertheless both threatened and threatening to a degree not witnessed for well over a half-century. 'Threatened', because of its own internal contradictions and its total incapacity to resolve the fundamental problems which plague societies today; 'threatening' because of the very manifestation of what it stands for (and has always stood for), and because, even more worrying, it is a hegemonic order that is increasingly donning the guise of those even worse 'spectres' of racism and chauvinism.

Where the lyrical, almost poetical, condemnation of this hegemonic order is second to none, and where it is firmly grounded in 'corporeal' empiricism, one certainly cannot say the same when it comes to a Derridean account of how this hegemony can be actively and effectively countered. Marxism, we are told, is certainly to be an important, crucial element of a counter-hegemonic strategy. But for Derrida, there are many contradictory Marxism*s*. Moreover, since he rejects *'almost everything'* (his emphasis) from the different spectres of these Marxisms (retaining only its spirit of radical critique), one cannot help but conclude that this 'new' affirmation of allegiance to Marx leaves too many questions unanswered. More significantly, we are also told that the main desire is to see the creation of a 'New International' one which, while still being 'discreet', is nevertheless becoming more and more visible, which can establish 'a link of affinity, suffering and hope', and which will have as its main task the production of 'critiques' of such phenomena as the current state of international law, as well as such concepts as state and nation.[9] What we are *not* told, however, is undoubtedly far more substantial and far more significant. Who, for example, are envisaged to be the real deconstructionist agents of change? Who are the social forces which would be the nucleus of a counter-hegemonic strategy? In what precise way is a counter-hegemonic force (presumably in the guise of this new International) to be actually constructed? What is the actual agenda of change? What will keep the counter-hegemonic force united for any length of time (other than a negative basis of opposition to real existing capitalism)? Where is the mobilisationary capacity of deconstruction? We know from many of Derrida's earlier works that he has no real positive conception of the agency of social class, considering it to have been 'ruined by capitalist modernity', and as something thoroughly outdated, unless conceived and used in a considerably 'differentiated' manner;[10] this antagonism towards class identification is repeated in his *Specters*. We also have a reiteration of an intrinsic hostility to the form and structure of a political party, which is more and more becoming 'suspect', Derrida tells us, and radically unadapted and unsuited to the contemporary era. In short, another mechanism ripe for an irrevocable deconstruction. But it is not just social classes and political parties which are being deconstructively spirited away. Derrida's counter-hegemonic force is to have no coordination, no country, no community, no co-citizenship. Like everything else that he sees around him in the world today, it too, even at the level of a desire, is 'out of joint', 'an untimely link, without status, without title, and without name'.[11] Indeed, at one point, Derrida makes no attempt to disguise the fact that it 'belongs only to anonymity'.[12]

The only thing for certain that we can say of this new International, this counter-conjuration, is that it will be very intellectual in scope. If it comprises anyone, it is those few writers (in the Derridean mould naturally), who have been brave enough [sic] 'to resist a certain hegemony of the Marxist dogma, indeed of its metaphysics, in its political or theoretical forms'.[13] Even leaving aside the question of the accuracy of this self-depiction of his own role and position over the past years, one can hardly be forgiven for thinking that what Derrida is proposing in practice is something resembling a very closed, elitist and cloistered order, perhaps as Aijaz Ahmad has put it, something that 'has the quality, more or less, of a Masonic order'.[14] Indeed, there is undoubtedly a strong sense of pious, (religious?) mysticism and explicit messianism in all of Derrida's language here – not so much a deconstructionist Third Way as perhaps a Second Coming.

What is more certain is that what we have here is a very narrow, abstract form of counter-hegemonic critique and agenda, an 'important gesture of defiance', to be sure, but nothing much besides. Like a modern-day Socrates,

Derrida is a very effective, ever-questioning critic of everything he observes around him. But he is totally unable, it seems, to offer something positively concrete in its place. He can certainly deconstruct, but he cannot *construct*. In one passage in the *Specters,* he takes enormous delight in a statement from a group of Soviet philosophers who insist that the best translation of the term *perestroika* was always 'deconstruction'. Yet he is totally oblivious of the bitter irony in this conceptual affiliation in terms of the outcome and consequences of this form of deconstruction.[15]

Nor is it just a question of the overwhelming *paralysing* effect of deconstructionism. Although all acts of deconstruction are intrinsically critical and *appear* to be intrinsically subversive, there is nevertheless a sense in which they can never do away with the phenomena they are criticising. As John Ellis has commented, the actual logic underpinning all forms of deconstructionist engagement (be it in the literary, philosophical or overtly political domain) is to question, subvert, undermine and then *retain* 'in order that we [the spectator] can focus on the act of subversion itself, which, however, does not constitute a final rejection'.[16] The compelling allegiance at the heart of deconstructionism, then, is to a notion of neither/nor, and this creates a kind of symbiosis between deconstructionism and conservatism 'in which the two feed on each other; and thus ideas [or structures] that deserve to die will not be allowed to do so'.[17]

In some of his earlier works, Derrida himself is more than well aware of the contradiction, whereby an act of opposition will often end up confirming the very thing that it has sought to question, precisely because it is unable or refuses to go beyond the critical norms and limits of the thing itself; that is to say, the criticism is tolerated, or in many cases even authorised and sanctioned, precisely because it is not 'bothersome' to its own circumscribed limits.[18] By his own reckoning, therefore, one can surely see this paradox at work in his *Specters of Marx.* As was once said of Nietzsche, is it not the case here that the nature of the critique ends up *consuming* the critical, subversive impulse itself? Or as Ahmad notes, recasting the Shakespearean context of Derrida's spectral analysis, should we not at least conceive the possibility that what we would end up with here is 'a mere Fortinbras – a "new" order that is a variant of the very old one, a systemic restoration that comes about through a process that neither his ghost nor Hamlet could anticipate or survive'?[19] After all, let us not forget Derrida's great fondness for paleonyms.[20]

There is, then, a tragic feel to Derrida's *Specters of Marx.* One of the reasons for proposing this title, he tells us, was to demonstrate that: 'At a time when a new world disorder is attempting to install its neo-capitalism and neo-liberalism, no disavowal has managed to rid itself of all of Marx's ghosts.

Hegemony still organizes the repression and thus the confirmation of a haunting. Haunting belongs to the structure of every hegemony.'[21]

Another reason for Derrida's title choice was to analyse the prominence of spectres in many of Marx's own major works, not least, of course, *The Communist Manifesto*. However, whereas Marx's own notion of 'spectre' is always of a presence, of an apparition, to come, that is, something not yet corporeal but which must become a *living* reality, Derrida's 'spectre' conjures up totally different visions. Following Jacques Lacan here, we get instead an overwhelming sense of a spectre that is now bearing witness to a total retreat, a final and irreversible withdrawal.

Forward to the New Middle Ages?

Up until now the argument has concentrated on the lack of a real, viable *counter*-hegemonic potential within the projects promoted by the likes of Laclau, Mouffe and Derrida. Whilst it is true that none of them would strictly class themselves as 'postmodernists', all three of them do undoubtedly share much of the broad postmodern agenda and have essentially used their works to promote many key aspects of it. In answer to the main question posed at the head of this chapter, one would thus far answer: yes, hegemony does have a postmodern future, but only in its established liberal-capitalist form. To this extent, Ralph Miliband was almost certainly correct when he wrote just before his untimely death: 'Hegemony [nowadays] depends not so much on consent as on resignation.'[22] And as Zygmunt Bauman has asserted: there 'is no conceivable way a realistic Left program could be patched together out of postmodernist theory'.[23] It is simply too much a philosophy of surrender, resignation and futility. It would reduce – *has reduced?* – the left promoting a series of concerns, which for all their importance, could only ever exist in the interstices of the hegemonic dominion:

There can be no Left as counter-culture, i.e., a positive and effective critique of neglects, drawbacks, and mismanagements in implementing the cultural promise of a better society, without the conviction that this cultural promise is viable and in principle realizable. There can be no Left without the belief that society can be improved and history brought to our side. There can be no Left without the idea that among different things, some are good and some are wrong, and that the first can be made more numerous than the latter. Postmodern theory is an invitation to intellectuals to make the best of their freedom bought at the price of irrelevance. Whatever else the Left can be, it cannot, by definition, be irrelevant.[24]

In short, the left still needs many of the metanarratives of modernity. It needs a redemptive politics. It still needs a strong structural interpretation of the social pervasiveness of class relations. It needs a centred, not a de-centred, social strategy. It even needs, I would argue, a utopianism, albeit perhaps shorn of some of its old-type messianism. And just as importantly, given these needs, it also requires the theoretical underpinning of a thinker such as Gramsci who has not been waylaid by the advocates of postmodernism. It is one thing for the likes of Andrew Ross to argue that 'a postmodernist politics must complete the Gramscian move to extend the political into all spheres, domains and practices of our culture'.[25] It is another thing entirely, however, to attempt this at the expense of ignoring the pivotal importance Gramsci attributed to the role of class or diluting Gramsci's primary concern of transcending the capitalist order.

Attempts to portray Gramsci as the fundamental precursor, let alone exponent, of postmodern politics are simply without foundation. Throughout his writings there is an emphasis upon all the key hallmarks of modernist thought: generality, universality, constructive understanding, the rationality of reality, the autonomy of reason, the temporal understanding of history, as well as the attempt to understand the actual via ahistorical norms. It is true that Gramsci may have recognised the pessimism of the intellect in his own times, but he certainly never went so far as to do what most 'left-leaning' postmodernists do today: espouse the pessimism of the will as well. As Terry Eagleton has so evocatively put it (in a related context of defending Gramsci): there is too often these days a soft-focusing of Gramsci, the creation even of a fictional Gramsci who amounts to nothing more than a 'Sardinian version of a London polytechnic lecturer in discourse theory, complete with enlightened opinions and pluralist politics, more interested in organising signifiers than auto-workers'.[26] What has happened, Eagleton asks, of the real-life Gramsci who helped to arm the Italian workers in 1920 and who organised Red Guards and factory councils?

To be fair to some of the theorists who have been operating within post-modern paradigms, there has been a growing recognition in recent times that the thoroughgoing suppression of all articles of absolute faith has proved so paralysing as to no longer be sustainable. Constantly to de-create, disintegrate, deconstruct, de-centre, displace, differentiate, discontinue, disjuncture, make disappear, decompose, de-define, demystify, de-totalise and de-legitimate – which are the recognised and oft-promoted essential characteristics of postmodernism – is all well and good, but there does come a time when one cannot help but ponder whether one has thrown out too many living babies with the dirty bath water. For a number of such theorists, then, the more recent ambition has been to try to retain what they see as being the critical gains of the postmodern approach – the celebration of fragmentation, particularity and difference, and the acceptance of the contingent and the apparent – while not suppressing all attachments to very specific values and goals, or what Judith Squires has called 'principled positions'.[27]

Just how well such critical theorists are really able to achieve a new kind of dialectical synthesis between old (modern) and new (postmodern), however, is very much open to question. In seeking to navigate a new set of contingencies *beyond* postmodernism (into a new realm, one assumes, of post-postmodernism), one is perhaps most struck by the way in which most of them simply regress to the very essences of modernity.[28] Still, the attempt to steer such a course will at least prove an interesting spectator sport. Having disparaged postmodernism so much, there is certainly a willingness to recognise that there are some aspects of the approach that one should not (or might not be able to) evade entirely – for good or for ill. As an actual *strategy* of counter-hegemonic opposition for the left, the notion of postmodernity, as I have already tried to show, has little to offer; or at least, what it does have to offer is totally insufficient, bordering as it does on outright submission. As a means of understanding and conceptualising some of the key changes that have affected the world we currently inhabit, it does perhaps have more to offer.

Without doubt, the most interesting and the most insightful areas of postmodern studies have been carried out by those theorists who are not just interested in the cultural shift of postmodernism, but who have also recognised and diagnosed a close, almost symbiotic, relationship between the emergence of this cultural paradigm and the unfolding of a new logic of capitalism. And while it is entirely correct that fierce critics such as Ellen Meiksins Wood should raise doubts as to whether these changes are of such a degree that they should warrant the designation 'an *epochal shift* in capitalism's development',[29] nevertheless no one can really question the profundity of the changed appearance of capitalism in recent decades. Certainly no one can question the assertion that the essential logic of this new era of capitalism now has a depth of penetration hitherto unseen.

What, then, is the fundamental nature of the (postmodern) systemic changes that capitalism has undergone in recent years? And, more significantly for our purposes, what impact have these changes had on capitalism's own intrinsic hegemonic capabilities? If there is no real counter-hegemonic force sufficiently strong enough to oppose capitalism at the moment, are there forces at work *within* this new era of capitalism which might at least provide us with a certain degree of optimism?

One of the first, and undoubtedly one of the most influential accounts of the nature of capitalism in an increasingly postmodern age was that of Fredric Jameson and his pioneering study *Postmodernism, or, the Cultural Logic of Late Capitalism*. Stripped of all its superfluities, the notion of the postmodern for Jameson essentially comprises two main themes: first, the appearance of a new or at least a 'different' stage of capital, and second, a series of very significant cultural modifications. For Jameson, these are not separate phenomena, but highly interconnected and interdependent ones. Postmodern*ity* (in its strictly social sense) represents first and foremost a designated 'mode of production' rather than a specific or autonomous cultural category. Postmodern*ism* (in its strictly cultural sense) is the ideological hegemonic vehicle for this mode of production, labelled by Jameson (following Ernest Mandel) as 'late capitalism'.

Representing a third, undoubtedly *purer*, historical stage of capital, one of the main essential features of late capitalism is undoubtedly its penetration and colonisation of hitherto uncommodified areas. Influenced in particular by Henri Lefebvre's understanding of spatial dimensions, Jameson asserts that the new space of late capitalism is not only able to suppress earlier restrictions of distance, but is now capable of relentlessly saturating all remaining voids and empty places. Similarly, in terms of the dimension of time, late capitalism is also able to fragment time into a series of 'perpetual presents', thereby giving it enormous penetrative scope and hegemonic advantages over its earlier incarnations. As a result, this has created 'a more homogeneously modernized condition' than ever before. As Jameson himself puts it: 'we no longer are encumbered with the embarrassment of non-simultaneities and non-synchronicities. Everything has reached the same hour on the great clock of development or rationalization (at least from the perspective of the "West").'[30] The organisational capacity of capital, the very 'Being of Capital', is now absolute. Virtually everything has been submerged in the space now occupied by capital. There is little or no scope left to occupy a critical distance outside of this space. Even Nature, that pre-capitalist enclave, which before at least offered an 'extraterritorial and Archimedian foothold for critical effectivity' has now been triumphantly assimilated to the dynamics of the system.

Capitalism has become stronger because it no longer requires a particular realm or type of consciousness or even argument – an ideology – to perpetuate and reproduce itself. Following Adorno, the commodity has become its own ideological category. The practice of consumption has replaced the old type of ratiocination. It does not need justifying because there is no longer any real awareness attached to the act of consumption. As Gilles Deleuze and Félix Guattari similarly argued, the unconscious is also a colony of this new era of capitalism. Apart from anything else, we are bound in a libidinal way to the present system.[31] Similarly, Jameson would also go along with Deleuze and Guattari's formulation of the schizo-phrenic breakdown of the subject. The fact that anxieties may periodically be engendered by the logic of capital, or that it may generate feelings of hostility, is no longer a threat but an advantage. Capitalism has in effect ceased to doubt itself. The more it creates schizophrenic complexes, the more it can feed on the contradictions which arise.

Last, but not least, there is the increasing depth of reification which accompanies this process. For Jameson (continuing the work of Lukács), a primary feature of late capitalism is its overwhelming capacity to efface virtually any trace of production from the commodity. From the point of view of the consumer, it is essential that they are freed of any last vestige of guilt which might be aroused if they were to contemplate the actual work that goes into making their commodities, especially when that work is per-formed by Third World slave labour.

If Jameson has given us the image of a much strengthened late capitalist hegemony, he has also, no matter how tentatively, offered us at least a potential strategy for resistance in the guise of 'cognitive mapping', what he essentially defines as 'a code word for "class consciousness" of a new and hitherto undreamed of kind'.[32] What is immediately striking about the notion of cognitive mapping is the obvious connection it has with the Althusserian and Lacanian understanding of ideology which prioritises the individual's *imaginary* relationship to the real conditions of existence which they see all around them. Its task, Jameson asserts, is 'to enable a situational representation on the part of the individual subject to that vaster and properly unrepresentable totality which is the ensemble of society's structures as a whole'.[33] Unrepresentable here does not mean that one can-not understand the totality in an abstract or even scientific form. Its logic is accessible, but as it is not directly experienced in its totality, a suitable, definable, representable image of it in its entirety is therefore not possible. This in itself, however, should not act as a hindrance or constraint. What is ultimately important is to engage in a cultural politics which is capable of overcoming our neutralised condition of spatial and social confusion in our specific environment by (re)inventing an oppositional space with a clearly defined set of social and political concerns, designed to stimulate open and active forms of struggle. And lest it be thought that this is tanta-mount to a vote of support in favour of the new social movements and their strategy of micro-politics, Jameson is quick to recoil at even the mer-est hint of the suggestion. As far as he is concerned, such types of resistance are nothing more than an 'obscene' celebration of contemporary capitalist pluralism and democracy: 'the system congratulating itself for producing ever greater quantities of structurally unemployable subjects'.[34]

Notwithstanding his own conviction to continue opposing the hegemony of late capitalism, one certainly does not come away from reading Jameson with the most optimistic feelings. It is true that one could apply the kind of critical line that Mike Davis has adopted by simply retorting that the contemporary capitalist structures of accumulation depicted by Jameson are not so much signs of triumph, so much as symptoms of global crisis,[35] a point that will be taken up below. But the substance of Jameson's arguments are certainly very convincing, and if there is a theoretical weakness it is more likely to be found in his resistance strategy of cognitive mapping, more than anywhere else.

What is most useful in Jameson's approach is, I think, spelt out very well in the opening lines of his study where he asserts the need today 'to grasp the concept of the postmodern as an attempt to think the present historically in an age that has forgotten how to think historically in the first place'.[36] And indeed he does demonstrate where late capitalism has arrived from, and more importantly how it has arrived still in possession of most of the baggage it had with it when it first started out on its journey; to put it somewhat differently, the contents are largely the same even if the quality of the case has been substantially improved. Similarly, as Stanley Aronowitz has commented, the fact that Jameson does not use his Marxist convictions *against* postmodernism, but instead invokes its categories to *explain* the phenomenon also has many positive attributes.[37] The eclecticism of his arguments may not always work, but the attempt to mobilise key features of modernity against certain perceived intangible features of postmodernity is a very useful approach.

Of all the theorists who have shown an interest in the relationship between capitalism and the emergence of a postmodern condition, no one has perhaps expressed more forcefully the new-found hegemonic depth of capitalism than Zygmunt Bauman. No matter what prefix one applies to contemporary capitalism, he writes, one should be absolutely clear about one central fact: it is in extremely 'good health', and any apparent signs of crisis are nothing more than wishful thinking. Its future, moreover, *'looks more secure than ever'*.[38]

Addressing the reasons for this predictive boldness, Bauman concentrates on a series of very specific defining features of the consumerist phase of capitalism. First, the consumer culture of the contemporary era is both self-perpetuating and self-reproducing, dependent as it is on nothing outside of its own remit. 'Consumer culture', as he succinctly puts it, 'is a culture of men and women integrated into society as, above all, consumers.'[39] Because of this, following Pierre Bourdieu, one can say that the mode of domination today is not repression, but *seduction*. If the system appears to make demands, at least they are demands promising nothing but unadulterated pleasure as we 'surrender' ourselves to the consumer delights that are on offer all around us. Small wonder, then, that '[w]ith such duties, one hardly needs rights', and that the very process of social control 'becomes easier and considerably less costly'.⁴⁰ Not that one would have any kind of conception of 'domination', 'surrender' or 'control' because another attribute of the consumer-dominated market economy is that it is seen as a perfected realm of freedom, the pure 'embodiment of liberation', in short, 'a post-modern ideology to put paid to all ideologies'.⁴¹

Due to its self-reproductive features, it can likewise now cope with any manner or degree of cultural variety, heterogeneity of styles and different belief systems. Indeed, to this extent, the actual specific notion of 'cultural hegemony' is almost an irrelevance, which in turn is akin to arguing that the sociocultural realm in general has been reduced virtually in its entirety to the economic. As Hans Bertens has thus pointed out, given this conception of the relationship of the social to the economic, one is clearly implying that the system also 'no longer needs traditional politics to perpetuate itself [either]'.⁴² This is certainly an allegation that Bauman would be hard pressed to dispute. As he himself has explicitly argued, the state today is effectively nothing more than an instrument of the market's need for constant re-commodification. One only needs to look at the present-day relationship with civil society to see this at work.

Civil society now 'is increasingly colonized by the state as the sphere of reproduction of consumers, i.e. men and women whose interests in autonomy are permanently re-directed to fit the needs of the market'.⁴³ As consumers rather than citizens, there is an increasing tendency to seek any kind of redress for grievances one might feel in the marketplace rather than from the state. As a consequence, the state is increasingly becoming emancipated from its citizens and from any real degree of democratic control, leaving the state bureaucracy (in almost Hegelian fashion) 'to colonize the everyday world, thereby rendering their own domination permanent'.⁴⁴

Bauman, Jameson, and many others notwithstanding, if there is one theorist who has thus far monopolised the postmodern interpretation of the nature of contemporary capitalism, it is Jean Baudrillard. Indeed, it is Baudrillard, particularly the early Baudrillard of the late 1960s and very early 1970s, who is really the major reference point for all those interested in conceptualising the nature and depth of capitalist hegemony in its consumerist guise.

Based on a semiological approach – the dominance of signs and codes, whereby both use and exchange values are now exploited by the new (postmodern) culture of consumption which privileges the image, and especially the status value derived from the image, over substance – it is Baudrillard who brings together really for the first time all of the key descriptive features of capitalism's unsurpassed degree of control and power: its new depths of commodified absorption unhindered by any boundaries or rigid determinations, the functionalisation of the consumer within the system and the psychological monopolisation of all needs, and the sense in which consumption is now the primary, almost even the *sole*, reason for living, devoid of a relationship any longer with a primitive instinct to devour, to satisfy desires or to engage in some kind of psychologically determined process of emulation.[45] For Baudrillard, the hegemony of the code or sign that he depicts is one where the sign can be everything, nothing, or anything in between – or even all these things at once. Everything is now indifferent to everything else, he writes, yet at the same time equivalent to everything else. Only death has the capacity to escape this totalising power of absorption, although even here one is left with the feeling that the tentacles of consumerist capitalism will soon be within reach.

Here as well in these early works is the Baudrillard who is keen to *adapt* the essence of (neo) Marxist explanatory logic to the new 'late' capitalist era: to explain the mystification of the primary values underpinning consumerism and its self-professed claims to freedom, justice, equality, and fulfilment; to decry the claims of those theorists from outside the Marxist heritage who claim that this new 'Age of Consumption' has no genealogical roots in the earlier 'grievous and heroic Age of Production', and to demonstrate that for all the appearance of revolutionary change, this is an internally determined substitution of processes within capitalism, which has left the basic intrinsic motivations of the system 'essentially unchanged', amounting in effect to little more than 'an imposed mediation of the system's reproduction'.[46]

Where the early Baudrillard, however, paved the way for later theorists to provide even more details and expand our understanding of late capitalist hegemony, the Baudrillard of the mid-to-late 1970s and beyond shifted ground radically. Especially in the works of, what he himself called, his extreme 'nihilist' and intellectual 'terrorist' phase, the image that we are now given of the social realm around us, and the hegemonic basis of that realm, is fundamentally different. Indeed, in this new world of 'hyperreality' and 'simulacra', the very notion of hegemony, not to mention its very existence, is not only pushed to its 'unendurable limits', it is effectively *dissolved* completely. All the foundation stones and building blocks which have come to be associated with hegemony (in its myriad guises) have been entirely dismantled in these later works. If nothing else, hegemony hitherto had been always intrinsically connected with the imposition of meaning and representation. In Baudrillard's hyperreality, however, there is simply no longer any meaning and representation.

For Baudrillard, hyperreality is in essence a world where the signs and the codes have reached such a point of significance that they have become *self*-referential. Whatever material anchors they might previously have had, they are now floating in a dematerialised void. To have a conception of meaning, one at least requires a certain foundation, a certain depth. As this is no longer there, meaning has therefore lost its own *raison d'être* – meaning without meaning. Indeed, in the realm of hyperreality, warns Baudrillard, whoever tries to live by meaning will surely perish by meaning.[47]

Hyperreality is in turn a totally decontextualised, as well as by implication, a depoliticised space. Now that the signs and images of this hyperreality have become self-referential, they can have no contextual source. Moreover, as the transition is completed from an existence where signs dissimulated something, to one where they dissimulate that there is nothing, so one moves from the age of ideology and politics (with their 'theological' notions of truth and secrecy), to an age of simulacra and simulations in which 'there is no longer any God to recognise his own, nor any last judgement to separate true from false [and] the real from its artificial resurrection, since everything is already dead and risen in advance'.[48]

Similarly, it follows for Baudrillard that within the realm of hyperreality there can no longer be any notions of 'power', 'social' or 'relational'. Once again, his radicalised logic of semiurgy would insist that all these notions require 'perspective space'. As this is not to be found in hyperreality, they are thus further concepts to be discounted for their ephemerality. Last, but not least, there can be no effective resistance. As there is no longer a signified social realm or social subject, there is likewise no scope for an emancipatory dialogue to appear.[49] With the foundation stones dismantled, then, hegemony (as well as counter-hegemony) can take their places alongside their conceptual brethren in the ephemeral world of modernity. One should remember them, implies Baudrillard, with 'nostalgia', but nothing more. In the postmodern, hyperreal world we now inhabit, all our energies are required to make what we can of our imploded, undifferentiated, simulated existence.

Intellectual terrorist or not, in any critical assessment of Baudrillard one would have to say that in these later works, one is not so much witnessing the disappearance of hegemony in the way that he is adumbrating (perhaps even celebrating), so much as its absolute *perfection* under capitalism. The truth of the matter is not that capitalism in its real, existing, materialised state has been dissolved in hyperreality; it is that Baudrillard's conception of hyperreality has simply made an *interpretation* of capitalism totally inaccessible, and the two things, of course, are poles apart. In effect, this inaccessibility of capitalist criteria in Baudrillard's later thinking must perforce *strengthen* capitalism. To exist, but to be inaccessible to interpretation, and, therefore, resistance and transformation, must surely represent the highest potential of hegemonic control.

Having made the considerable effort to enter the realm of hyperreality in the first place, let us at least take this opportunity to linger there for a little while longer. Indeed, let us take an excursion into some of its deepest recesses with an alternative travel guide to Baudrillard – Umberto Eco.

If Baudrillard can be said to conjure up the image of a 'demented fourth century philosopher, unhinged by the imminent demise of a classical era of reason, who capers around the self-immolation of a whole epoch',[50] Umberto Eco is someone who gives off a totally different persona. There is certainly nothing 'demented' or 'unhinged' about him. On the contrary, he simply revels in the new age of pastiche, and in his own 'travelogue of hyperreality' there is a relaxed *jouissance,* a *jeux d'esprit* – many would say 'sarcasm' – which one would rarely find in the staid Baudrillard. Anyway, to take the comparison even further, Eco would not be seen dead in the shabby attire of the fourth century, preferring instead the much more refined, much more distinguished, style of the later Middle Ages. It is, after all, his popularisation of the Middle Ages, and his belief in an impending *New* Middle Ages, that has become one of his intellectual and literary trademarks.

The starting point of this parallel between the new and the old Middle Ages is the total disaggregation and collapse of a 'Great Pax', of an era of peace that had long reigned supreme, beginning to break down, and whose effects are felt across the whole military, civil, social, economic, political and cultural domain. In particular, the New Middle Ages is signified by the demise of a great international power which had once sought to unify the world 'in language, customs, ideologies, religions, art and technology', but which has now reached a state of 'ungovernable complexity' and excess.[51] In its place a vacuum – or what Alain Minc, another New Middle Ages theoretician has called a 'black hole'[52] – has been created, and on its borders all manner of 'barbarian hordes' are lurking in the wings ready to fight (and pick) over the remains of the old order.

Not surprisingly, given such a starting point, the major motifs here are crisis, disorder, chaos, anxiety and insecurity, and not just from an external perspective. Internally, for example, the collapse of the old order is most evident in the increasing 'ghettoisation' of towns and cities. 'Clans' are formed, which are unwilling to integrate and fuse with each other. Their neighbourhoods are inaccessible to 'outsiders'. Consensus is no longer possible or desirable as the social body becomes totally fragmented. For those who can afford it, migration out of the cities into specially constructed, purpose-built, self-sufficient enclaves is the only answer. In the most extreme cases (although what is extreme today will be standard practice tomorrow), the richer 'ghettos' will seek to defend themselves against possible outside aggression. Buildings and residences will more and more take on the appearance of fortresses, with the necessity for armed protection that goes with it.[53] For those left inside the cities, meanwhile, there will be a slow process of suffocation, not so much through the lack of things, as through their *excess:* population, transportation, communication, pollution, refuse and especially impoverished immigrants and refugees. As Eco puts it: destruction 'through a paroxysm of activity'.[54]

When it comes to the remit of state power and control, this will be increasingly narrowed. With the multiplication of these ghettos, or what Minc calls 'grey zones', the exercise of any kind of open, legitimate authority is well-nigh impossible. In contrast to the past few centuries of state expansion and encroachment, we are once again in an age of state withdrawal and abandonment, just as we were in the first Middle Ages. In many of the suburbs of all major cities, the state is essentially not present or off-limits. Whatever 'potentates', 'suzerains' and 'vassals' there are, they are more often than not under the control of drug barons and Mafia groups. And in strictly social terms as well, even the new 'lumpenproletariat' of today's ghettos essentially do not look to the state for any kind of support or amelioration. Under circumstances not necessarily chosen by themselves, they have opted for a strategy of outright autonomy towards the state and society. In other words, they have simply lost a desire for any kind of social reintegration.

In this ever-increasing 'Age of Insecurity', impending disasters are commonly perceived to be just around the corner, while 'mendicant orders' of all different kinds flourish, offering all manner of mystical salvation and happiness. In short, this medievalist resurgence is fostering the collapse of reason and the dominance of superstition. In place of our long-standing rationalist vision of historical optimism, irrationality and abject pessimism are beginning to rule again. For both Eco and Minc alike, therefore, the new age of disorder, which is destined to sweep everything away in its path, will in turn lead to a new dawn of revolution, one more genuinely revolutionary than anything witnessed before because of its utter and complete sense of *indeterminacy*. The Liberal has already perished, as far as Eco is concerned, and the notion of 'civilised capitalism' which went with it is not far behind. Today, there is simply no longer the adhesive social space that once underpinned their earlier hegemonic existence.

Of course, it is not stretching credulity too far to believe that such prognoses contain nothing more than the hallmarks of a fin-de-millennium, media-inspired fad – dressed up, packaged and hyped for a half-an-hour slot on a late-night television show (with subsequent guest appearances guaranteed). Such cynicism notwithstanding, it is increasingly noticeable just how many of these ideas are being taken up in a whole range of very serious scholarly researches. In the final part of his historical *magnum opus* on the last two centuries, for example, Eric Hobsbawm is likewise convinced that the language of chaos, disorder, anxiety and insecurity is the most appropriate for the world we currently live in; he too writes of a world that has 'lost its bearings' and which has eroded its previous forms of normative regulation.[55] In such a condition, he argues, capitalism is indeed unable to prevent itself being engulfed by a 'landslide'. Admittedly, the landslide is not as big as the one that swallowed up Soviet communism, but it is a landslide that is getting more powerful by the day as the intrinsic contradictions of late capitalism's existence begin to show themselves more and more, unfettered as they are now, ironically enough, by any competitive systemic restraints.

A similar conclusion, if one reached by a different route and a different method, is also very apparent in Giovanni Arrighi's study *The Long Twentieth Century*.[56] One can also locate it in Immanuel Wallerstein's study of contemporary capitalist civilisation, which, he writes, currently finds itself in 'the autumn of its existence', reaping the abundant harvest of seeds sown long ago, but nevertheless in the full knowledge that the winter frost will soon be upon it.[57]

What is perhaps of most significance about all of these works – especially given the ideological pedigree of the authors – is the fact that their 'doom and gloom' prophecies of capitalism's future are no longer equated with any kind of outside pressure being forced upon it from a countervailing left-inspired social force. Each, in their different ways, concentrates almost exclusively on the internal contradictions which capitalism is finding increasingly impossible to cope with. More significantly, there is likewise no conception of a post-capitalist world which would make any kind of recognisable left-wing agenda the major beneficiary of capitalism's self-destruction. Of the three possible post-capitalist scenarios very briefly outlined by Wallerstein, for example, only one, the remotest, has anything at all positive to say about the future from a left perspective. The implications of the other two, meanwhile, largely speak for themselves, labelled as they are by Wallerstein as 'neo-feudalism' and 'democratic fascism'.

Whether the findings by these highly respected authors are due to some kind of 'generational lament' or not, it is perhaps too hard to say.[58] Nevertheless, whatever we call the new age waiting to greet us, it is almost certain that it will be an age of tremendous upheaval. Jean-François Lyotard's concern that '[h]idden in the cynicism of innovation is surely a despair that nothing further will happen', is surely misplaced.[59]

Hegemony and the Nation State

Ever since Gramsci, few would want to take issue with the claim that the contextual, *spatial* remit of hegemony has been primarily defined by the contours of the nation state. This can be seen, I think, in two essential ways. First, there was Gramsci's pivotal argument that any successful search for hegemony must always transcend narrow class corporatism so as to include a much broader form of collective will, embodied in what he called the 'national-popular'. The terrain of this national-popular was the nationally constituted civil society, and the key task of any aspiring hegemonic force was to embody a 'national energy'. Here, in particular, was the foundation stone for many of Gramsci's lifelong concerns: in the necessity of a unified, national language; in the historical disinterestedness of the masses during the time of the Risorgimento; in the non-existence of a national-popular literature in Italy at this time; in his abiding interest in matters of national folklore and why there was never a period of Italian romanticism, and last, but not least, his constant dismay at the failings of Italian intellectuals in the national-popular realm in general.

The second way in which the nation state has very much defined – although in this case *re*-defined would be more appropriate – the contextual remit of hegemony is from the perspective of its territorial, and especially its institutional, parameters. To borrow the terminology of Anthony Giddens, whatever else the nation state has represented, it has first and foremost been regarded as a 'power container' of the most dominant kind.[60] Through its level of institutional control, it has represented the key arena for the channelling of power and the dissemination of social reality. It has defined the way in which the entire social space under its remit was coordinated, and it has likewise been the foremost realm of social unification. Certainly no modern capitalist structure has emerged without the accompanying cocoon of a nation state to at least consolidate its existence. And it was precisely because of its capacity to provide a universal type of legitimate 'binding authority'[61] over a given social space that the notion of hegemony (as formulated by Gramsci) was able to take on a totally different conception from its earlier incarnation as something synonymous with nothing more than an explicit form of coercive domination; a definition of hegemony which in many instances is still the most appropriate one in an *international* context. It is for this reason, then, that the nation state is often considered one of the foremost icons of modernity.

If we now turn our attention back to the notion of postmodernity, we are immediately struck by a profound difference of emphasis. A constant feature of just about all descriptions of the postmodern condition has been the emphasis on the nation state's perceived irrepressible decline, at least in its classically constituted form. The key issue here has been a concerted focus on the kind of *spatial restructuring* which has been occurring in recent decades, a phenomenon which has been particularly well captured in David Harvey's account of 'time-space compression'.[62] In the light of such analyses, then, the issue to be addressed in this final section is this: if indeed we are witnessing the gradual demise of the nation state, what effects will this have on the traditional understanding and remit of hegemony?

The *if* in the question is absolutely vital. As one would expect on such an issue, there is certainly no universal consensus that the nation state is experiencing some kind of diminution in its role or status. Passions also tend to run high on both sides of the debate, and emotive- as well as reason-laden arguments are regularly resorted to. As for the specific arguments themselves, these have been so well rehearsed over recent years as to warrant little attention here.[63] Suffice it to say at this point that it is one of those debates which is certainly not helped by an almost total lack of conceptual agreement. And it is almost certainly one of those instances when the most accurate response lies somewhere in the middle of the two extremes. As Karl Deutsch has argued, it is almost undeniable that given the nature of recent changes in the world, the nation state has been found wanting and inadequate in its capacity to respond. At the same time, however, there is still a degree of indispensability about it which will almost certainly ensure its longevity in a reasonably recognisable modern form.[64]

Aristotelian logic notwithstanding, there is nevertheless a good deal of truth in the argument that a number of critical aspects of the modern nation state *are* being seriously compromised. As Tony McGrew has succinctly put it, its competence, its form, its autonomy and ultimately its very authority and legitimacy are undoubtedly under threat.[65] What is more, its besiegers are coming at it from on high as well as from below in the twin guises of globalisation and regionalisation. To make matters even worse for the besieged nation state, there is an undoubted unholy alliance amongst its twin belligerents. Although the two forces which have been thrown together have every objective appearance of intrinsic contradictoriness, Étienne Balibar is surely correct when he argues that the essence of the contradiction is a classically Hegelian one. Each is stimulated by the other by a dialectical antagonism which neither is able to resolve by itself.[66] Rather than benefiting from this, the position of the nation state in the middle is made considerably worse. As Ernest Gellner has also put it, rather than obliterating the ancient prejudices which have always lurked beneath the surface of the nation state, the advance of globalisation (in its capitalist form) is instead helping to incite those prejudices to ever-increasing levels of intensity.[67]

What for Gellner are ancient and venerable prejudices are for others, of course, bona fide attachments to a form of community, the likes of which the increasingly anchorless nation state cannot possibly conceive. On the broad 'regionalisation' front, then, *community* is the privileged, quintessential feature. It is meant to evoke tightness of construction, a privileging of cultural and social ties over territory, and organicity over extraneousness. As the nation state is slowly but surely being dispossessed of its earlier primary functions (particularly in the realm of the economy), so the community is increasingly seen as a natural remedy for the ensuing ontological insecurity which is felt by more and more people. Moreover, as the old centre collapses, and with it a sense of systemic unity, so the very nature of coordination changes with it.

All of this, then, cannot help but have a dramatic impact on the modernist conception of hegemony. With the dispersal of the logic of hegemony to myriad communities, the old notion of a clearly delineated centre, a power centre which claimed a universal privilege, is no longer feasible. What was once made functionally complementary in the coordinated space of the nation state is now beginning to break apart. Similarly, in place of the nation state as a largely homogenous 'moral community' which produced a high degree of conformity, one is now faced by a daunting fragmentation of morality and values. As Bauman notes, 'Loyalties must [now] be negotiated anew and priorities within multiple allegiances rearranged.'[68] In the process, however, Derrida is surely right when he asserts that this kind of renegotiation will always take place under the protective cover of a self-enclosed language, 'idiolects' which are profoundly jealous of each other, and even more profoundly untranslatable.[69]

It is perhaps not so much the relocation and fragmentation of authority downwards, so much as its relocation upwards and outwards, however, which has really been at the forefront of the debate concerning the future of the nation state. If the claim can be made that the realm of the new-style community is a long way from being the nation writ small, so it is even more true that the new realm of the 'global' is a long way from being the nation writ large. The effect of globalisation on the logic of hegemony is therefore equally, if not considerably more, profound.

As with notions of nationhood, statehood and community, the phenomenon of globalisation, and the extent to which we inhabit a global society, is subject to enormous empirical and conceptual contestation. For the purposes here, globalisation will be taken to refer to those activities which take place at a *trans*national level, rather than at a purely national-international level. Where the latter still very much relies on the state as a key, innovatory agency, this is not the case in the former. The state may well continue to play a role in transnational activities, but it no longer has a dominant, or even a crucial role.[70]

Given this conceptual framework, there is clearly only one place to commence an analysis. If the imagery of a transnational, even 'borderless', world applies to any realm of activity, the economic surely takes pride of honour. In an age of global communications, global technology, global finance and global markets, the old-style pivotal role of the nation state in key areas such as exchange rates, trade balances, trade flows and industrial policy is becoming increasingly seen as an 'archaic remain' of an earlier civilisation. No longer the economic power container that it once was, the nation state has had to adapt to the appearance of new power containers which are the complete negation of its own sense of exclusive territoriality and spatial functionality. These new power containers, of course, are the transnational corporations (TNCs). And what makes them the real epitome of the globalisation phenomenon is not just their capacity to challenge the old role of the nation state, or even to supplant it. What really gives them the edge is their ability to *ignore* the economic *modus operandi* of the nation state in many of the most crucial domains.

To talk of a modern-day TNC is to talk of an institution which has a larger economic capacity than whole countries the size and status of Denmark. More significantly, these are corporations which are effectively stateless in international legal terms. As Mathew Horsman and Andrew Marshall have pointed out, because they are not subject to constraints of space and time, they therefore have little requirement for sovereignty in the old sense of the concept. Last, but not least, with a membership of employees (and increasingly *temporary* employees) rather than citizens, they likewise have little or no need of any real sense of accountability.[71]

Nor are the TNCs an alternative power container in the purely economic domain. Increasingly, through the function of sponsorship (not least in the educational domain, for example), they are acquiring highly significant degrees of overt social and political power, a feature undoubtedly assisted by their greater capacities of flexibility in comparison with government operations at a purely national level. For all these reasons, it is small wonder that the heads of many of the largest TNCs are more and more referred to as the real 'modern Princes' of the contemporary era.

Given the ontological nature of the TNCs in the wider remit of the globalisation process, arguably the most profound effect of their role and existence has been the way in which the general realm of the economy has increasingly become *disconnected* from the general realm of politics in a manner not witnessed since probably the 1920s. Certainly the rhetoric of the globalist ideology is very much dominated by anti-political creeds. There is now a profound aversion to the old kind of political constraints which were once imposed on the economic realm by the territorially constrained nation states. What the TNCs most desire, and what they are able to achieve in a whole range of areas, is a complete liberation from such encumbrances.

This has likewise had a profound effect on the nature of the state within the national context. For analysts such as Robert Cox, one of the main features of the globalisation process has been the way in which the state has slowly but surely been converted 'into an agency for adjusting national economic practices and policies to the perceived exigencies of the global economy'.[72] Having previously acted as the main bulwark protecting the domestic economy from external incursions, the state, he argues, has now become nothing more than a virtual 'transmission belt', mediating in favour of the global economy in the national domain. Other commentators, such as Leo Panitch, have strongly disagreed with this line of analysis, and have instead tried to identify ways in which the global economic actors are still very much embedded in national state structures, leading to the conclusion that capitalism has yet to escape the full confines of the state.[73] Nevertheless, one must surely concur with those who conclude that in terms of the state's capacity to wield any real degree of political authority over the economic realm, one is at least witnessing a declining trend. Both the location and the primacy of authority, in other words, is drifting away from the state, and this has undoubtedly made the notion of power far more shadowy.

Following on from this, one can also say that another consequence of globalisation on the logic of hegemony concerns the way it has very much 'compromised the traditional pact between citizens and the nation state'.[74] That is to say, the *mediating* role of the nation state is a far cry from what it once was. Once again, this is clearly most visible in the economic realm. At the same time, however, one should not underestimate the *social* consequences of this as well. In many ways, the very notion of 'society' – treated, as it nearly always was, as a synonym of the nation state itself – is increasingly becoming dislodged as the traditional social boundaries of our existence and our experience are more and more redrawn in an ever-increasing plethora of ways.

Finally, one must also draw attention to the kind of effects that globalisation has had (and will continue to have) on the realm of culture. As most commentators will point out, one can certainly not say that there is a 'global culture' in existence at the moment which is in any way equal with the levels of development reached by a global economy. To this extent, globalisation is an asymmetrical process. Developments in the economic realm are running way ahead of developments elsewhere on a global level. Quite simply, a global culture does not exist because there is as yet little or no indication of a concerted homogeneous or totalised production of meaning in the very specific realm of culture. What instead exists is a uniform process, or more accurately speaking, a series of uniform processes, purposely designed to adapt and interact with the cultural myriad of the modern world. In other words, there is undoubtedly a uniformity to the *logic* of cultural globalisation, but it is one that is taking place in conjunction with a desire to preserve, and even enhance, culturally diverse outcomes.[75]

The non-existence of a homogeneous global culture notwithstanding, the effects of globalisation on the cultural realm are likely to have profound consequences on our future understanding of the hegemonic process. First, and this ties in with the brief analysis given above of regionalisation and the challenge of the new 'communities', there is undoubtedly a sense in which the traditional seams of nationally-based cultures are now becoming 'de-spatialised', and therefore seriously weakened, to the point, according to Jonathan Friedman, of virtual 'de-hegemonisation'.[76] Second, and in conjunction with this, at the level above the nation state, the very logic of globalisation will likewise produce a realm of culture 'situated in panoramic space', to use the terminology of Anthony Smith, which will be very much bereft of any real roots. As Smith goes on to assert, this will be a culture which will be inevitably 'tied to no place or period', timeless, memoryless, and without context, 'drawn from everywhere and nowhere'.[77] Above all, it will be 'borne upon the modern chariots of global telecommunications systems', and it will be driven by a technocratic intelligentsia whose 'culture of critical discourse', argues Alvin Gouldner, 'replaces the social critique of its earlier humanistic counterparts'.[78]

As the nation state has come under ever greater onslaught from antagonistic forces around it, what has perhaps been most interesting to observe is the way in which increasing elements of the left have felt obliged over the years to take up the struggle in its defence. Rather than engage with the forces of transnational capitalism in the global arena itself – which in principle at least should be the left's own preferred arena – what we seem to be seeing is an almost complete withdrawal from this terrain of struggle, and the waging instead of some kind of 'guerrilla warfare' within the old terrain of the nation state. That is to say, the left is itself utilising more and more the nationalist language of the nation state as the primary weapon in its resistance struggle against the vagaries of capitalist globalisation. What, then, is the basis for this strategy, and the much more positive approach to the nation state? Is it yet another sign of some kind of intrinsic sympathy the left always seems to have for 'endangered species', or, perhaps even worse than that, 'lost causes'? Or is there something else at work here? Are there in fact very strong principles underpinning this stronger, more committed affection for the nation state?

If there is one attribute which appears more than any other in this left-wing defence of the nation state against globalisation, it is almost certainly that of *authenticity,* particularly (but not exclusively) in its application to the realm of 'popular culture'. Benedict Anderson, in his seminal work on *Imagined Communities* was undoubtedly the main trend-setter here with his extremely powerful and evocative celebration of national customs, and in particular, language – a heavily imbued romanticist celebration of these forces which clearly showed little sympathy for some of the more over-determined tenets of classical Marxism. Given the closeness of the correlation between nationhood and the birth of vernacular languages in all their particularistic guises, Anderson is convinced that the key distinguishing feature of a community is determined by the style in which it is imagined. As a consequence, it is the cultural products of nationalism – in the shape of poetry, prose fiction, music and the visual arts – which creates the truest sense of belonging and attachment. 'What the eye is to the lover, language … is to the patriot',[79] and in both cases the attachment produced is often of the most profound self-sacrificial kind. In short, Anderson sees in the nation state 'the beauty of gemeinschaft', and by implication this is a depth of communal belonging which simply cannot be re-created at a transnational, global level. The powers of imagination, and consequently, the potential for forms of solidarity, so crucial to the left, are heavily circumscribed by the borders of the nation.

The historian Raphael Samuel likewise captured a sense of popular cultural authenticity which was firmly and exclusively embodied in the materiality of nationhood. Through the (re)construction of what he generically termed 'theatres of memory', he too attempted to evoke a depth of tradition which would always be lacking in the more artificial and non-material realm of the global.[80] Samuel's principal aim was to excavate, what he called, the 'nether world' of national, historical imagination. This was partly achieved by an unravelling of folklore, and by a recuperation of notions of romanticism. What characterised Samuel's work above all, however, was his desire and search for roots and for content – undoubtedly the key attributes of any notion of authenticity.

Another theme that runs throughout his work was the strong conviction that the kind of past which is rooted in the nation should not just be seen as a prelude to the present, but more importantly 'as an alternative to it'. For Samuel, the very notion of popular culture had an inherent 'subversive potential' which the left, again within the framework of the nation, must always be looking to exploit to the full. In short, there is a spirit and romance of place attached to the nation, and because of that a sense of dignity, as well as warmth, which is simply nowhere to be found in conceptions of globalisation, or, for that matter, universalist conceptions as a whole.[81]

Of all the contemporary left-wing advocates of a nationalist approach, however, it is arguably Tom Nairn who most stands out for his strength of commitment and allegiance. According to Nairn, as we look out at the world which is developing around us now in a state of utter sobriety, there are few, if any, options open to the left:

> [S]ocialists will have to decide what type of capitalists they will become, and internationalists will have to decide what sort of nationalists they will become.
>
> Some may regard this choice as the hangman's noose, but I believe they are wrong. It is wrong if we attend to the generous, imaginative side of the old internationalist credo, rather than to its rigid, elitist, quasi-metropolitan side.[82]

For Nairn, we are 'all nationalists now', and long may it remain so. Nor is this a stance exclusively defined by his own distinctive context of belonging to a (pre-devolution) Scottish nation subjugated by English domination of the United Kingdom. On a more broader front, one gets the sense that it is almost as though in the new global environment we now inhabit, virtually all nations are essentially reduced to being subjugated colonies, and in the face of such a status the primacy of nationalist resistance is therefore universally legitimised.

Underpinning the very positive assertions of the nation made by the likes of Anderson, Samuel, and (in a somewhat different context) Nairn, is an overwhelming conviction that any kind of 'global popular' to match a

Gramscian-conceived 'national-popular' is clearly inconceivable. Invoking (even if only implicitly) Gramsci's support for a modern-day defence of the nation state against the forces of globalisation, however, must obviously be carried out with a great deal of circumspection. Notwithstanding the vital importance which he attributed to the nation state as the pivotal realm of hegemony, Gramsci was always keen to differentiate his own conception of national-popular with outright nationalism. In particular, Gramsci was acutely conscious of just how ambivalent any conception of nationalism could be in terms of its practical consequences. He was always adamant that the left should never concede the national terrain to opposing political forces, but at the same time the intrinsic contradictions of a national orientation always had to be faced head-on.

For Gramsci, the national-popular orientation he gave credence to was never more than a means to an end. It was certainly never an end in itself. What ultimately mattered was the way in which the conception of the national-popular was actually utilised by a political force in an ongoing hegemonic struggle in the social domain. Any potential unifying features of the nation, in other words, were never allowed to dominate, contain, or worse still *deny*, the antagonisms stemming from the social domain, which is precisely what it can do when national*ism* is utilised as an end in itself. Stressing the importance of the particular (in the form of national cultures and traditions) was always dialectically linked with a classical Marxist belief in universalism. A sense of awareness and appreciation of one's distinctive national identity did not in itself detract from being a good internationalist. Gramsci certainly believed in a loyalty to the *patria*. No one knew, or respected, or loved Italy more than him, and no one knew better than him how to utilise such attachments and sentiments in the political struggle. But Gramsci's ultimate loyalty was to a '*patria*' of the left, which could only be defined by the universal values of freedom and social justice for all mankind. As he wrote in his article 'Russia and the International' in *L'Ordine Nuovo* (9 January 1921), just as the victory of the Russian revolution would only be guaranteed by the victory of the 'universal revolution', so the same formula would apply to the Italian revolution, no matter how different the form of that revolution might ultimately be. In short, Gramsci's approach to national consciousness was epiphenomenalist.

Last, but not least, as Aijaz Ahmad has so cogently put it (clearly in the spirit of Gramsci), given the recent disintegration of the international communist movement, there is almost certainly little effective choice but to envision and struggle for 'an alternative [to the present-day global supremacy of capitalism] at the level of the individual nation states within which one works'.[83] Notwithstanding this lack of choice, however, one must always be careful not to overvalue the arena of the nation state and any accompanying nationalism as a resistance strategy to the current form of imperialism, which masks itself in the guise of globalisation. The more the left reneges on its commitment to principles of universalism and its corollary of egalitarianism, the more its own version of nationalism will become dangerously prone to revanchist and aggressive tendencies, irrespective of how much it is couched in supposedly positive, romanticist tones.

Conclusion: The Hegemonic Landscape After the Battle

> The Spectre is the Reasoning Power in Man, and when separated from Imagination and closing itself as in steel in a Ratio of the things of Memory, It thence frames Laws and Moralities to destroy Imagination, the Divine Body, by Martyrdoms and Wars.
>
> William Blake, *Jerusalem*

1

When we come to look at the prospects for a left hegemony in Russia today, what is the landscape that we see before us? The first thing that we immediately see is a country ravaged by the vagaries of its Western-inspired economic transition, one which has been underpinned by the so-called dictates of globalisation and the West's firm intention of not tolerating a 'special' or 'Cubanised' Russia. Within the space of just a few years since the collapse of the old Soviet communist order, Russia's industrial and manufacturing decline has been far in excess of the economic contraction suffered by America and other countries during the Great Depression. As for its agricultural sector, such has been the decimation here that it has left the country overwhelmingly dependent on Western food items, which often have to be purchased at *above*-average world prices.

We see a country where, on the one hand, the external indebtedness is equivalent to over one thousand dollars for every man, woman and child in Russia and where, on the other hand – if we look hard enough – we can see that the ill-gotten gains of capital accumulation by the new financial elite are being deposited in offshore havens at an estimated (conservative) average of 20 billion dollars per year; this figure is some six to seven times larger than the total amount of incoming foreign investment and official aid.

We see a country in which the social consequences of this transition are not just making themselves known in the usual (sic) phenomena of structural unemployment, homelessness, dire levels of poverty and malnutrition. They are also making themselves manifest in the reappearance of once-forgotten diseases such as typhoid, diphtheria and tuberculosis. And a short sideways glance will reveal to us the very noticeable decline in population, caused by such things as lower birth rates, a considerably reduced life span and dramatically higher numbers of suicides and murders.

Last, but not least, we see a country where the institutions of the state have become nothing more than a parasite feeding off the few remaining resources left to it; perhaps the most visible sign of this parasitic existence is the depths to which it is the state itself which is most blatantly the major source of phenomenal levels of bribery and corruption, not least through its cooperation with myriad Mafia organisations, many of which it helped to spawn. As one commentator has remarked, the only thing that the Russian state knows how to create these days is crises, and given its tradition of resolving crises by gorging itself on its favourite food – blood – one can only hope that its hunger is not insatiable.[1]

Taken together, of course, many of these different elements have all the hallmarks of a fairly coherent Western approach to Russia's economic transition. A decimated manufacturing base offers no real competition to Western producers, and has the added benefit that if there is ever a greater commitment to taking over Russian firms, it can be achieved at rock-bottom prices in conditions of almost certainly debilitated labour hostility to new work practices. In the new trading climate, the West now has very extensive access to the Russian domestic market, and is able to guarantee itself relatively cheap energy supplies, thereby tying Russia into a position of subservience in the global division of labour. For the new oligarchic elite of Russia, meanwhile, any residual notions of national 'dependency' are more than compensated for by their new-found enjoyment of an unlimited access to Western consumer goods, as well as their own increasing integration into the realms of global finance capital. And as for the condition of the state institutions, this at least converges very well with the demands of global financial speculators who can virtually hold the debt-ridden government to ransom over such things as the terms for issuing bonds. In short, what one sees when one looks at Russia is the clearest intention (if not reality itself yet) of Western-dominated globalisation striving to be the newest (perhaps the highest) stage of (neo) imperialism.

If we go on to view the new Russian landscape from a slightly different perspective, using a deeper, sharper lens, the other phenomenon which most comes into focus is the extent to which society is succumbing to a whole range of almost feudal-like tendencies. Far from advancing in a time-space continuum, Russia is in some crucial ways regressing.

Part of the logic at work in this apparent temporal anomaly has been interestingly conceptualised by Mikhail Epstein. When communism collapsed in the Soviet Union, it did not just signify the end of a system or an entrenched set of beliefs; perhaps even more than that it represented the end of the 'future', at least in the one and only way that Russians had been taught to conceptualise the future for the last three-quarters of a century.

All of a sudden, the interminable future had disappeared, vanished in the wind, and with it the whole framework of time was turned on its head. A sense of the future no longer existed, only the present and the past remained. Of these two dimensions, however, in what sense could one be sure that there was a present? As Epstein notes:

> In the trinary system of time, the present normally represents authentic reality, whereas the past and future appear as its long-distance projections. Not so in Russia. Here, the present has almost never enjoyed its own worth, but rather was perceived as an echo of the past or a step toward the future.[2]

This, then, left only the past with any resemblance of real existence. Having for so long been in the avant-garde of historical and cultural time, Russia now finds itself the embodiment of its *arrière-garde*. It is not at the 'end of history', but back at the beginning, and while the communist future has itself become a thing of the past, what now approaches Russia 'from the direction where [one] had expected to meet the future' are the relics not so much of a bourgeois past, but something more distant than that: feudalism. Russia has entered 'the stage of [the] "pre-future"'.[3]

What, then, are the main features of this return to feudalist tendencies?[4] To provide just a few illustrations, there is firstly the almost symbiotic relationship between property and power in Russia today, to the point at which whole districts have been turned into nothing more than personal fiefdoms. Second, there is the greater importance of personal connections rather than other types of interaction based on more formal (or institutionalised) relationships in the political, social and economic realm – characterised in Russian by the all-pervading notion of *krysha*. If vassalage best describes the relationship amongst the rulers themselves, below this sphere it is dominated by patron–client relationships centred around a whole series of clans.

Next is the all-pervading dominance of barter relations, not just in the economic realm of non-pecuniary exchange – where workers, for example, if they are paid at all are invariably paid in kind with the items that they themselves produce – but also in the sociopolitical realm of exchanging favours. Fourth, a level of violence exists throughout society which has forced people to rely on their own resources for protection, up to and including the creation of private armies; this has given rise to traditional feudal notions of *commendation* (the demand for protection from the new 'lords' and 'barons' in the face of the dangers posed by roving armed bands in return for a promise of near-total servitude).

Fifth, the 'provincialisation' of the country has taken place, and the almost complete breakdown of any meaningful political, economic, social and cultural integration. In conjunction with this, there is a classic 'divide and rule' policy from the central authorities as the only means of exercising any real degree of control and authority over the affairs of the country. By means of this approach to its 'vassals', however, the state generates enormous degrees of animosity and instability, and can rely on little or no degrees of trust. Sixth, there is the incapacity to achieve compromise or consensus in the political domain as the personal stakes involved in the game of intrigue and power are too high. Related to this is the fact that political 'parties' and associations have a far greater tendency to be the vehicles and conduits for private, personal promotion rather than anything more articulatory or representative in nature. And, in addition, one can also see the creation of a 'state within a state' at the highest echelons of power as a means of trying to achieve some degree of security as well as personal economic well-being.

For Vladimir Shlapentokh, the major effect of all these tendencies is particularly noticeable in the way in which the social and political life of the country has become 'privatised' in the extreme. Over the course of Russia's entire history, he asserts, and irrespective of the mode of production which was dominant, a conviction of the superiority of public over private interests has effectively reigned supreme. This is most decidedly no longer the case, and in the process has had an enormous impact on the nature of 'patriotism' which had hitherto been embodied in a fundamental concern about the collective (national) welfare of the country as a whole. Really for the first time, then, ordinary individuals now 'find themselves socially "naked" … Russians today have the strong conviction that the only realm which matters is their private lives, and public life is viewed as irrelevant.' As a consequence, with such perpetual insecurity all around them, they 'are wholly absorbed with survival in a … society' which is barely recognisable to most of them.[5]

It does not take too much foresight, then, to see that it is here – with the breakdown of many of its old traditions and the resulting injustices and inequalities that have been produced – that any remaining opportunities for the left in Russia to make its own distinguishing mark on the post-communist transition process still exists. Nor does it take much foresight to see that a dominant plank of any political strategy would almost certainly base itself on a strong nationalist orientation. The real question is: what is the fundamental nature of any nationalist orientation which has thus far been pursued and what are its real (counter) hegemonic potentialities?

2

The main embodiment of the appropriation of nationalism as the dominant mobilisationary force in the hegemonic struggle that has been taking place in Russia since the collapse of the old Soviet order has been the Communist Party of the Russian Federation (CPRF). And since it is clear (at the time of writing at least) that this is the one and only organisational forum which the Russian left has in engaging in any kind of realistic struggle for power, what I have to say on this issue will be almost exclusively restricted to the CPRF alone.

A desire to blend communism with nationalism is, of course, nothing new in the Russian context, and it is as well to stress this right from the outset. For all the internationalist rhetoric of Soviet communists, few observers have ever really questioned the prioritising of a nationalist agenda. Stalin's vision of 'socialism in one country' – that 'ideological monstrosity', as Sartre was later to call it, 'because it said *more* than was necessary'[6] – was the formalisation of this union. But the nationalist priorities really had been in vogue for a long time before this. Indeed, for some, what ultimately emerged as the ideology of Marxism-Leninism was the perfect incarnation of nationalism – nothing more, nothing less. Nevertheless, the essence and nature of the current blend of these two forces seems to me to give off a different aroma altogether. And without doubt the role of the CPRF's leader, Gennadii Zyuganov, has been absolutely crucial here.

When the re-foundation congress of the Communist Party of the Russian Federation elected Gennadii Zyuganov as its leader in February 1993, it was certainly not in ignorance of his political outlook. His radical nationalist credentials were second to none, both in terms of organisational affiliations as well as in what was already at that time a significant corpus of theoretical writings, all of which had largely been devoted to the long-standing question of Russia's supposed superior uniqueness and exceptionalism as against the rest of Western civilisation.[7]

At its core Zyuganov's approach has been based on the overriding premise that in the aftermath of the 'overthrow' of the old order, the Russian communist faith can only be defended through the mechanism of nationalism and patriotism. To sustain this approach, he has consistently tried over the last few years to bridge what, in some cases at least, were nearly always considered to be unbridgeable divides.

No one has done more than Zyuganov, for example, to try to create a dialectical synthesis out of the Civil War divide between Reds and Whites, and out of the later division between Reds and Browns, seeking to overcome the division by imbuing the mutual belief of these forces in the nation with a degree of sacredness rarely found before in a communist leader. Based on the largely Hegelian-inspired ideas of Lev Gumil'ev (amongst many others), Zyuganov is adamant that the ethnos or nation is the main 'agent of history'. In the Eurasian realm, this is recognised even more cogently by the existence of a *super-ethnos*, which has historically fused the Slavs, Tatars and Mongols. For Zyuganov, if there is to be any vilification of the actions of past political figures in Russian history, the greatest vilification must be reserved for the likes of Trotsky and other old Bolsheviks for their supposed 'perverse' and 'cynically cosmopolitan betrayal' of Russia; this charge is likewise levelled at the 'outrageous neo-Trotskyite' architects and foremen of *perestroika*.

In another attempt to overcome the dimensional barriers of time, no one has done more than Zyuganov to correlate *post*-communism with *pre*-communism. In particular, few have laboured longer and harder to sustain the conviction that the 'Russian Idea' – that phenomenon which is 'so mysterious and incomprehensible to the West' – is a profoundly socialist idea.[8] Like Berdyaev and Dostoevsky before him, Zyuganov readily acknowledges the 'contradictory properties' of the 'Russian Idea'. But he is also adamant that whatever else one can say about the Russian character or 'soul', one thing is for sure: it has never been 'bourgeois' and is totally unsuited to be bourgeois, not least because up until the present time Russians have been 'innocent of the sin of ownership'. While socialism, therefore, is based on deep-rooted atavistic sentiments, capitalism simply cannot be an organic part of the flesh and blood, the life, the customs and psychology of Russian society. Similarly, there is an inseparable linkage here between the notion of communism and the Russian term *obshchina* (community), where priority has always been given to common, collectivist and community-driven interests, as distinct from private, egoistic and individualist ones.

Perhaps most crucially of all, no one has done more than Zyuganov to construct a symbiotic connection between communism and religion, with Islam and Buddhism on the one hand, but most importantly of all with that most dominant of all of Russia's religions – Orthodox Christianity. The relationship can be seen in practical terms, where there has been no greater defender of the interests of Orthodoxy against the infiltration of Western (alien) sects of one kind or another than the Communist Party. It can be seen in the attempts to create ideological, theoretical parallels between notions of communist collectivism and Orthodox conciliarism *(sobornost')*. It can be seen in the attempt to create historical, genealogical parallels between the two, based on the notion that communism is also two thousand years old 'because of its compatibility with the teachings of Christ'. And it can also be seen in the explicit religious imagery which fills all of

Zyuganov's keynote speeches and texts, often with accompanying icons of Jesus Christ and the Mother of God in permanent tow. A very common refrain, for example, is the appeal for Russian people 'to see the light' (as he himself has done); communists are often labelled 'secular Christians' whose sense of morality is perfectly compatible with the Ten Commandments; capitalism is by nature the 'anti-Christ' compared with communism's ability to rise, Lazarus-like, from the grave; ex-President Yeltsin is frequently portrayed either as 'the beast from the abyss sent by the Devil' or as Judas (with the latter character slur also being used in a much broader sense as a personification of the 'ideal' citizen of the new capitalist Russia); there are regular 'Bible readings' particularly from Zyuganov's favourite Book of Revelations, and there are frequent sermons on the way in which Russians, as befits one of 'God's chosen people', possess a depth of sacredness unmatched by any other national group. In short, what one frequently witnesses is effectively the transformation of ideology into *theology*. Not unlike Nicholas Berdyaev at the beginning of the century – who ironically, of course, along with Vladimir Solov'ev, was already prophesying a new Middle Ages for Russia[9] – Zyuganov seems to have visions of a new religious-based collectivity that will sweep away all the old remnants of humanism, individualism and liberalism. And again, like Berdyaev, such a view of 'progress' is not so much underpinned by the forces of irrationalism, so much as a belief in a kind of theocratic *super-rationalism*. Whatever the underpinning, however, opium, so it seems, has a far more pleasing affect at the very end of the twentieth century than it did, at least for Marx, in the mid-nineteenth century.

Here, in outline, are the kind of basic nationalist and exceptionalist images which have become the essential fulcrum of the CPRF's counter-hegemonic collective will. More to the point, there can be little doubt that Zyuganov's long-term aim is to have his understanding of national-patriotism accepted as an official state ideology. In order to assess the tactical, hegemonic acumen of this approach, to see whether it arises from concrete exigencies, to gauge how progressive and healthy it is, and to understand whether it should be considered more as a malady than a remedy for the tasks facing the Russian left over the coming years, it is clearly essential, at this stage at least, not to prejudge the CPRF as automatically guilty of the sin of some kind of intrinsic left heresy or apostasy. Indeed, Tom Nairn's advice here is very sound: one should always avoid an overly *moralising* perspective when assessing the different positive and negative ambivalences of a nationalist outlook, particularly in the kind of circumstances facing Russia today.[10] Let us, then, pursue such positive and negative ambivalences in as rational a manner as possible, and let me at least offer my apologies in advance for any emotional strain which might creep into the analysis.

If one was to provide a case for the defence here, that is to say, if one was to support the strategic line offered by the CPRF in recent years, there are at least six key arguments or testimonies that one would want to highlight. The first argument is in the form of a response to those critics who think that a nationalist perspective for any communist organisation is some kind of gross 'blasphemy' against everything considered 'sacred' in Marxist theory. As Zyuganov himself has argued:

> The ... question giving rise to the most serious disputes is the question of the need to consider Russia's historical uniqueness in the Communist Party's activity and programme goals. People ask whether there is not nationalism and a betrayal of the class-based approach here. If you identify a class-based approach with vulgar sociology, then yes ... But the Marxist theory of sociohistorical development never taught us to view countries and peoples as a blank sheet of paper on which the impersonal economic laws write history. So we believe that the attempt to consider the uniqueness of the Russian way, to reveal its 'socialist predisposition', so to speak, is in the mainstream of the scientific methodology of historical analysis.[11]

One could perhaps go further and also argue that it would be almost impossible to accuse the communists of a theoretical deviation here because, to put it quite crudely, there is simply no definable Marxist theory of nationalism to deviate against in the first place. It could be contended, of course, that *The Communist Manifesto* is without a shadow of doubt a powerful anti-nationalist tract, and that, at least as far as Marx himself was concerned, he rarely, if ever, wavered in his deep-seated antagonism to the possible nationalist contamination of the working-class movement. Nevertheless, all these claims could be, and frequently have been, challenged by equally virulent and justifiable antithetical claims. Moreover, even accepting that there might be a sufficiently uncontested Marxist approach to nationalism, one would perhaps still have to recognise that ultimately it is such an intrinsically instrumental approach as to be of service to virtually any stance which might be adopted by a communist leader in any given context.

Second, and following on from this, a strong case could be made along the following lines: because the Russian masses undoubtedly have a much stronger identification with the nation than they do with class, it would therefore be pure folly on the part of the CPRF not to use this in their strategic and programmatic considerations. As Boris Kagarlitsky, for example, has so cogently argued, Russian society for most of this century has effectively been *declassed*.[12] In such circumstances, it is hardly surprising that there are very few genuine, or at least consistent, feelings of class consciousness and attachment in any of the social groups in present-day Russian society. One can hardly blame the communists, many would claim, for not waging a class struggle if the objective conditions for that struggle are not there in the first place.

Moreover, in the face of all the destructive, disaggregative tendencies brought about by the past decade of change, the close identification with a nationalist agenda by the CPRF has at least provided people with a positive sense of collective identity and belonging. It has fulfilled, if only in a psychological sense, what many would regard as an absolutely crucial internal need of Russian society at this point; it has given the Russian people a renewed sense of pride and hope. And perhaps, after all, the advocates of nationalism are correct: it is only in the form of a 'people', not classes, that the masses enter the political domain and make history. As Marx himself said, this making of history always carries with it the weight of tradition of a nation's dead generations. Few have captured this psychological need better than Frantz Fanon. To believe in one's national culture 'is in fact an ardent, despairing turning towards anything that will afford ... secure anchorage'.[13] The style might necessarily be harsh, vigorous, and yes, violent. But it is also rhythmic, full of life, colour and images which can liberate previously unconscious energies, scattering them over all the surrounding meadows.

A third argument for the defence is that the national-patriotic emphasis of the CPRF represents the definitive rejection of Bolshevik-style voluntarism. At long last, it is contended, the intellectual bias of this thoroughly idealist, vanguardist approach to political activity has now been replaced by an emphasis on the instincts and values of the ordinary man and woman in the street. Zyuganov's ideas may not bear the hallmark of intellectual originality, let alone internal consistency. They may even amount to nothing more than an extremely primitive 'propagandistic myth'. But this is beside the point. For all the didactic simplicity and eclecticism of his approach, he has nevertheless succeeded in the one major task that has otherwise alluded all the other self-professed forces of the democratic left in Russia, replete as they are with all their grand ideas and words. He has succeeded in actually mobilising opposition segments of the Russian population and he has at least made some indentations into that previously impenetrable apathy that has so characterised the ordinary Russian masses since the heady days of the late Gorbachev period.

Another argument stressing the tactical acumen of the communists and their nationalist agenda concerns the affect this has had on their most vociferous political enemies. In a country such as Russia, so the argument goes, nationalism is not a force which can be left in the hands of the forces of the xenophobic and chauvinistic right. The communists have therefore been absolutely correct to occupy this terrain of struggle as the most effective means of keeping such forces at bay. By their success, they have not only carried out a great service to Russia, but to the whole of Europe.

Boris Kapustin is one Russian commentator who has promoted this line very strongly. If Zyuganov deserves credit for anything, it is the way that he has outstandingly ensured the predominance of the 'left-wing modernisers' in the patriotic debate. True, Zyuganov has left himself open to charges of 'conservatism'. According to Kapustin, however, this is a very mild-mannered form of conservatism in the mould of Karl Mannheim or, perhaps on occasion, even Edmund Burke. It is about appreciating how features of the present era have their roots in the past, and how we should understand and savour those roots, an approach which is diametrically opposed to the much more radical and dangerous type of 'fundamentalist nationalism'. Above all, it is about the desire to retain symbols that still have meaning for so much of the population, hence the reason why Zyuganov has been adamant in preserving the name 'Communist' for the party. For all these reasons, Kapustin is at least happy to call Zyuganov a 'left conservative' and to acknowledge the positive benefits of, what Zyuganov himself often calls, 'creative conservatism'.[14]

Kapustin in his article also goes on to make the point that the communists are perfectly well aware of the dangers of playing the nationalist game. Again, however, the argument is very forcefully made that it is a game which they have little choice but to play, and up until now at least, they have played it on their own terms – that is to say, they have at least accentuated the positive social values of the so-called 'Russian Idea'. Whatever else their nationalism consists of, it is not a narrow-minded ethnic form of nationalism. They have at least tried to use nationalist rhetoric to define the kind of society Russia should be.

Indeed, this brings us to one of the strongest defences of the CPRF under Zyuganov's tutelage. If nationalism is what it takes to elect the communists and oust the current despised regime, then so be it. Just think of all the positive consequences that would stem from this. From a domestic point of view (assuming we can accept the promises made by the CPRF), it would mean increased social welfare provisions for schools and hospitals, and greater state help for the most deprived social groups – the unemployed, the homeless, the elderly, the infirm and the very young. It would mean increased state subsidies for Russia's manufacturing and technological base, as well as agriculture, leading in turn to better prospects for the workers and peasants. It would mean a halt to the iniquitous process of capital accumulation. It would lead to a clamp-down on Mafia activities and social evils such as prostitution and pornography. It would also lead to radical political changes in the balance of legislative–executive relations, with promises to curtail the ever-increasing absolutist powers of the Presidency and the unaccountable personal administration which has been built up alongside it. From a more international perspective, meanwhile, it would bring a highly welcome stronger form of opposition to NATO imperialism, and would almost certainly stop the discussions about the viability of including former Soviet republics in any intended expansion drive. It would likewise open up the possibilities for a much stronger form of reintegration of Russia with the old 'fraternal' republics of the USSR. And who knows, a CPRF victory in Russia might well inflict serious damage on the economic hegemony of neo-liberalism, with positive knock-on effects elsewhere in the developing and developed world.

Having raised an *international* dimension here, this brings us to the final major argument for the defence, which can likewise frequently be heard in left-wing discussion forums inside and outside Russia. For many defenders – or at least sympathisers – of communist nationalism, there is a tendency to view this development within the *global* framework of anti-imperialism. Within this framework, Russia can be viewed as a potential bastion of opposition to the global, imperialist ambitions of Western capitalist hegemony. In the process, Russia almost becomes transformed into a 'Third World' outpost. With its levels of underdevelopment, but with its potential for colonisation by global capitalism, the nationalist resistance of the communists takes on the increasing appearance of a 'romantic' struggle for *self-determination*. The atavistic dangers of past forms of Russian nationalism thereby become submerged in this broader anti-imperialism of the present. To use the words of Tom Nairn, it becomes a justifiable 'compensatory reaction on the periphery' of capitalist imperialism,[15] and for the left at least, such a peripheral form of nationalism can always be much more tolerated, forgiven, or excused than a 'core-area' nationalism. In short, it is perceived as the only route out of dependency and must therefore be supported at all costs, for it is the only 'antithesis' of the forward march of global capitalism and, by its 'organic' linkage of the community and the state, the only real antidote to the all-pervasive power of Western individualism and social atomism.

The notion that the left can make positive use of nationalism, and that there is even a necessity for a nationalist agenda, has a long theoretical as well as practical pedigree. Think of all the great revolutionary causes over the past couple of hundred years of the modern era, and this is immediately, even strikingly, apparent. Indeed, as was outlined in Chapter 5, as the years have progressed, some of the most eloquent works written by left-wing theorists and activists have been precisely in this domain of accentuating the positive (usually *culturally*-based) tenets of nationalism.

The conviction that there can be extremely progressive understandings and uses of nationalism by left-wing forces is not the issue here. What is at issue, certainly for any critic of this phenomenon, or, at least, for anyone trying to make use of a Gramscian perspective on hegemony, is more the actual manner in which the appeal to nationalism is constituted and then applied in practice. As an essential framework for judging the nationalist predominance in the CPRF, it is hard, to put it no more harshly than this for the time being, not to experience some very grave misgivings and anxieties. Is perhaps the communist nationalism of the CPRF masking a more sinister notion of national communism/socialism, an updated version of Ustrialovism?[16]

Turning to the case for the prosecution, then, the first of the major criticisms is rooted in a fear of the history of nationalism in the Russian context. Notwithstanding a hint of exaggeration, there is a very strong argument that, given the historical experience of Russian nationalism, this in itself is sufficient reason to behove the Russian left never to resort to this tactic. To use Seton-Watson's designation, Russian nationalism has always been an *official* nationalism.[17] It has always existed as the creation from above of a power group, fearful of its own self-imposed exclusion from the popular will of the masses. While suitably camouflaged in an unfathomable veneer of mysticism, it has always been designed to be used in highly conservative and reactionary ways to serve exclusively the interests of an all-powerful, absolutist state. Moreover, so all-pervasive is this legacy that the left should not even attempt to tame it, because no matter what virtuous intentions it might start out with, it will always end up reproducing its impure, pathological and phantasmatic excesses – precisely one of those instances, in other words, when the baby should indeed be thrown out with the dirty bath water.

If there is an excessive degree of fatalism in this understanding of the penetrative depth of official nationalism, there is at least sufficient empirical evidence to incriminate the CPRF as an accessory to the crime of wilfully perpetuating its pernicious influence. More worryingly, one cannot even produce much mitigating evidence to show how the best intentions of Zyuganov and the CPRF in their efforts to tame the worst features of the nationalist beast have gone astray. Taming it was never on Zyuganov's agenda. Instead, he chose to ride the beast, and has been much enjoying the ride.

Judging from many of his speeches, there can be little doubt that Zyuganov is an ardent admirer of the political figure who really invented official nationalism in Russia – Count Sergius Uvarov, Tsarist Minister for Education in the 1830s and 1840s. First, there is his unstinting belief in the notion of *derzhavnost'* – a form of Great Power statism which intrinsically subordinates all other issues and concerns to its own primacy. Second, there is his strong attachment to a messianic understanding of nationalism, the constant promotion of Russia's sense of special destiny, which in turn promotes the constant search for, and need of, a saviour. This likewise explains the growing positive reappraisal of Stalin emanating from many sections of the CPRF, not least Zyuganov himself, who brackets Stalin with the likes of Ivan the Terrible and Peter the Great for his redoubtable state-strengthening and state-conquering achievements. And third, there is Zyuganov's enduring faith in the mysticism underpinning nationalist convictions in the Russian tradition. This partly explains, for example, his desire to achieve a reconciliation with Orthodox Christianity which always acted as the main mythogenesis of the old Tsarist state. It likewise explains his strong affinities with thinkers such as Konstantin Leont'ev, Vladimir Solov'ev, Nicholas Berdyaev and Lev Gumil'ev.

All of this, then, could not be further from any notion of a 'progressive' left nationalism. If, following Régis Debray, we understand a progressive, healthy form of nationalism as one which promotes the maxim 'cultivate and accentuate the positive and decry the negative in your country's culture and tradition',[18] this is not easily applied to Zyuganov and the CPRF, who too often seem to delight in turning the maxim on its head. Likewise, by emphasising the nationalist primacy of the state, it is certainly not adhering to that other main feature of progressive nationalism: a promotion of the popular-cultural traditions of the people. Individual 'saviours' like Stalin are seemingly worth more than all the grass-roots democratic traditions of the (early) soviets in communist rhetoric.[19] As for Zyuganov's mystical faith in his country, while one should not necessarily begrudge him this, there must surely be some limits here. As the poet Maria Avakkumova wrote in a belated reply to Fyodor Tyutchev's famous rendition about the inability to grasp Russia by the rational mind, because only profane, spiritual belief in Russia would suffice: yes, 'But just how much can one only believe!!'

Given the commitment Zyuganov has to the notions of *derzhavnost'*, messianism, mysticism and so forth, Aleksandr Tsipko – in contrast to the aforementioned views of Boris Kapustin – would not hesitate to identify

Zyuganov's 'conservatism' with a far more right-wing, rather than left-wing tradition. While it is 'red in form', it is far more 'white in content', embodied as it is in the right-wing cocoon of an all-powerful Russian state.[20] Tsipko's views here also raise a far more disturbing allegation against the CPRF. Whilst it is undeniable that the CPRF has done the whole of the European continent an invaluable service in seeing off (for the time being at least) the challenge posed by the far right, to what extent have they done this by simply colonising much of the same rhetoric and values?

Perhaps most disturbing of all is the appropriation of a whole range of nationalist imagery by Zyuganov and other leading members of the CPRF which anyone even loosely associated with the left should find intrinsically distasteful: the chauvinism, for example, of much of the nationalist rhetoric of the CPRF, the xenophobic need to find all manner of scapegoats to blame for the country's 'unjust' predicament, the allusions to fears that the supposedly unique 'genetic composition' of the Russian people is once again being threatened, the implicit and explicit anti-Semitism of Zyuganov and many others which simultaneously blames nearly all aspects of the economic transformation in Russia today on the culture and ideology of a 'Judaic Diaspora, whose influence is consistently growing by the day, even by the hour'. Last, but not least, a great deal of the nationalist rhetoric of the CPRF is too often tied in with a sense of *humiliation*. We hardly need to be reminded of the lessons of the 1920s and 1930s to appreciate that there are enormous inherent dangers in grounding a nationalist conviction in sentiments of this nature, which essentially sees the nation as a victim. All of this imagery, then, if it cannot be eradicated entirely from the political scene because of the existence of fascist elements, should at least have no 'positive' role to play in the language of the left. Exactly the contrary.

Another criticism of the nationalism and patriotism of the CPRF is that it is too much rooted in the past. Not unlike the damned in Dante's *Divina Commedia,* the present-day Russian communists seem to have their heads turned permanently backwards. Perhaps in itself, this is not too much of a bad thing, and a lot of political capital can be gained from this approach, allowing one to portray the past and those associated with it in heroic, glorious and selfless terms. If taken to extremes, however, it can clearly have many serious adverse affects, as even Zyuganov himself has at times acknowledged.[21] In short, it is a form of nationalism which allows little or no space for the posing of the most important question 'where is Russia going?', because it prefers concentrating on the question 'where has Russia come from?'

Notwithstanding the general legitimacy of the argument, especially in the present Russian context, that there might be a stronger identification with the nation than with class, this should not detract from the powerful criticism that the CPRF is undoubtedly missing enormous opportunities to strengthen a sense of class awareness and class-based affiliation in the social and economic domain of struggle. That is to say, there is too often an 'over-valorisation' of nationalism – to use the terminology of Aijaz Ahmad – as a strategy of resistance. As a consequence, it is closing off too many other avenues of resistance which should be the overriding domain of any genuine left-wing strategy.[22]

The limits of this constant narration of an 'over-valorised', unitary experience of national oppression can be seen, for example, in the party's whole attitude to the nature of capitalist transformation affecting the country. The essence of the party's antagonism is not an attack on capitalism as such, but an attack almost exclusively directed at *'comprador'* capitalists and the moral perversity of the *nouveaux riches*. By far the worst attribute of the *compradors*, according to Zyuganov, is that they constantly refer to Russia in the most impersonal way as 'this country'. What he really wants are capitalists who call it 'my country', and preferably ones who have an affinity to the ancient traditions of 'Holy Rus', rather than the excessively modern Russia. Certainly in tone and essence, some of the economic programmes of the CPRF have not been all that different from their opponents. To be sure, the tax system would be used in stronger ways to ensure some degree of greater redistribution, but as Zyuganov has been making abundantly clear for a considerable time, there would be no real attack on the new private owners. What Zyuganov wants is an emphasis on 'national capitalism' with 'native *(otechestvennye)* entrepreneurs', and this is by far the main reason why he has been able to retain a social democratic faction within the party, while so many other (more left-wing) tendencies have been forced to leave.

It is thus very hard to ignore the criticism that the CPRF's approach to an emerging Russian capitalism is barely left-wing at all. If it represents anything, it is far more a right-wing critique rooted in a desire to protect the patriarchal masses. By giving such priority to nationalist concerns, the party has clearly failed to maximise the positive potential of the fundamental social contradictions and antagonisms currently existing in Russia. Indeed, in many ways, it has been socially regressive in helping to *contain* these problems, leaving many of the most deprived sectors of society feeling that whoever and wherever they turn to for political assistance, they will always end up being duped. As political cannon-fodder, the deprived have their uses, and politicians of all kinds, especially if willing to play the nationalist card for all its worth, will always need their fears and prejudices.

Taking stock of all these criticisms, the case for the prosecution can perhaps best be concluded in the following way: as always in politics it is a question of means and ends. For Zyuganov, on the very limited occasions he gives vent to socialist causes, it is absolutely clear that this is nothing more than a tactical ploy to help boost the ultimate ends he is striving for, the re-emergence of Russia as a *derzhava* – a Great Power defined in nationalist, messianic terms. Zyuganov is first and last a nationalist, and everything else is oriented around this. In any clash between his socialism and nationalism, the pretences of the former would very quickly be sacrificed on the altar of the convictions of the latter.

On balance, therefore, it would be hard to deny that the shortcomings and weaknesses of the nationalist counter-hegemonic strategy of the Russian communists outweigh the advantages and strengths. More importantly, the shortcomings and weaknesses are extremely serious, as well very *dangerous,* ones from a whole manner of perspectives. Having earlier cited an argument of Frantz Fanon for the defence, let us not forget the warnings that he appended to his celebration of national cultures. Instead of trying to rehabilitate anything of substance in a previously forgotten, ignored or subsumed national consciousness, those engaged in this task will all too often let themselves 'be hypnotized by … mummified fragments'[23] – fragments, moreover, which are invariably static and which in reality are nothing more than symbols of negation and outworn contrivances. Zyuganov would do well to remember that culture abhors all attempts at simplification. Where such attempts are made, one cannot help end up being mired in the mud of demagogy and opportunism, listening to the harsh tones of fly-by-night late-comers.

In addition to the implicit dangers of this kind of orientation, one must also surely note a sense of deep regret, if not despair. A bitter disappointment that out of the collapse of the old Soviet order, no better, no more principled left-wing alternative and vision was able to sustain itself on the political arena in Russia. To borrow the sentiments of one of Robert Rozhdestvensky's poems, once again we have all been in a state of frozen anticipation over the last few years, residing in a perpetual waiting room, looking out with a heightened sense of both expectation and dread at where Russia was about to jump to next.[24] Indeed, what other country has provided us with so many paradoxes? Here is a country which has stirred the political imagination of the left far more than any other over these past few decades. Here is a country which has done more than any other to resist the onslaught of world capitalist hegemony. Here is a country which is still the key potential terrain of resistance to that capitalist globalisation. And here is a country which may well determine the nature of developments in Europe and beyond long into the twenty-first century. Yet notwithstanding all of this, what other country has so consistently shattered the dreams of the international left? It seems it is the country's destiny to touch the extremes of left-wing optimism and pessimism. Perhaps the most uncanny thing of all is that it does so almost simultaneously.

3

If there is a final conclusion to be made of this study on the interaction of hegemony between East and West over the course of the last century, one would have to say that at the present juncture Russia and the West are separated far more in time than in space, a temporal disparity the extent of which it would be hard to find a historical parallel. Not even Pyotr Chaadayev – who, in the first half of the eighteenth century wrote of the stifling, fatal obsessiveness and oppressiveness of Russia's embrace of time, and of how Russia had hitherto been divorced from the temporal and spatial dimensions of universal existence[25] – could have foreseen the even greater temporal disjunctions to come and which now characterise East-West interactions.

As we enter the dawn of a new century, the West is congratulating itself on its transition to postmodernity, while in Russia there is a backward movement towards pre-modernity. In the latter case, time has turned back on itself. A 'political retrovirus' is at work which, as Alain Touraine rightly points out, 'looks to a mythical past to compensate for a present which has no future'.[26] Most disconcerting of all, it is a political retrovirus which has contagiously spread and deeply infected the Russian communists, along with many others. How else can one explain the nationalist and patriotic offerings of the present-day Communist Party other than by references to pre-modern *demotic* ideas of community? How else can one explain their cultural historicism other than by references to pre-modern notions of didacticism?

According to Liah Greenfeld, Russian nationalism (in both its Westernist and Slavophile forms) has always been characterised by *ressentiment* – an existential envy of the West.[27] Perhaps the most dominant subconscious characteristic of the contemporary version of nationalism, however, is that of *shame*. Shame that the modern rational attributes of liberty, (social) justice, equality (and not forgetting fraternity as well) have never properly been faced up to in Russia. Because rationality – and with it, modernity – are so unpalatable, it hence follows that they must be rejected. In their place, one is reduced to falling back on the only thing which is left – sentiment and feeling. As Greenfeld goes on to note, however, there has always been so much inexpressible, unlimited and hyperbolic reliance on such attributes as these that one cannot help but end up choking on them. In light of this, it is certainly not to be wondered that Zyuganov is so regularly (and disparagingly) portrayed as a product of traditional Russian peasant society – a man of the rural, feudal past.

Moreover, in light of the cultural-civilisational aspirations of the Russian communists, one should also express no surprise at the way in which Samuel Huntington's counsel of despair on the coming 'Clash of Civilisations' – for all its confusion, idiosyncrasies, incoherence and perniciousness – could so quickly displace Fukuyama's triumphalist 'End of History' thesis as the current guiding light of many Western intellectual and policy-making circles.[28] Zyuganov, of course, has turned out to be the perfect knave to Huntington's fatalism – a position he shares with Islamic fundamentalists and 'jihadistes'. And along with his much vaunted popularisation of earlier admired civilisational soothsayers and doom-mongers – Danilevskii, Leont'ev, Spengler and Toynbee – he is desperately doing everything possible, it seems, to turn Huntington's diatribe into a self-fulfilling prophecy.

In terms at least of left aspirations, the present situation is a world apart from that which existed at the beginning of the twentieth century. At that time one could say of the Russian and the Western left, admittedly with a few doubts and hesitations, that like Janus, they were often looking in somewhat different directions, but nevertheless a single heart was beating in them; a single heart, moreover, was beating for one overriding purpose – a common desire to attain the full developed fruits of a thoroughly modern form of socialism. Likewise, one could also say that the evolving notion of hegemony was a pivotal feature and strategic ambition of this common desire.

With the prevalence of a pre-modern nationalism on the Russian left and a postmodern apoliticism on much of the Western left, one is left these days not so much with a common desire, so much as a common disease, perhaps the worst political (and anti-hegemonic) disease possible for the left – *escapism*. With such ersatz ideologies as now abound in East and West, we are increasingly witnessing a 'dialectic of devaluation' (to use a Habermasian term) of the left. It is the present author's hope, however, that on both sides of the new temporal iron curtain separating East and West, a desire for a qualitatively rejuvenated critical project of socialist modernity will again become the shared hegemonic task. For this to happen, of course, the dialogue of negation and reciprocal exclusivity which has so pervaded the actual relations between the Eastern and Western left throughout so much of the past century will itself have to be negated; a Marxian double negation – negation of the negation – which will take us down the far more constructive and creative road of affirmative unity. As Gramsci always demonstrated in both thought and deed, the perpetual search for the unity of constituent elements and the transcendence of contradictory tensions is surely the very essence of what it means *to be* on the left, an intrinsically unavoidable existential condition of socialist hegemony.

Notes and References

Preface

1 Jeremy Lester, *Modern Tsars and Princes: The Struggle for Hegemony in Russia* (London: Verso, 1995).
2 Louis Althusser, *For Marx*, trans. Ben Brewster (London: Verso, 1990), p. 114, n. 29.

Introduction: Hegemony and the Project of Modernity

1 The review is by Martin Dewhirst in *International Affairs*, Vol. 72, No. 3, 1996, p. 619.
2 Pinochet's warning was expressed in an interview with *Komsomol'skaya pravda*, 30 September 1992, p. 3.
3 Renate Holub, *Antonio Gramsci: Beyond Marxism and Postmodernism* (London: Routledge, 1992), p. 104.
4 In addition to Pinochet's own warnings, one can also cite the warnings contained in the so-called Santa Fe reports on the political situation inside Latin America. Written for the American State Department and other government organisations by a number of academics and at least one General (who collectively call themselves the Committee of Santa Fe) the documents have continually made references to the strong Gramscian influence on Latin American opposition movements and the absolute necessity to combat this influence in all possible areas. For details, see Enriqueta Cabrera (ed.), *Respuestas a Santa Fe II* (Dia en Libros, 1989. Seccion Testimonios y docs. 35).
5 Benedetto Fontana, *Hegemony and Power. On the Relation between Gramsci and Machiavelli* (Minneapolis: University of Minnesota Press, 1993), p. 160.
6 Ibid., p. 24.
7 See both the 'Introductory Essay' and the 'Postscript' by Stuart Hall in Roger Simon, *Gramsci's Political Thought: An Introduction* (London: Lawrence and Wishart, 1991), pp. 7–10 and 114–30.
8 Michel Foucault, *The Archaeology of Knowledge*, trans. A.M. Sheridan Smith (London: Routledge, 1995).
9 Victor Ehrenberg, *The Greek State* (London: Methuen, 1969), p. 92.
10 *The Politics of Aristotle*, trans. with notes by Ernest Barker (Oxford: Clarendon Press, 1948), p. 375.
11 William Scott Ferguson, *Greek Imperialism* (London: Constable, 1913), pp. 99–100.
12 See Kurt von Fritz and Ernst Kapp (trans and intro.), *Aristotle's Constitution of Athens and Related Texts* (London: Hafner Press, 1950), pp. 94 and 168.
13 An ardent supporter of panhellenism and the conviction that all Greeks should unite under the *shared* hegemony of both Athens and Sparta, it should be remembered that in his views on the power of discourse, Isocrates was not himself a sophist. More significantly for our purposes, Isocrates was also a very powerful advocate of the original meaning of hegemony which sought to endow a sense of mutual stability through a foundation built solidly on

general consent. See, in particular, Isocrates' key work *Panegyricus*, ed. and trans. S. Usher (Warminster: Aris and Phillips, 1990).

14 Ferguson, *Greek Imperialism*, p. 26.

15 Ibid., p. 36.

16 For Alcuin's *Versus de Patribus Regibus et Sanctis Euboricensis Ecclesiae*, see Peter Godman (ed.), *The Bishops, Kings, and Saints of York* (Oxford: Clarendon Press, 1982).

17 Peter Gay, *Style in History* (London: Jonathan Cape, 1975), p. 90.

18 On the connections between Ranke, his notion of hegemony and later German foreign policy, see Ludwig Dehio, *The Precarious Balance: The Politics of Power in Europe 1494–1945* (London: Chatto and Windus, 1963).

19 As leader of the Piedmontese government from December 1848 to March 1849, Gioberti was in a prime position to see the mistakes, failures and illusions of this abortive revolutionary period at first hand.

20 Vincenzo Gioberti, *Del rinnovamento civile d'Italia*, ed. Widar Cesarini Sforza (Bologna: Nicola Zanichelli, 1943), Vol. 2, p. 302.

21 Ibid., p. 384.

22 Quintin Hoare and Geoffrey Nowell Smith (trans. and eds), *Selections from the Prison Notebooks of Antonio Gramsci* [hereafter *SPN*], (London: Lawrence and Wishart, 1971), p. 104.

23 In conjunction with this praise, one must not forget that in general terms Gramsci constantly refers to Piedmont's position at the time of the Risorgimento as a classical illustration of dictatorship *without* hegemony.

24 Ernesto Laclau and Chantal Mouffe, *Hegemony and Socialist Strategy: Towards A Radical Democratic Politics* (London: Verso, 1985).

25 Ibid., p. 8.

26 Ibid., p. 7.

27 Ibid., p. 18, original emphasis.

28 Ibid., p. 7.

29 Ibid.

30 Fernand Braudel, *Grammaire de Civilisations* (Paris: Les Editions Arthaud, 1987).

31 *SPN*, p. 447.

32 Ibid., p. 448.

33 Henri Lefebvre, *Introduction to Modernity*, trans. John Moore (London: Verso, 1995), p. 29. Lefebvre, of course, was referring to the way in which language was used as a tool of Soviet officialdom and ideological orthodoxy. Nevertheless, it is clearly an observation which still merits a critical analysis in these post-Soviet times. It should also be pointed out that Lefebvre could appreciate the 'indisputable superiority' of the language of the East, as against that of the West, which was far more suited, but therefore limited, to the realm of discussion.
      Similar kinds of conclusion about the excessive linguistic abstractness of Western Marxism, in comparison with Russia, was also noted by Walter Benjamin during his brief stay in Moscow. See Walter Benjamin, *Moskauer Tagebuch* (Frankfurt am Main: Suhrkamp Verlag, 1980).

34 Perry Anderson, 'The Antinomies of Antonio Gramsci', *New Left Review*, 100, November 1976–January 1977, pp. 44–9.

35 Ibid., p. 50.

36 See, for example, H. Stuart Hughes, *Consciousness and Society* (Brighton: Harvester Press, 1979), p. 101.

37 Laclau and Mouffe, *Hegemony and Socialist Strategy,* p. 3.

38 It is worth reiterating in this context a very valuable point first made by Stuart Hall: 'We mustn't *use* Gramsci (as we have for so long abused Marx) like an Old Testament prophet who, at the correct moment, will offer us the consoling and appropriate quotation.' Nevertheless, Hall continues, it certainly is possible to 'think' through problems and situations in a Gramscian way: 'Gramsci gives us, not the tools with which to solve the puzzle, but the means with which to ask the right kinds of questions ...', Hall, 'Postscript', in Simon, *Gramsci's Political Thought*, pp. 114 and 116.

39 Perry Anderson, *Considerations on Western Marxism* (London: Verso, 1989), p. 80.

40 Holub, *Antonio Gramsci: Beyond Marxism and Postmodernism*, p. 7.

41 For an early, very critical perspective on modernity, see Antonio Gramsci, 'Modernità', *Avanti*, 18 March 1918.

42 Valentino Gerratana (ed.), *Antonio Gramsci: Quaderni del Carcere* (Torino: Einaudi, 1975), Vol. 3, Notebook 21, § 13, p. 2133. The passage is also cited in Holub, *Antonio Gramsci: Beyond Marxism and Postmodernism*, pp. 113–14.

43 Lefebvre, *Introduction to Modernity*, pp. 1–2. For Adorno's opposition to any kind of distinction between 'modernity' and 'modernism', see his 'Ästhetische Theorie' in *Gesammelte Werke* (Frankfurt: Suhrkamp, 1970), Vol. 7, p. 45.

44 See, for example, Jürgen Habermas, *The Philosophical Discourse of Modernity,* trans. Frederick Lawrence (Cambridge: Polity Press, 1995), p. 7.

45 Jacques Derrida, *The Other Heading: Reflections on Today's Europe,* trans. Pascale-Anne Brault and Michael. B. Naas (Indianapolis: Indiana University Press, 1992), p. 42.

46 Jay Bernstein, *The Fate of Art: Aesthetic Alienation from Kant to Derrida and Adorno* (Cambridge: Polity Press, 1992) p. 4.

47 Zygmunt Bauman, *Intimations of Postmodernity* (London: Routledge, 1992), p. 180.

48 Marshall Berman, *All That Is Solid Melts Into Air: The Experience of Modernity* (London: Verso, 1983), p. 15.

49 Ibid., pp. 15, 23 and 86.

50 See Jeffrey C. Alexander, 'Modern, Anti, Post and Neo', *New Left Review*, 210, 1995, p. 83.

51 Lefebvre, *Introduction to Modernity*, p. 228.

52 Albert Camus, *The Myth of Sisyphus*, trans. Justin O'Brien (Harmondsworth: Penguin Books, 1988), pp. 109 and 11.

Chapter 1: The Russian Origins of Hegemony

1 See, for example, Johann P. Arnason, *The Future That Failed: Origins and Destinies of the Soviet Model* (London: Routledge, 1993), p. 43.

2 As cited in Tibor Szamuely, *The Russian Tradition* (London: Fontana, 1988), p. 66.

3 Perry Anderson, *Lineages of the Absolutist State* (London: Verso, 1989), p. 356.

4   Tim McDaniel, *Autocracy, Capitalism and Revolution in Russia* (Berkeley: University of California Press, 1988), pp. 42–7.

5   Szamuely, *The Russian Tradition*, p. 209.

6   Ibid., p. 234.

7   As cited in Samuel H. Baron, *Plekhanov: The Father of Russian Marxism* (London: Routledge and Kegan Paul, 1963), p. 68.

8   See, in particular, Marx's letter to *Otechestvenniye Zapiski* (Saltykov-Shchedrin) in November 1877 in K. Marx and F. Engels, *Collected Works* (London: Lawrence and Wishart, 1989), Vol. 24, pp. 196–201; his letter (and previous drafts) to Vera Zasulich in March 1881 in *Collected Works*, Vol. 24, pp. 346–71; and Engels' letter to Zasulich in April 1885 in *Werke* (Berlin: Dietz Verlag, 1967), Vol. 36, pp. 303–7. For an excellent appraisal of Marx's changing attitude to the Russian commune and the prospect of an immediate transition to socialism, see Teodor Shanin (ed.), *Late Marx and the Russian Road: Marx and 'the peripheries of capitalism'* (London: Routledge and Kegan Paul, 1983). In light of this exchange of ideas, it was perhaps not surprising that Plekhanov kept the contents of Marx's reply to Zasulich quiet.

9   G. Plekhanov, *Selected Philosophical Works* (London: Lawrence and Wishart, 1961), pp. 122–399.

10 Ibid., p. 371.

11 Ibid., pp. 371–2.

12 Ibid., p. 347.

13 In Engels' *The Peasant War in Germany* which, as we have seen, Plekhanov quoted from at length, there are a couple of passages in which Engels himself makes reference to notions of hegemony and the kind of conditions which are required to underpin its viability. It is almost certain that Plekhanov's first encounter with the notion of hegemony was this.

14 See Baron, *Plekhanov*, pp. 75–6.

15 Plekhanov, *Selected Philosophical*, Vol. 1, p. 60.

16 Ibid., p. 239

17 See Baron, *Plekhanov: The Father of Russian Marxism*, pp. 107–12.

18 Plekhanov, *Selected Philosophical*, Vol. 1, p. 117.

19 Ibid., pp. 117–18.

20 Baron, *Plekhanov: The Father of Russian Marxism*, p. 155.

21 See Lenin's letter to Plekhanov in January 1901 in V.I. Lenin, *Collected Works* (London: Lawrence and Wishart, 1977), Vol. 34, pp. 55–7.

22 See Baron, *Plekhanov: The Father of Russian Marxism*, pp. 229–30.

23 Lenin, *Collected Works*, Vol. 5, p. 387.

24 Ibid., p. 391.

25 Ibid., Vol. 2, pp. 331 and 333–4, original emphasis.

26 Ibid., Vol. 34, pp. 28–31.

27 Ibid., Vol. 22, pp. 185–304.

28 As cited in Perry Anderson, 'The Antinomies of Antonio Gramsci', *New Left Review*, 100, November 1976–January 1977, p. 16.

29 Lenin, *Collected Works*, Vol. 5, pp. 373–97.

30 As cited in Baron, *Plekhanov: The Father of Russian Marxism*, p. 250.

31 As cited in Christine Buci-Glucksmann, *Gramsci and the State*, trans. David Fernbach (London: Lawrence and Wishart, 1980), p. 178.

32 See, for example, Leon Trotsky, *History of the Russian Revolution* (London: Pathfinder 1980), and 'The Proletariat and the Russian Revolution' and 'Our Differences' in Leon Trotsky, *1905* (London: Penguin Books, 1973), pp. 299–333.
33 Lenin, *Collected Works*, Vol. 6, pp. 49 and 51, original emphasis.
34 Buci-Glucksmann, *Gramsci and the State*, p. 179.
35 Ibid.
36 As cited in ibid.
37 Ibid., p. 182.
38 Ibid., pp. 182–3.
39 Neil Harding, *Lenin's Political Thought. Volume 2: Theory and Practice in the Socialist Revolution* (London: Macmillan, 1986), Ch. 13, *passim*.
40 See, for example, Nikolai Bukharin 'Teoriya permanentnoi revolyutsii', *Pravda*, 28 December 1924, pp. 5–7; Joseph Stalin, 'The Foundations of Leninism' in *Works*, (Moscow: Foreign Languages Publishing House, 1953), Vol. 6, p. 107.
41 Buci-Glucksmann, *Gramsci and the State*, p. 260.
42 As cited in ibid., p. 254. See also Stephen Cohen, *Bukharin and the Bolshevik Revolution: A Political Biography 1888–1938* (London: Wildwood House, 1974), pp. 107–22.
43 As cited in Buci-Glucksmann, *Gramsci and the State*, p. 262.
44 Ibid.
45 Ibid.
46 Lenin, *Collected Works*, Vol. 27, p. 464.

Chapter 2: The Gramscian Legacy

1   Antonio Gramsci, *Lettere dal Carcere* (Turin: Einaudi, 1975), p. 501.
2   Quintin Hoare and Geoffrey Nowell Smith (trans and eds), *Selections from the Prison Notebooks of Antonio Gramsci* [hereafter *SPN*], (London: Lawrence and Wishart, 1971), p. 462.
3   See Christine Buci-Glucksmann, *Gramsci and the State* trans. David Fernbach (London: Lawrence and Wishart, 1980), p. 338.
4   *SPN*, p. 351.
5   Ibid., pp. 402–3.
6   Walter L. Adamson, *Hegemony and Revolution: A Study of Antonio Gramsci's Political and Cultural Theory* (Berkeley: University of California Press, 1980), p. 124.
7   *SPN*, p. 344.
8   Louis Althusser, 'La Filosofia, la Politica e la Scienza', *Rinascita*, 15 March 1968, pp. 23–4.
9   *SPN*, p. 445.
10 Ibid., p. 412.
11 Ibid., pp. 180–1.
12 A. Showstack Sassoon, *Gramsci's Politics* (London: Croom Helm, 1980), p. 185.
13 *SPN*, pp. 181–2, emphasis added.
14 See Sue Golding,'The Concept of the Philosophy of Praxis in the *Quaderni* of Antonio Gramsci', in C. Nelson and L. Grossberg (eds), *Marxism and the Interpretation of Culture* (London: Macmillan, 1988), pp. 543–58.
15 *SPN*, p. 126.

16 Buci-Glucksmann, *Gramsci and the State*, p. 235.

17 Antonio Gramsci, 'The Revolution Against "Capital"' in Quintin Hoare (ed.), *Antonio Gramsci: Selections from Political Writings 1910–1920* (London: Lawrence and Wishart, 1977), pp. 34–5.

18 *SPN*, pp. 262–3.

19 Ibid., p. 12.

20 Ibid., p. 244.

21 See Norberto Bobbio, 'Gramsci and the Conception of Civil Society' in Chantal Mouffe (ed.), *Gramsci and Marxist Theory* (London: Routledge and Kegan Paul, 1979), pp. 21–47.

22 Jacques Texier, 'Gramsci, Theoretician of the Superstructures' in Mouffe (ed.), *Gramsci and Marxist Theory*, p. 71.

23 Bobbio, 'Gramsci and the Conception of Civil Society', p. 40.

24 Adamson, *Hegemony and Revolution*, p. 178.

25 *SPN*, p. 366.

26 Adamson, *Hegemony and Revolution*, p. 177.

27 *SPN*, p. 377.

28 See note in *SPN*, p. 54.

29 Ibid.

30 Buci-Glucksmann, *Gramsci and the State*, p. 274.

31 *SPN*, p. 418.

32 Ibid., p. 13.

33 Hoare (ed.), *Selections from the Prison Notebooks*, pp. 10–11.

34 Ibid., pp. 12–13.

35 Showstack Sassoon, *Gramsci's Politics*, pp. 25–6.

36 *SPN*, p. 97, emphasis added.

37 See Joseph Femia, *Gramsci's Political Thought: Hegemony, Consciousness and the Revolutionary Process* (Oxford: Clarendon Press, 1981), p. 132.

38 *SPN*, p. 349.

39 Ibid., p. 129.

40 Ibid., p. 235.

41 Ibid., p. 238.

42 Showstack Sassoon, *Gramsci's Politics*, p. 193.

43 *SPN*, p. 238.

44 Ibid., pp. 235–8.

45 Ibid., p. 210.

46 Ibid., p. 195.

47 Ibid., p. 210.

48 Ibid.

49 Ibid., p. 211.

50 Christine Buci-Glucksmann, 'Hegemony and Consent: A Political Strategy', in Anne Showstack Sassoon (ed.), *Approaches to Gramsci* (London: Writers and Readers Publishing Cooperative Society, 1982), p. 117.

51 *SPN*, p. 90.

52 Femia, *Gramsci's Political Thought*, p. 38.

53 Ibid., p. 37.

54 As cited in ibid., p. 42.

55 As cited in Steven R. Mansfield, 'Introduction to Gramsci's "Notes on Language"', *Telos*, No. 59, 1984, p. 126.

56   See ibid.
57   *SPN*, p. 349.
58   Ibid., p. 323.
59   Ibid., pp. 333–4, emphasis added.
60   Ibid., p. 367.
61   Femia, *Gramsci's Political Thought*, p. 187.
62   *SPN*, p. 365.
63   Ibid., pp. 323–4.
64   Ibid., pp. 193–4.
65   See ibid., p. 350.
66   Ibid., pp. 237–8.
67   Perry Anderson, 'The Antinomies of Antonio Gramsci', *New Left Review*, 100, November 1976–January 1977, p. 50.
68   *SPN*, p. 238.
69   Anderson, 'The Antinomies of Antonio Gramsci', p. 50.
70   Ibid., p. 51.
71   Ibid., p. 55.
72   Derek Boothman (trans. and ed.), *Antonio Gramsci: Further Selections from The Prison Notebooks* (London: Lawrence & Wishart, 1995), p. 282.
73   Anderson, 'The Antinomies of Antonio Gramsci', p. 50.
74   Fabio Frosini, 'Dall'ottimismo della volontà al pessimismo dell'intelligenza', in Giorgio Baratta and Andrea Catone (eds), *Antonio Gramsci e il 'Progresso Intellettuale di Massa'* (Milan: Unicopli, 1995), p. 188.
75   Boothman, *Antonio Gramsci: Further Selections from the Prison Notebooks*, p. 307.
76   Ibid., p. 306.
77   Anderson, 'The Antinomies of Antonio Gramsci', p. 76. Anderson, however, is right when he points out that Gramsci's criticisms of Trotsky as an advocate of permanent adventurism were based on misunderstandings and misconceptions of Trotsky's position throughout the 1920s and 1930s.
78   See, for example, Domenico Losurdo, *Antonio Gramsci dal liberalismo al 'comunismo critico'* (Rome: Gamberetti, 1997), pp. 244–7.
79   Giuseppe Tamburrano, 'Fasi di sviluppo del pensiero politico di Gramsci', in Alberto Caracciolo and Gianni Scalia (eds), *La città futura: Saggi sulla figura e il pensiero di Antonio Gramsci* (Milan: Feltrinelli Economica, 1977), p. 47.
80   Carl Boggs, *The Two Revolutions: Antonio Gramsci and the Dilemmas of Western Marxism* (Boston, MA: South End Press, 1984), p. 291.
81   For an English translation of the main letters, see Quintin Hoare (ed.), *Antonio Gramsci: Selections from Political Writings 1921–1926* (London: Lawrence and Wishart, 1978), pp. 426–41. For the most comprehensive analysis of the significance of the letters, along with new documents recently located in Soviet archives, see Chiara Daniele (ed.), *Gramsci a Roma, Togliatti a Mosca* (Torino: Einaudi editore, 1999).
82   Ibid., p. 440, original emphasis.
83   Christine Buci-Glucksmann, 'State, Transition and Passive Revolution', in Mouffe (ed.), *Gramsci and Marxist Theory*, pp. 219 and 20.
84   For more background details, see Felice Platone, 'Relazione sui Quaderni', *Rinascita*, 1944, pp. 181–90.
85   *SPN*, p. 268.
86   Ibid., emphasis added.

87   Giuseppe Vacca, *Appuntamenti con Gramsci* (Roma: Carocci editore, 1999), p. 214.

88   It is known that Gramsci read the manual following its publication in France in 1929. The full title was *Précis d'èconomie politique: L'èconomie politique et la théorie de l'èconomie soviétique* (Paris: Editions sociales internationales), and the translation was by Victor Serge.

89   Vacca, *Appuntamenti con Gramsci,* p. 215.

90   Francesco Benvenuti and Silvio Pons, 'L'Unione Sovietica nei *Quaderni del carcere',* in Giuseppe Vacca (ed.), *Gramsci e il Novecento* (Roma: Carocci editore, 1999), pp. 101–102.

91   Vacca, *Appuntamenti con Gramsci,* p. 222.

92   See, for example, G. Fiori, 'Non ho taciuto né omesso nulla', as cited in Guido Ligouri, *Gramsci conteso: Storia di un dibattito 1922–1996* (Roma: Editori Riuniti, 1996), p. 127, and the testimony of Ercole Piacentini in Cesare Bermani (ed.), *Gramsci raccontato* (Roma: Edizione Associate, 1987), p. 168.

93   See D. Forgacs and G. Nowell-Smith (eds), *Antonio Gramsci: Selections from Cultural Writings* (London: Lawrence and Wishart, 1985), p. 108.

94   Vacca, *Appuntamenti con Gramsci,* p. 225.

95   Régis Debray, 'Schema for a study of Gramsci', *New Left Review,* 59, January–February 1970, p. 51.

Chapter 3: From Monologue to Dialogue: Gramsci's Reception in Soviet Russia

1   Interview with Giuliano Gramsci in Moscow, 4 June 1994.

2   It is true that not longer after Gramsci's arrest, the Soviet Government officially supported the idea of a prisoner exchange, involving Gramsci's release from prison and subsequent exile to the Soviet Union in exchange for the release and exile of a Soviet citizen (Urusova) who had spied for the fascists. The fact that the exchange never happened was largely because of the intransigence of Mussolini. Nevertheless, one cannot help thinking that if Gramsci had been exiled to the Soviet Union, would he have survived the brutal years of Stalin's purges? This point, of course, was vilely and unashamedly made by Mussolini himself in an article in *Il popolo d'Italia* (31 December 1937) only a few months after Gramsci's death.

3   'Skonchalsya tov. Gramshi', *Pravda,* 29 April 1937, p. 5.

4   Interview with Giuliano Gramsci. See also Evghenii Ambarzumov, 'Studi gramsciani nell'Unione Sovietica', *Critica marxista,* No. 3, 1967, pp. 150–2; Ilia Levin, 'Come si parla di Gramsci in URSS', *Rinascita,* No. 4, 30 January 1980, p. 16.

5   As cited in Giuseppe Vacca, *Togliatti sconosciuto* (Roma: l'Unità editrice, 1994), pp. 144–5.

6   The selections were edited by Carolina Misiano and the extracts represented about one-quarter of the complete notebooks. On the Soviet side, the publication was 'supervised' by Dmitrii Shevliagin, an important functionary in the party's Central Committee. On the Italian side, Ambrogio Donini was personally charged with the task of supervision by Togliatti himself. To this day, it is not known whether the initiative came from the Soviet or Italian

Communist Party. It has often been suggested, however, that the publication was a form of compensation for the Italian party's decision to remain a member of the Cominform.

7 B.R. Lopukhov, *Antonio Gramshi* (Moscow: Izdatel'stvo Akademii Nauk SSSR, 1963).
8 Ambarzumov, 'Studi gramsciani nell'Unione Sovietica', p. 152.
9 A.S. Golemba, *Gramshi* (Moscow: 1968).
10 Interview with Giuliano Gramsci.
11 Ibid. See also Levin, 'Come si parla di Gramsci in URSS', p. 16.
12 See, for example, Zoya Meleshchenko, 'Nekotorye voprosy istoricheskogo materializma v "Tyuremnykh tetradyakh" Antonio Gramshi', *Vestnik Leningradskogo universiteta*, Vol. 2, No. 11, 1958, pp. 35–44.
13 For details of the conference, see Ambarzumov, 'Studi gramsciani nell'Unione Sovietica', pp. 157–69.
14 Ibid., p. 169.
15 G. Vodolazov, 'Esteticheskoe nasledie Gramshi', *Novyi mir*, No. 1, 1968, p. 259.
16 Ambarzumov, 'Studi gramsciani nell'Unione Sovietica', p. 157.
17 See, for example, V.A. Bogorad, 'Antonio Gramshi: k 80-letiyu so dnya rozhdeniya', *Voprosy istorii KPSS*, No. 1, 1971, pp. 108–10.
18 I.V. Grigor'eva, *Istoricheskie vzglyady Antonio Gramshi* (Moscow: Izdatel'stvo Moskovskogo universiteta, 1978).
19 M.N. Gretskii, *Antonio Gramshi – Politik i Filosof* (Moscow: Izdatel'stvo Nauka, 1991), p. 143.
20 Boris Kagarlitsky, *The Thinking Reed: Intellectuals and the Soviet State from 1917 to the Present*, trans. Brian Pearce (London: Verso, 1988), p. 285.
21 Kagarlitsky mentions in particular the journal *Varianty*, four issues of which appeared in the period 1977–80. Ibid., p. 284.
22 It should perhaps be stressed, however, that no Russian translation of 'The Revolution Against "Capital"' has ever appeared.
23 As cited in I.D. Mitel'man, 'Vydayushchiisya myslitel' – revolyutsioner', *Voprosy istorii KPSS*, No. 7, 1987, p. 125.
24 See, for example, A.S. Popov, 'A. Gramshi o partii i politicheskom rukovodstve', *Voprosy istorii KPSS*, No. 5, 1987, pp. 86–98; V.O. Mushinskii, 'Antonio Gramshi o gosudarstve', *Sovetskoe Gosudarstvo i Pravo*, No. 8, 1986, pp. 98–107; Svetlana Sokolova, 'Antonio Gramshi o roli chelovecheskogo faktora v zhizni obshchestva', in Materialy konferentsii, *Rol' chelovecheskogo faktora v uskorenii nauchno-tekhnicheskogo progressa* (Pavlodar: 1987), pp. 46–48
25 L.B. Popov and G.P. Smirnov, 'Aktual'nost' idei Antonio Gramshi', *Kommunist*, No. 6, 1987, pp. 102–9.
26 See, for example, V.O. Mushinskii, *Antonio Gramshi: Uchenie o gegemonii* (Moscow: 1990), p. 124.
27 Boris Kagarlitsky, *The Dialectic of Change*, trans. Rick Simon (London: Verso, 1990), p. 343; *The Thinking Reed*, p. 359.
28 Gretskii, *Antonio Gramshi*, pp. 62–3.
29 For Gretskii, the Soviet system had previously given rise to three different types of historical blocs correlating to three specific socioeconomic formations: war communism, NEP and the command-administrative system. Ibid., p. 82. Needless to say, the emergence of new historical blocs in the early 1990s was of a fundamentally different order.

30   Ibid., pp. 3 and 141–3.

31   As cited in ibid., p. 97.

32   This term is used by Kagarlitsky who also goes on to state (writing as he was in the final stages of the Brezhnev era): 'Without the contribution to science made by ... Gramsci the new culturology would have been as impossible as if Bakhtin had never existed. However, it is risky to talk openly about that in some circles', *The Thinking Reed*, p. 282.

33   Craig Brandist, 'Gramsci, Bakhtin and the Semiotics of Hegemony', *New Left Review*, 216, March–April 1996, p. 94.

34   See V.N. Voloshinov, *Marxism and the Philosophy of Language*, trans. L. Matejka and I.R. Titunik (London: Seminar Press, 1973), p. 41. According to Franco Lo Piparo, it is almost certain that Gramsci's notion of hegemony derived from his linguistic studies, and that it was this which determined his later hegemony-oriented approach to politics and culture. Franco Lo Piparo, *Lingua Intellettuali Egemonia in Gramsci* (Roma: Laterza, 1979).

35   Michael Holquist, *Dialogism: Bakhtin and his World* (London: Routledge, 1990), p. 30.

36   Ibid., p. 52.

37   See, for example, L. Gozman and A. Etkind, 'Kult vlasti', in *Osmyslitkult Stalina* (Moscow: Progress, 1989), pp. 365ff.

38   Caryl Emerson (trans. and ed.), *M.M. Bakhtin: Problems of Dostoevsky's Poetics* (Minneapolis: University of Minnesota Press, 1984).

39   As cited in Katerina Clark and Michael Holquist, *Mikhail Bakhtin* (London: Harvard University Press, 1984), pp. 348–50.

40   Michael Holquist (ed.), *The Dialogic Imagination: Four Essays by M.M. Bakhtin*, trans. Caryl Emerson and Michael Holquist (Austin: University of Texas Press, 1981), p. 346, original emphasis.

41   Brandist, 'Gramsci, Bakhtin and the Semiotics of Hegemony', p. 109.

42   Ibid., p. 108.

43   Ibid., pp. 108 and 109.

Chapter 4: Post-Gramscian Debates on Hegemony in the West

1   See Colin Mercer, 'Revolutions, Reforms or Reformulations? Marxist Discourse on Democracy', in Alan Hunt (ed.), *Marxism and Democracy* (London: Lawrence and Wishart, 1980), p. 117.

2   I have used the English translation of Bobbio's address to the 1968 Cagliari Congress on Gramsci which appeared under the title 'Gramsci and the Conception of Civil Society', in Chantal Mouffe (ed.), *Gramsci and Marxist Theory* (London: Routledge and Kegan Paul, 1979), pp. 21–47.

3   Ibid., p. 30.

4   Ibid., p. 31.

5   Ibid., p. 32.

6   Ibid., p. 36.

7   Ibid., p. 41.

8   Texier's response was originally published in *La Pensee* in June 1968. An English translation appears under the title 'Gramsci, Theoretician of the Superstruc-

tures', and is also contained in Mouffe (ed.), *Gramsci and Marxist Theory*, pp. 48–79.

9   Ibid., p. 49.
10 Ibid., p. 51.
11 Ibid., p. 55.
12 Perry Anderson, 'The Antinomies of Antonio Gramsci', *New Left Review*, 100, November 1976–January 1977, pp. 5–78.
13 Ibid., pp. 12–13, original emphasis.
14 Ibid., pp. 26–9.
15 Ibid., p. 32, original emphasis.
16 Ibid., pp. 33–4.
17 Ellen Meiksins Wood, *Democracy Against Capitalism: Renewing Historical Materialism* (Cambridge: Cambridge University Press, 1995), p. 255.
18 No one can doubt, however, that Althusser was always very ill at ease when making any kind of direct criticism of Gramsci. Take, for example, his remarks in *Reading Capital* where he analyses historicism. Having said that unfortunately he has no choice but to include Gramsci in his critical framework, he goes on to remark: 'I do not do so without profound misgivings, fearing not only that my necessarily schematic remarks may disfigure the spirit of this enormously delicate and subtle work of genius, but also that the reader may be drawn against my will to extend to Gramsci's fruitful discoveries in the field of *historical materialism*, the theoretical reservations I want to formulate with respect only to his interpretation of *dialectical materialism*', Louis Althusser and Étienne Balibar, *Reading Capital* (London: New Left Books, 1970), p. 126, original emphasis.
19 See, in particular, his essay 'Contradiction and Overdetermination', in Louis Althusser, *For Marx* (London: Allen Lane, 1971), pp. 107–111.
20 Louis Althusser, 'Ideology and Ideological State Apparatuses (Notes Towards an Investigation)', in *Lenin and Philosophy and other Essays* (London: New Left Books, 1977), p. 138.
21 Gregory Elliott, *Althusser: The Detour of Theory* (London: Verso, 1987), pp. 228–9.
22 As cited in ibid., p. 229.
23 Ibid., original emphasis.
24 Althusser, *Lenin and Philosophy*, p. 139.
25 E.P. Thompson, *The Poverty of Theory and other Essays* (London: Merlin Press, 1980), p. 369.
26 John Keane, *Democracy and Civil Society* (London: Verso, 1988), p. 227.
27 Terry Eagleton, *Ideology: An Introduction* (London: Verso, 1991), p. 147.
28 Elliott, *Althusser: The Detour of Theory*, p. 232.
29 Ted Benton, *The Rise and Fall of Structural Marxism: Althusser and His Influence* (London: Macmillan, 1985), p. 105.
30 See, in particular, Nicos Poulantzas, *Political Power and Social Classes* (London: New Left Books, 1973), pp. 39; 124–5; 138–9 and 200–1.
31 Ibid., p. 139.
32 Nicos Poulantzas, 'The Problem of the Capitalist State', in R. Blackburn (ed.), *Ideology in Social Science*, (London: Fontana, 1972), pp. 252–3, original emphasis.

33 Poulantzas, *Political Power and Social Classes*, p. 140.
34 Bob Jessop, *Nicos Poulantzas: Marxist Theory and Political Strategy* (London: Macmillan, 1985), p. 194.
35 See Christine Buci-Glucksmann, *Gramsci and the State*, trans. David Fernbach (London: Lawrence and Wishart, 1980), pp. 58–9.
36 Jessop, *Nicos Poulantzas: Marxist Theory and Political Strategy*, pp. 112; 139; 140 and 144.
37 As quoted in ibid., pp. 145–6.
38 Nicos Poulantzas, *State, Power, Socialism* (London: New Left Books, 1978), p. 256.
39 Nicos Poulantzas, 'Le Risposte che è difficile trovare', *Rinascita*, 12 October 1979, pp. 25–6, emphasis added.
40 Ibid., p. 26.
41 See Z.A. Pelczynski, 'Solidarity and "The Rebirth of Civil Society"', in John Keane (ed.), *Civil Society and the State* (London: Verso, 1988), pp. 361–80.
42 Ivan Szelenyi, 'Socialist Opposition in Eastern Europe: Dilemmas and Prospects', in Rudolf L. Tokes (ed.), *Opposition in Eastern Europe* (London: Macmillan, 1979), p. 204.
43 See Jean L. Cohen and Andrew Arato, *Civil Society and Political Theory* (Cambridge, MA: MIT Press, 1994), pp. 142–74.
44 The original title of Lukács's work was *Demokratisierung heute und morgen*. The English translation and change of title to *The Process of Democratization* was done by Susanne Bernhardt and Norman Levine (New York: State University of New York Press, 1991).
45 Ibid., p. 118.
46 See the 'Introduction' by Norman Levine, in ibid., p. 31.
47 See Renate Holub, *Antonio Gramsci: Beyond Marxism and Postmodernism* (London: Routledge, 1992), p. 15.
48 See ibid., pp. 199–201.
49 As cited in Barry Smart, 'The Politics of Truth and the Problem of Hegemony', in David Couzens Hoy (ed.), *Foucault: A Critical Reader* (Oxford: Basil Blackwell, 1991), p. 166. See also R. Radhakrishnan, 'Toward an Effective Intellectual: Foucault or Gramsci', in Bruce Robbins (ed.), *Intellectuals: Aesthetics, Politics, Academics* (Minneapolis: University of Minnesota Press, 1990) pp. 59–99.
50 See, for example, Pierre Bourdieu, *Outline of a Theory of Practice* (Cambridge: Cambridge University Press, 1977).
51 Terry Eagleton (ed.), *Raymond Williams: Critical Perspectives,* (Cambridge: Polity Press, 1989), p. 6.
52 Holub, *Antonio Gramsci: Beyond Marxism and Postmodernism*, p. 104.
53 Fernando Ferrara, 'Raymond Williams and the Italian Left', in Eagleton (ed.), *Raymond Williams,* p. 105.
54 Raymond Williams, *The Long Revolution* (London: Chatto and Windus, 1961), p. 48.
55 Ibid., p. 51.
56 Ibid., p. 52, original emphasis.
57 Raymond Williams, *Politics and Letters: Interviews with New Left Review* (London: Verso, 1981), pp. 133–6.
58 See E.P. Thompson, 'The Long Revolution', *New Left Review*, 9/10, 1961, pp. 24–33 and 34–9; Stuart Hall, 'Politics and Letters', in Eagleton (ed.), *Raymond Williams*, pp. 61–3.

59 Raymond Williams, *Marxism and Literature* (Oxford: Oxford University Press, 1977), p. 94.
60 Ibid., p. 165.
61 Ibid., p. 61.
62 Ibid., p. 166.
63 See Eagleton (ed.), *Raymond Williams*, p. 8.
64 Williams, *Marxism and Literature*, pp. 133–4, original emphasis.
65 Raymond Williams, *Problems in Materialism and Culture* (London: Verso, 1980), p. 37.
66 According to Eagleton, Williams deliberately sought to provide an excessively crude interpretation of ideology so as to provide hegemony with a 'straw-target'. What emerges out of Williams' writings is a notion of hegemony as some kind of 'super-ideology'. See Eagleton (ed.), *Raymond Williams*, pp. 170–1.
67 Williams, *Marxism and Literature*, p. 111.
68 Williams, *Problems in Materialism*, p. 43.
69 Ibid., pp. 40–42; see also *Marxism and Literature*, pp. 121–7.
70 Williams, *Marxism and Literature*, p. 115.
71 Eagleton, *Ideology*, p. 115.
72 Nowhere is this ingrained optimism of Williams better demonstrated than in one of his final works, *Towards 2000* (London: Chatto and Windus, 1983), where the notion of 'Resources for a Journey of Hope' is given full scope.
73 Jan Gorak, *The Alien Mind of Raymond Williams* (Columbia: University of Missouri Press, 1988), p. 125.
74 Raymond Williams, *Resources of Hope: Culture, Democracy, Socialism,* ed. Robin Gable (London: Verso, 1989), p. 75.
75 Ernesto Laclau and Chantal Mouffe, *Hegemony and Socialist Strategy: Towards a Radical Democratic Politics* (London: Verso, 1985), p. 136.
76 See, for example, Ernesto Laclau, *New Reflections on the Revolution of Our Time* (London: Verso, 1990), pp. 93–4.
77 Laclau and Mouffe, *Hegemony and Socialist Strategy*, p. 71.
78 Ibid., p. 136.
79 Ibid., p. 70, original emphasis.
80 Chantal Mouffe, 'Hegemony and New Political Subjects: Toward a New Concept of Democracy', in C. Nelson and L. Grossberg (eds), *Marxism and the Interpretation of Culture* (London: Macmillan, 1988), p. 90.
81 Laclau, *New Reflections on the Revolution of our Time*, p. 29, original emphasis.
82 Laclau and Mouffe, *Hegemony and Socialist Strategy*, p. 137.
83 Ibid., pp. 95–6.
84 Eagleton, *Ideology: An Introduction*, p. 206.
85 Ibid., p. 214.
86 Laclau and Mouffe, *Hegemony and Socialist Strategy*, p. 58.
87 Eagleton, *Ideology: An Introduction*, p. 215.
88 See, for example, Ellen Meiksins Wood, *The Retreat From Class: A New 'True' Socialism* (London: Verso, 1986), p. 63.
89 Laclau, *New Reflections on the Revolution of our Time*, p. 232, emphasis added.
90 Wood, *The Retreat from Class*, p. 75.
91 Norman Geras, 'Post-Marxism?', *New Left Review,* 163, May–June 1987, pp. 42–3.
92 Wood, *The Retreat from Class*, p. 61.

93 See Nicos Mouzelis, 'Marxism or Post-Marxism?', *New Left Review*, 167, January–February 1988, pp. 116–17.
94 Esteve Morera, *Gramsci's Historicism: A Realist Interpretation* (London: Routledge, 1990), p. 180.
95 Erik Olin Wright, *Classes* (London: Verso, 1989), pp. 31–2.
96 Ibid., p. 32.
97 See Ellen Meiksins Wood, 'The Uses and Abuses of "Civil Society"', in R. Miliband and L. Panitch (eds), *The Socialist Register 1990* (London: Merlin Press, 1990), pp. 60–84.
98 Ibid., pp. 65–6.
99 Ibid., p. 77, original emphasis.
100 Ibid., emphasis added.

Chapter 5: Does Hegemony Have a Postmodern Future?

1 Ernesto Laclau and Chantal Mouffe, *Hegemony and Socialist Strategy: Towards a Radical Democratic Politics* (London: Verso, 1985), p. 188.
2 See Ernesto Laclau, *New Reflections on the Revolution of Our Time* (London: Verso, 1990), p. 229.
3 Laclau and Mouffe, *Hegemony and Socialist Strategy*, p. 181.
4 Ibid., p. 182.
5 Ellen Meiksins Wood, *The Retreat From Class: A New 'True' Socialism* (London: Verso, 1986), p. 68.
6 Ibid., p. 17.
7 Jacques Derrida, *Specters of Marx: The State of the Debt, the Work of Mourning, & the New International*, trans. Peggy Kamuf (London: Routledge, 1994), p. 35, original emphasis.
8 Ibid., pp. 51–2.
9 Ibid., pp. 85–6.
10 See, for example, Michael Sprinker, 'Politics and Friendship: An Interview with Jacques Derrida', in E. Ann Kaplan and Michael Sprinker (eds), *The Althusserian Legacy* (London: Verso, 1993), p. 204.
11 Derrida, *Specters of Marx*, p. 85.
12 Ibid., p. 90.
13 Ibid.
14 Aijaz Ahmad, 'Reconciling Derrida: "Spectres of Marx" and Deconstructive Politics', *New Left Review*, 208, 1994, p. 104.
15 Derrida, *Specters of Marx*, p. 88.
16 John M. Ellis, *Against Deconstruction* (Princeton: Princeton University Press, 1989), p. 71.
17 Ibid., p. 89.
18 See, for example, 'The Ends of Man', in Jacques Derrida, *Margins of Philosophy*, trans. Alan Bass (London: Harvester Wheatsheaf, 1982), p. 114.
19 Ahmad, 'Reconciling Derrida', p. 105.
20 Derrida defines paleonomy as: 'the "strategic" necessity that requires the occasional maintenance of an *old name* in order to launch a new concept ...', Jacques Derrida, *Positions*, trans. Alan Bass (London: The Athlone Press, 1987), p. 71, original emphasis.

21 Derrida, *Specters of Marx*, p. 37.
22 Ralph Miliband, *Socialism for a Sceptical Age* (Cambridge: Polity Press, 1994), p. 11.
23 Zygmunt Bauman, 'The Left as the Counter-Culture of Modernity', *Telos*, No. 70, 1986/7, p. 86.
24 Ibid.
25 Andrew Ross (ed.), *Universal Abandon? The Politics of Postmodernism* (Minneapolis: University of Minnesota Press, 1988), p. xv.
26 Terry Eagleton, 'The Hippest', *London Review of Books*, 7 March 1996, p. 5.
27 Judith Squires (ed.), *Principled Positions: Postmodernism and the Rediscovery of Value* (London: Lawrence and Wishart, 1993).
28 See, for example, David Harvey, 'Class Relations, Social Justice and the Politics of Difference', in Squires, *Principled Positions*, pp. 85–120.
29 Ellen Meiksins Wood, 'Capitalism or Modernity?', a paper given at the Socialist Scholars Conference, New York, April 1996, original emphasis.
30 Fredric Jameson, *Postmodernism, or, the Cultural Logic of Late Capitalism* (London: Verso, 1991), p. 310.
31 See, in particular, Gilles Deleuze and Félix Guattari, *Anti-Oedipus* (Minneapolis: University of Minnesota Press, 1983).
32 Jameson, *Postmodernism*, p. 418.
33 Ibid., p. 51.
34 Ibid., p. 320.
35 Mike Davis, 'Urban Renaissance and the Spirit of Postmodernism', in E. Ann Kaplan (ed.), *Postmodernism and its Discontents: Theories, Practices* (London: Verso, 1988), p. 83.
36 Jameson, *Postmodernism*, p. ix.
37 Stanley Aronowitz, 'Postmodernism and Politics', in Ross (ed.), *Universal Abandon? The Politics of Postmodernism*, p. 51.
38 Zygmunt Bauman, *Intimations of Postmodernity* (London: Routledge, 1992), p. 51, original emphasis.
39 Zygmunt Bauman, *Legislators and Interpreters: On modernity, post-modernity and intellectuals* (Cambridge: Polity Press, 1987), p. 166.
40 Bauman, *Intimations of Postmodernity*, p. 51.
41 Bauman, *Legislators and Interpreters*, p. 186.
42 Hans Bertens, *The Idea of the Postmodern: A History* (London: Routledge, 1995), p. 233.
43 Bauman, 'The Left as the Counter-Culture of Modernity', p. 92.
44 Ibid.
45 See, in particular, Jean Baudrillard, *Le Système des objets* (Paris: Gallimard, 1968); *La Societé de consommation* (Paris: Gallimard, 1970).
46 Jean Baudrillard, 'Consumer Society', in Mark Poster (ed.), *Jean Baudrillard: Selected Writings* (Cambridge: Polity Press, 1988), p. 50.
47 Jean Baudrillard, 'On nihilism', *On the Beach*, No. 6, 1984, p. 39.
48 Jean Baudrillard, *Simulations*, trans. Paul Foss, Paul Patton and Philip Beitchman (New York: Semiotext(e), 1983), p. 12.
49 In Baudrillard's case, no resistance may well be better than a strategy of resistance. His recommendation, for example, to seek to abolish the capitalist system by pushing it into 'hyperlogic' – consuming ever more and more in ever-increasing absurd ways – in order to inflict a brutal amortisation was

hardly designed to cause the dominant capitalist classes too many sleepless nights.

50 David Ashley, 'Critical Theory and the Modern Project', in Bryan S. Turner (ed.), *Theories of Modernity and Postmodernity* (London: Sage, 1993), p. 90.
51 Umberto Eco, 'Living in the New Middle Ages', in *Travels in Hyperreality* (London: Picador, 1987), p. 74.
52 Alain Minc, *Le nouveau Moyen Âge* (Paris: Gallimard, 1993).
53 As Mike Davis has argued with reference to Manhattan's Trump Tower, this 'medievalized Bonaventure' clearly signals 'the coercive intent of postmodernist architecture in its ambition, not to hegemonize the city in the fashion of the great modernist buildings, but rather to polarize it into radically antagonistic spaces', 'Urban Renaissance and the Spirit of Postmodernism', pp. 86–7.
54 Umberto Eco, 'Living in the New Middle Ages', p. 77.
55 Eric Hobsbawm, *Age of Extremes: The Short Twentieth Century 1914–1991* (London: Michael Joseph, 1994), Part 3, *passim.*
56 Giovanni Arrighi, *The Long Twentieth Century: Money, Power and the Origins of Our Times* (London: Verso, 1994).
57 Immanuel Wallerstein, *Historical Capitalism* with *Capitalist Civilization* (London: Verso, 1996), p. 141.
58 See Michael Mann, 'As the Twentieth Century Ages', *New Left Review,* 214, 1995, p. 113.
59 Jean-François Lyotard, 'The Sublime and the Avant-Garde', *Art Forum,* April 1984, p. 43.
60 Anthony Giddens, *A Contemporary Critique of Historical Materialism* (London: Macmillan, 1995), p. 193.
61 See Bauman, *Intimations of Postmodernity,* p. 60.
62 David Harvey, *The Condition of Postmodernity* (Oxford: Basil Blackwell, 1990), pp. 201–308.
63 If there is one overriding framework to the debate, it is between those advocates who essentially view the nation state as a 'natural' and, therefore, permanently autonomous realm of social existence, as distinct from those who regard the nation state as nothing more than a product of late modernisation whose autonomous status will sooner or later be made obsolete.
64 Karl Deutsch, 'Learning-state and the self-transformation of politics', in M. Campanella (ed.), *Between Rationality and Cognition* (Torino: Albert Meynier, 1988), p. 54.
65 Anthony McGrew, 'A Global Society?', in Stuart Hall, David Held and Tony McGrew (eds), *Modernity and its Futures* (London: Open University Press, 1992), p. 87.
66 Étienne Balibar, *Masses, Classes, Ideas* (London: Routledge, 1994), pp. 198–9.
67 Ernest Gellner, *Nations and Nationalism* (Oxford: Basil Blackwell, 1983), Ch. 8, *passim.*
68 Zygmunt Bauman, 'Searching for a Centre that Holds', in Mike Featherstone, Scott Lash and Roland Robertson (eds), *Global Modernities* (London: Sage, 1995), p. 153.
69 Jacques Derrida, *The Other Heading: Reflections on Today's Europe,* trans. Pascale-Anne Brault and Michael B. Naas (Indianapolis: Indiana University Press, 1992), p. 44.

70 See Leslie Sklair, *Sociology of the Global System* (London: Prentice Hall, 1995), Ch. 1.
71 Mathew Horsman and Andrew Marshall, *After the Nation-State: Citizens, Tribalism and the New World Disorder* (London: HarperCollins, 1994), pp. 200–15.
72 Robert W. Cox, 'Global Perestroika', in Ralph Miliband and Leo Panitch (eds), *New World Order? Socialist Register 1992* (London: Merlin Press, 1992), pp. 30–31.
73 Leo Panitch, 'Globalisation and the State', in Ralph Miliband and Leo Panitch (eds), *Between Globalism and Nationalism. Socialist Register 1994* (London: Merlin Press, 1994), pp. 60–93.
74 Horsman and Marshall, *After the Nation-State*, p. 172.
75 See Mike Featherstone, 'Global Culture: An Introduction', in Mike Featherstone (ed.), *Global Culture: Nationalism, Globalization and Modernity* (London: Sage, 1995), pp. 1–14.
76 Jonathan Friedman, *Cultural Identity and Global Processes* (London: Sage, 1994), pp. 233–53.
77 Anthony D. Smith, 'Towards a Global Culture?', in Featherstone (ed.), *Global Culture*, p. 177.
78 As cited in ibid.
79 Benedict Anderson, *Imagined Communities: Reflections on the Origin and Spread of Nationalism* (London: Verso, 1983), p. 140.
80 Raphael Samuel, *Theatres of Memory* (London: Verso, 1994).
81 Ibid., pp. 259–73.
82 Tom Nairn, 'Internationalism and the Second Coming', in Gopal Balakrishnan (ed.), *Mapping the Nation* (London: Verso, 1996), pp. 274–5.
83 'Nationalism, Post-Colonialism, Communism', an interview with Aijaz Ahmad, *Radical Philosophy,* No. 76, 1996, p. 38.

Conclusion: The Hegemonic Landscape After the Battle

1 Sergei Kovalev, 'Russia After Chechnya', *New York Review of Books,* Vol. XLIV, No. 12, 17 July 1997, p. 28.
2 Mikhail N. Epstein, *After the Future: The Paradoxes of Postmodernism and Contemporary Russian Culture,* trans. and intro. Anesa Miller-Pogacar (Amherst: University of Massachusetts Press, 1995), p. xii.
3 Ibid., p. 331.
4 For a more detailed analysis of Russia's feudal tendencies see Vladimir Shlapentokh, 'Early Feudalism – The Best Parallel for Contemporary Russia', *Europe-Asia Studies,* Vol. 48, No. 3, 1996, pp. 393–411; Jeremy Lester, 'Feudalism's revenge: the inverse dialectics of time in Russia', *Contemporary Politics,* Vol. 4, No. 2, 1998.
5 Shlapentokh, 'Early Feudalism', p. 397.
6 Jean-Paul Sartre, 'Socialism in One Country', *New Left Review,* 100, November 1976–January 1977, pp. 147–8.
7 The most important of these writings are: *Drama vlasti* (Moscow: Paleia, 1993); *Derzhava* (Moscow: Informpechat', 1994); *Za Gorizontom* (Orel: Veshnie vody, 1995); *Rossiya i sovremennyi mir* (Moscow: Informpechat', 1995).

8   Gennadii Zyuganov, *Za Gorizontom*, p. 162.
9   See Nicholas Berdyaev, *The End of Our Time*, trans. Donald Atwater (London: Sheed & Ward, 1933).
10 See Tom Nairn, 'The Modern Janus', *New Left Review*, 94, 1975, p. 5.
11 *Sovetskaya Rossiya*, 24 January 1995, p. 2.
12 Boris Kagarlitsky, *The Disintegration of the Monolith*, trans. Renfrey Clarke (London: Verso, 1992), pp. 13–26.
13 Frantz Fanon, *The Wretched of the Earth*, trans. Constance Farrington (Harmondsworth: Penguin Books, 1990), p. 175.
14 Boris Kapustin, 'Levyi konservatizm KPRF i ego rol' v sovremennoi politike', *Nezavisimaya gazeta*, 5 March 1996, p. 5.
15 Nairn, 'The Modern Janus', p. 14.
16 For a detailed study on Ustrialov (the main Russian theorist of national bolshevism at the time of the revolution) see M. Agurskii, *Ideologia natsional-bol'shevisma* (Paris, 1980).
17 Hugh Seton-Watson, *Nations and States: An Enquiry into the Origins of Nations and the Politics of Nationalism* (Boulder, CO: Westview Press, 1977).
18 See his interview with *New Left Review*, 105, September–October 1977.
19 For an attempt to formulate a different culture-based strategy of left opposition in Russia, drawing on the popular, democratic, participatory legacy of the early soviets, see Jeremy Lester, 'Remembrance of Things Past … The 1905 Soviets and their Contemporary Implications', *Contemporary Politics*, Vol. 2, No. 2, 1996.
20 Aleksandr Tsipko, 'Pochemu partiya Gennadiya Zyuganova mozhet pobedit' na dekabr'skikh vyborakh', *Nezavisimaya gazeta*, 9 November 1995, p. 5.
21 See, for example, *Sovetskaya Rossiya*, 16 January 1996, pp. 2–3.
22 Aijaz Ahmad, *In Theory: Classes, Nations, Literatures* (London: Verso, 1994).
23 Fanon, *The Wretched of the Earth*, p. 180.
24 Robert Rozhdestvensky, 'Pered novym pryzhkom' [Before a New Jump], in Vladimir Markov and Merrill Sparks (eds), *Modern Russian Poetry* (London: MacGibbon & Kee, 1966), p. 803.
25 Pyotr Chaadayev, 'Philosophical Letters', in James M. Edie, James P. Scanlan and Mary-Barbara Zeldin (eds), *Russian Philosophy*, Vol. 1 (Chicago: Quadrangle Books, 1965).
26 Alain Touraine, *Critique of Modernity* (Oxford: Basil Blackwell, 1995), p. 360.
27 Liah Greenfeld, *Nationalism: Five Roads to Modernity* (Cambridge, MA: Harvard University Press, 1992), p. 250.
28 Samuel Huntington, *The Clash of Civilizations and the Remaking of World Order* (London: Simon & Schuster, 1997).

Index